LEADERSHIP IS WHAT?

The Importance of Vision, Integrity, and Developing Others

DAREN HANCOTT

Dedication

This book is dedicated to my lovely, dedicated, and supportive wife, Linda. To my mother, Isabel, for giving me some smarts, and to my father, Ernest, who gave me the stubbornness and drive to never give up.

To my pride and joy, sons Dyllan and Garrett, who make life and just being alive and healthy so very delightful. Even though I rarely am satisfied, I can honestly say I am truly blessed, so very happy, and forever grateful for my family and the love I know.

You are the love of my life, the wind beneath my wings, and all the inspiration I will ever need.

Thank you,
Daren

Contents

Preface xii

Introduction. xiii

What Is Leadership? 1

Are Leaders Born or Made? 3

Why Would You Want to Be a Leader? 8

Leadership versus Management: The Balancing Act 10

Role of a Leader. 13

Skills, Qualities, Characteristics, and Attributes of Leaders 16

Management Too Is About People. 30

The Corporate Structure with Leaders and Managers 31

A Synthesis of the Major Differences Between Leadership and
    Management. 33

Differences Between Management and Leadership in Time Spent
    on Core Activities. 35

The Pillars of Leadership and Management 36

Leadership, Management, and Cultural Change 39

Organizational Culture Defined 42

Main Components of Culture 47

Organizational Culture and Change: Why Are They Important? 50

The Role of Culture in Change and Organizational Performance 51

The Role of Leadership in Building Culture and the Change Process . 54

The Change Process and Leadership. 57

Why Transformation Efforts Fail. 59

Common Approaches to Organizational Change 60

Why People Resist Change: The Leader's Real Challenge 62

The Five C's of the Individual Change Process. 64

Types of Organizational Change 70

What Organizations Change 71

Achieving Organizational Change with Leadership 72

Changing the Culture of the Organization. 74

Integration of Change Theories: A New Framework. 75

The Role of Leadership in Change. 77

Strategic Change and Leadership. 78

Leading Change, Culture, and Performance: Do Public
    Universities Have It?. 81

Leadership, Change, and Culture in Universities of the Twenty-
    First Century. 83

Leaders of the Future 86

The Role of Leaders and Cultural Change within the Public
    University 88

Conclusion 96

Endnotes. 98

High Performance: Elusive Ideal or Possible Reality? 109

What Does a High-Performance Organization Look Like?. 111

Common Characteristics of Successful Companies 116

Comparative Analysis of Loblaws and Sobeys 117

Framework for Organizational Evaluations .119

Time Telling 121

Clock Building. 122

The Profit Myth. 125

Core Ideology. 127

Visionary versus Comparison 128

Drive for Progress 129

Cultlike Culture, Trying Something New, and Learning from
    Mistakes. 131

Promoting from Within: How Do They Do It? 132

Better Off Tomorrow than Today, and Organizational Alignment . . 133

Building the Vision 135

A Comparison of the Characteristics of Successful Companies 137

Culture and Characteristics of Learning Organizations and
    Relationship to Transformational Leadership 142

Learning, Knowledge, and Competitive Advantage 143

Differences between Knowledge and Learning 145

Importance of Organizational Learning. 148

Importance of Individual and Organizational Learning and
    Leadership. 150

Developing a Learning Organization 153

Importance of Creating a Learning Culture. 155

Relationship between Coaching, Learning, Culture, and
    Transformational Leadership 158

Transformational Leadership and Learning Organizations 160

Leadership, Coaching, Learning, and Performance. 162

Learning and Transformational Leadership 166

Transformational Leadership and Firm Performance 169

Possible Paradigm for Understanding the Relationship between
    Transformational Leadership, Organizational Culture,
    Competitive Advantage, and Performance. 172

Conclusion 173

Endnotes. 174

Analysis of Leadership Styles 185

Trait Leadership. 186

Situational Leadership. 187

Transactional Leadership 188

Transformational Leadership 189

What Is a High-Performance Organization? 191

Transformational Leadership and Organizational Performance 193

Integration of Change Theories and a New Framework for
    Performance 195

The Role of Leadership in Change and Performance. 197

Leadership, Culture, and Performance: Is There a Relationship? 198

High-Performance Companies and Leadership in the Twenty-First
    Century 200

New Competency Framework for Leading Complex Change and
    Obtaining Performance 202

Leadership Characteristics That Work Well in High-Performance
    Organizations (A Comparison of Angiotech Pharmaceuticals
    and QLT Therapeutics). 203

Leaders of the Future Can Create High-Performance Organizations 205

The Role of Leaders and the Performance of the Organization 207

Company Comparisons of Key Financial Ratios 215

Conclusion 217

Endnotes. 219

Appendix A: Discussion of New Competency Framework for
    Leading Complex Change and Obtaining Performance 223

Appendix B: Life Cycles of Organizational Development 224

Appendix C: Traditional versus High-Performance Organizations . . 225

Appendix D: QLT Inc. Background and Company Description 231

Appendix E: Angiotech Pharmaceuticals Background and
    Company Description 232

Concluding Thoughts 234

Some Findings From the Study of Transformational Leadership 234

Link to Motivation 235

Role in Change 235

Benefits of Transformational Leadership 236

Endnotes. 237

Glossary 238

References 241

Preface

In researching the topic of leadership, I became so overwhelmed with the number of volumes and information available I honestly did not know where to start. Even after I received my PhD in organization and management with a specialization in leadership, I found that most books on the subject were confusing, limited, or focused on management rather than leadership. So I decided to write a fun book on the topic for my enjoyment, from my perspective, and based solely on my experiences and insights, which I am sure are similar in many ways to yours (I hope!).

I tried to make it light with levity, content-rich, slightly academic (in case some MBA students want some higher-order thinking), and also very practical, in case readers and some of my MBA students and colleagues want to implement some of the ideas contained in my book.

This book defines leadership and management and compares and contrasts their core elements while discussing the core issues that leaders and managers face in today's rapid-paced, highly competitive, and often too-complex-to-understand business environment.

The goals were simple: to get the stuff off my chest, to try to clarify a complex subject, to have fun writing, and to try to help others in the process. I really hope you enjoy the content, and I sincerely hope it is insightful and helps you with the subject in some small way. Enjoy the read.

Introduction

I have never really understood what it is about leaders that makes people want to follow them and do things that they themselves would not normally do. I have been in the presence of some of these people over the past forty years, but when I try to understand what makes them tick, I find that numerous books and articles use management theory as a guise to talk about leadership. Many of these authors know very little about leadership. In fact, of the 1,100 or so leadership books available, I would submit that fewer than 100 are really about leadership, and even fewer than that are worthy of the investment and the time necessary to read them. I should know, as I've bought and read most of them over the past twenty years or so. They are comprised of so many lofty expectations and mistruths or opinions that very little of the information contained in them can be used by the average person (the person who represents the general population that produces great leaders). My personal belief is that anyone can learn to become a leader if they really want to. Make no mistake about it—many people do not want to become leaders because of the commitment, the pressure, and the basic lack of respect that we, as a society, have for leaders of any kind.

What has encouraged me to write this book on leadership is the numerous positive comments I have received from people I have met over the last fifteen years or so as I have progressed in my quest to become a leader. I try to help others wherever I can. I try to put others before myself whenever I can. I always try to find time, day or night, to mentor or speak to others who may be struggling with an issue, a concept, or an illness. I always try to understand the other person's perspective. I always try to keep a positive attitude, work hard, commit myself to an organization, and make it better. I try to improve the people of an organization through communication, regular meetings, training, and personal and professional development. I really try to understand what motivates them. None of this is easy to do, and in many cases, it is almost impossible. However, leaders must develop others so that they can rise to a level of maximum potential.

What you are about to read is a culmination of skills and practices that I have learned in over fifteen years of leading others (and being led myself). For over twelve years, I have been teaching these skills to others through seminars, university courses, and general staff training sessions. I have seen the "lights" go on in the eyes of many men and women; these "aha" moments have given me great satisfaction and the energy to continue to develop myself and become (I hope) more effective at leading others. Now I have the opportunity to share my successes and my ideas of what I think leadership ought to be.

The terms "leadership," "management," and "discontinuous change" have become overused in today's business jargon, but they are still misused and poorly understood by many people, even those who are leading large, complex companies. For many of these people, leadership is management, and management is lower-level leadership. For others, discontinuous change is just change that is different from the last change, perhaps in both magnitude and scope. Everybody likes to use these terms, and while many have a good understanding of what they mean, these terms are still frequently misunderstood. Not everyone wants to be a leader, and not everyone is trained to deal with discontinuous change. The real question that needs to be answered is: Can we learn to be successful leaders and managers, and can we learn to deal with discontinuous change? The good news is that the answer is an emphatic *yes*.

As you will see throughout this book, the core elements of leadership and management are different. So there is no wonder that people confuse the terms and their meanings. In this book I try to put these issues into perspective; talk about them in clear, easy-to-understand terms; and blend the theory or major views with my own views and experiences so that readers can hopefully learn and apply the concepts to their daily business problems. Upon reflection, I really wonder if this is entirely possible. Well, here goes anyway …

What Is Leadership?

Being a leader can be many things to many people. It can be exciting, rewarding, and motivating, as well as challenging, lonely, and frustrating. The saying "It can be lonely at the top" is a great one for many leaders. Leaders are torn between not getting too close to employees and being available to build and lead the team to accomplish the organization's objectives.

Almost everyone has an opinion on what good leadership is. However, for those whose responsibility is leadership, it is often much more difficult and complex than just stating an opinion on the subject. Every organization has its own unique culture and characteristics, and success depends upon one's ability to work well within a very unique, dynamic, entrepreneurial, and ever-changing environment. In all organizations in which I have worked—from Seafreez Foods in Newfoundland to Maple Leaf Foods in Vancouver—high expectations were the norm, and *what* needed to be done was often much simpler and clearer than *how* we needed to do it. There were no employee orientations, no probationary period, and no HR department to help with training, and budgets had to be met without guidance on how to achieve them. They were sink-or-swim situations that were often daunting and very frustrating.

I was employed as a vice president of Canadian operations and campus director of the University of Phoenix in Vancouver, British Columbia, Canada, the first successful international venture of Apollo Group (parent company of the University of Phoenix). Perhaps because the university itself was so unique, some of the challenges it faced—and the solutions that were found—were somewhat unique.

However, after leading this venture in Canada for over ten years, I would submit that it is not unlike any other organization for which I have worked or led except that it has an intense focus on policies and procedures, a fanatical focus on compliance because of scrutiny in the US market, and generally a market-leading approach to employee and managerial/leader development. Annually, every employee must complete thirty-five to forty hours of professional development that is either

1

supplied or fully supported by managers and the executive team. In addition, there is a very intense and long new-employee orientation that could last from thirty to sixty days. And finally, from the first day on the job, all employees receive free tuition to complete their bachelor's degree and/or master's degree, and 75 percent off the tuition for a doctoral degree. I know of few other companies that support their employees and their personal development to the extent that the University of Phoenix does. It is a wonderful organization that is fast-paced, entrepreneurial, intensely focused, and well managed. In terms of management and leadership, it truly does practice what it preaches almost all the time.

This book on leadership is meant to serve as an outline for further leader and managerial discussion on what leadership means, what a leader does, what a leader is, and how management is sometimes similar yet distinctly different. It is meant to provide a practical, relevant, succinct, and reflective framework for discussion; to act as a guide for self-assessment; and to be used as a tool for leadership development in conjunction with other necessary development tools, such as management and leadership courses. It is a compilation of past leadership research, current thoughts and ideas from leadership experts, and my observations over the last decade on my leadership experiences in Canada.

Are Leaders Born or Made?

As mentioned earlier, leaders are *made,* not *born.* Many current leaders started in entry-level positions and probably did not have leadership characteristics when they were hired but developed them over their careers. In business, education, medicine, and unions, most current leaders have worked their way from lower-level positions to the executive ranks.

Often discussions of leadership include the names of high-profile business or world-renowned leaders, such as Margaret Thatcher, Jack Welch, or Bill Gates. These leaders' influence, charisma, reputations, and legacies have been felt at all levels across organizations, time, and space, and they continue to possess power even when they are not in power. These leaders, no doubt, have influenced millions of people and, in some cases, have revolutionized business. However, it is likely that our lives will be touched, influenced, and changed by leaders whose names are largely unknown but whose influence is more profound and significant within the circles of our lives. Think about school principals, fathers, mothers, big brothers, church and civic leaders, and sports coaches to find examples of local leaders who touch us all and have profound effects on us throughout our lives.

The debate is still raging as to whether leaders are born or raised, and it will not end soon (such is the world of academia). However, much of the current literature seems to be heading toward the latter. In the mid-nineteenth and early twentieth centuries, commentators and writers on leadership advanced the idea that history is shaped by great men who are endowed with unique characteristics and qualities and that these qualities capture the imagination of the masses and initiate movement that changes the course of history. While the Great Man theory is a good and somewhat interesting theory, and in some cases it may have been true (even of some "born" leaders), over the last four to five decades, this has not been mainstream. Subsequently, trait-leadership theories such as those developed by Mann and Stogdill[1] were developed from the assumption that if, as the Great Man theory suggests, leaders are differentiated from followers by their naturally endowed superior qualities, then these qualities should be identifiable. Although empirical studies and evidence have not supported the trait-theory assumption that leadership effectiveness is dependent upon certain traits,[2] myriad studies have identified many characteristics as being descriptive of the various skills or attributes possessed by leaders. According to Bernie Bass, these traits are

> social and interpersonal skills, administrative skills, technical skills, intellectual skills, leadership effectiveness and achievement, social nearness and friendliness, emotional balance and control, a drive to exercise initiative in social situations, a readiness to absorb interpersonal stress, a willingness to assume responsibility and accept the consequences of his or her decisions, and an ability to influence others' behaviors, and ethical conduct and personal integrity.[3]

For most of us, these traits are common sense, and we find them in many people around us. We just don't spend much time analyzing people to determine whether they have these characteristics or attributes. Maybe we should consider this as a good place to start learning about leadership. Researchers have found that the possession of certain traits increases the likelihood of leadership effectiveness but does not guarantee it. And it has not been established that certain traits are absolutely necessary for leadership effectiveness.

Stodgill offers the following summary of a trait-profile characteristic of a leader:

> The leader is characterized by a strong drive for responsibility and task completion, vigor and persistence in the pursuit of goals, venturesomeness and originality in problem solving, drive to exercise initiative in social situations, self-confidence and sense of personal identity, willingness to accept consequences of decision and action, readiness to absorb interpersonal stress, willingness to tolerate frustration and delay, ability to influence other persons' behavior, and capacity to structure social interaction systems to the purpose at hand.[4]

4

Again, these characteristics are found in many people we know, we tend not to think about them as formal leaders but rather as friends and personal contacts. It is possible that this traditional view of leadership, as the influence of gifted people with special traits and abilities, influencing followers to achieve societal or organizational goals, is reflective of a more industrial model of leadership of the past. Future leadership will be more about involving teams, sharing power and responsibility, empowering others, and "seeking to influence others and the conditions in which they work, allowing them to perform to their full potential and thus both increasing the probability of realizing the vision and maximizing the organizational and personal development of all parties involved."[5] This is a gold nugget about leadership, in my humble opinion, because today, more than ever (due to increased competition, globalization, and the speed-of-light pace of change), the success of leaders and their organizations depends, to a great extent, on the abilities of followers and their level of commitment to the team/organization.

> The success of leaders and their organizations depends, to a great extent, on the abilities of followers and their level of commitment to the team/organization.

What seems apparent is that excellent leaders possess certain qualities and characteristics no matter the culture in which they live.[6] For some, these characteristics may be an inherent and natural part of their personality, while for many others, they may have to work hard at developing them and may never succeed in doing so.

Although leadership skills and attributes can be learned or developed by most, not everyone has the ability, desire, personality, or ambition to become a leader. Leadership is very hard work and does not come easily. One must decide if one has the traits, attributes, desire, and ambition to lead. This is another important point regarding leadership: wanting it determines, to a large degree, the effort put forward to acquire the skills and development necessary to become a successful leader. It does not just show up on the doorstep, knock

> Wanting it determines, to a large degree, the effort put forward to acquire the skills and development necessary to become a successful leader.

on the door, and come on a platter engraved with "Leader" on it. It takes learning, training, pushing, pulling, volunteering, scratching your head, figuring out people and complex problems, networking, helping others more than yourself, and working longer hours than you really want to while feeling like you are really in over your head. You need lots of energy, drive, passion, and commitment, and you require a belief in lifelong learning.

IS LEADERSHiP iN YOU?

Why Would You Want to Be a Leader?

Just thinking about the challenges facing today's leaders gives many people the shivers. As my grandfather Blake was fond of saying, "more shivers than a bowl of Jell-O"—leadership is difficult and demanding. It is a thankless task that requires tremendous amounts of time, effort, and personal and family sacrifice, and it requires a focus on the wants and needs of others, as opposed to "self." The energy and intensity required to be a leader means leadership is not for everyone. Leaders (and potential leaders) must be aware of the level of commitment required and have a realistic sense of what leadership entails. Leadership requires a willingness to do things that other people are often less willing or able to do, and it means having followers who end up doing something that they would not normally do. They work and end up achieving things they did not think were possible. And leaders have to be able to get them to do it while they are smiling along the way (my way of describing motivation for the journey)—no easy task.

Leadership is born of a desire, a passion, and a commitment to make a contribution to an organization or society and to make a difference. Leaders take charge and enjoy the responsibility and challenge of leading. This is who they are and what they enjoy doing. They "see no other option to achieving their vision and bringing about what they believe are significant and needed changes."[7] Leaders also understand and tend to enjoy the rewards and tremendous benefits of leadership. Simply put, they like people and what can be achieved through people. They value the satisfaction that comes from articulating a vision, helping others, changing lives, accomplishing tasks, and making a difference. They appreciate the additional rewards of power, position, respect, and financial gain that often accompany leadership positions, and most leaders would not change these things even if they could. These things are the soul food that true leaders crave, and they tend to want to give back to others, because they were "blessed" with good fortune.

When becoming a leader, one accepts the challenges, sacrifices, and commitments that go with it. As a leader, one's life will undoubtedly change dramatically from what it was like before. Leaders have to set examples for everything they do. They may have to give up some of the closeness they may feel toward peers, work longer hours, and dedicate more of their personal time to the demands of leadership and its accompanying responsibilities. Leaders recognize that the additional time, pressure, and responsibility required are most always offset by the intrinsic and extrinsic rewards of additional power, status, or money that may accompany the leadership position. Leaders also understand "the issue of balance pales in comparison to the power of possibly realizing a significant vision and influencing one's own destiny."[8]

In considering leadership, Bennis and Goldsmith[9] have identified four personal responsibilities of leaders, or demands that most constituents want from their leaders. They are: (1) purpose, direction, and meaning; (2) trust; (3) optimism; and (4) action and results. They suggest that leadership traits can be strengthened, and skills can be developed by each person who has a true desire to become a leader. However, being aware of the commitment and sacrifices that leaders must make may ensure that we do not all achieve the same level of success or even satisfaction as leaders. Sure, leaders must have purpose, direction, and meaning, but they must be able to articulate these things to others as well. Oddly enough, many successful leaders will tell you that while they possess these things, they had coaches, mentors, colleagues, and friends who helped them internalize and understand what it all meant before they became successful themselves. That is, *they learned a lot of what they know by watching, communicating, networking, following, trying, and practicing what others before them and around them were doing.* Yes, they learned what it took to be successful.

> They learned a lot of what they know by watching, communicating, networking, following, trying, and practicing what others before them and around them were doing.

Leadership versus Management: The Balancing Act

The debate over what leadership is, as compared to management, has been raging for decades, with no signs of slowing down. There are over a thousand books on the subject of leadership (over 1,500 by my count this year), so why another one? Good question. I think it is because I find most of them confusing and hard to put into context. So I decided to write my own, mostly for me and hopefully for you, so that the topic of leadership would be just a sliver more clear (the Newfoundlander in me coming through). Both leadership and management are essential to the success of organizations, and even though they are considered and discussed in the same context, there are distinct differences between the two. Management is generally considered to be about doing things *right*, while leadership is about doing the *right* things. Managing is about efficiency, and leading is about effectiveness. Management is tasked with the responsibility of accomplishing objectives, executing plans, and preparing budgets, while leadership is centered on the broad and encompassing role of providing the vision, direction, and inspiration for the organization. It is with the leader that the responsibility rests in looking to the future and assuring others that the organization is on the right course to success.

Bennis and Goldsmith[10] suggest that management is about systems, controls, procedures, policies, and structure, and that leadership is about innovation, initiation, trust, and people. Kotter,[11] a professor of leadership at the Harvard Business School, summarizes the role of management as (1) planning and budgeting, (2) organizing and staffing, and (3) controlling and problem-solving. Also, he explains that management is a set of processes that can keep a complicated system of people and technology running smoothly. Leadership defines what the future should look like. In addition, the role of leadership can be summarized as (1) establishing direction, (2) aligning people, (3) articulating vision, and (4) motivating, empowering, and inspiring. It is important to note that in offering this explanation, Kotter does not suggest that the two are mutually exclusive. In my dissertation, I argued that leadership and management are balanced like the stones of Stonehenge, and any out-of-balance elements causes one or both to fall. One relies on the other for organizational growth and mission execution (the lasting effect of the organization).

In fact, in today's fast-paced and ever-changing organizations, management often thinks in terms of "managing change," but 70 to 90 percent of successful transformation requires leadership and leadership skills. Kotter asserts that understanding the fundamental differences in the roles of managers and leaders is crucial to any successful change effort.

Although some leaders manage and some managers lead, the two are not synonymous. Leaders have specific roles and responsibilities, as do managers, and it is the *task* that defines the differences. Managing is really a much more complex process than just controlling, organizing, planning, and directing; a manager's effectiveness depends upon that person's ability to get things done through other people. Organizational size, as well as hierarchical level and structure, can certainly influence and define the role of the manager. The nature of the business, the environment within which it operates and the levels of the tasks performed, all influence the scope of each role, as well as the mix of managerial or leadership tasks required.[12]

According to Bennis, there are clear distinctions between the roles of managers versus those of leaders.

> The leader is charged with doing the right thing, the manager with doing things right. The leader takes the long view, the manager the short view. The leader concentrates on the *what* and *why*, while the manager focuses on *how*. The leader has the vision, the manager has the hands-on control. The leader thinks in terms of innovation, development, the future, while the manager is busy with administration, maintenance, the present. The leader sets the tone and direction, both inside and outside the company, while the manager sets the pace.[13]

Managers are more often involved in *how* things should be done and in managing the short term and the bottom line; leaders are involved in *what* should be done, and in the vision, mission, and strategic plan. Management generally has more to do with *efficiency* (systems and procedures), while leadership has more to do with *effectiveness* (vision and direction). Efficiency (management) has more to do with implementation, while effectiveness (leadership) is all about focusing the organization's energy in a particular direction. That being said, leaders have to be able to be both effective and efficient, and leadership needs to be involved in not only the vision but also the implementation. Although management may be characterized by efficiency and implementation, and leadership may be characterized by effectiveness and vision, they are not mutually exclusive, nor is one exclusively management and the other exclusively leadership. According to management gurus Ken Blanchard and James Bolt, both are the responsibility of the leader.[14]

According to Zaleznik,[15] leaders differ from managers with respect to their attitude regarding change. Those who embrace chaos become true leaders. Managers focus on creating and maintaining order, while leaders focus on new approaches and ideas. Leaders exert influence by shaping moods and ideas, evoking images, and establishing objectives, all of which determine the company's direction. Rather than conserving the existing order, leaders strive to alter organizational structures.

Although leadership is often defined in more ideal and lofty terms, and management is relegated to the more mundane and mechanistic, the role of management should never be discounted. Sometimes what an organization needs is not another vision or change in direction. The complex nature of managerial positions usually includes a broad range of responsibilities and requires a wide range of skill sets and knowledge. Many managerial positions involve responsibilities that are more leadership in nature than managerial. What begins to become clear from the literature is that the successful leaders of the future will have to be efficient and effective and have some managerial skills. Competitive and changing environments call for managers who have strong leadership skills and leaders who know how to manage.

See, I told you that everything would start to become clearer as you read. Yes, you say it is clear (clear as muddy water, right?). Okay, so what then is the role of the leader today? You will find out very soon. Trust me! Trust is necessary for leader and subordinate success.

Role of a Leader

Leaders do many things. Leaders create a vision and encourage others to follow them as they make the vision a reality. Leaders are able to convince followers that their vision is the right one for the organization and, in doing so, set the example for others as they lead the execution of the vision. There are so many books available on leadership, the role of the leader, and what makes a good leader that it is difficult to know where to start. Leadership experts define leadership in slightly different terms; however, most agree that the role of the leader includes the following: formulating and communicating a vision for the organization, adding value to their organizations, and leading an organizational imperative to inspire and motivate followers.[16] Management is more about the traditional activities revolving around and related to planning, organizing, directing, and controlling.[17]

A leader formulates and communicates a vision. In all the literature reviewed, the recurring theme focused on the responsibility of the leader to articulate, define, and put into action the core values of the organization. Leaders define a vision in terms that enable others to want to follow them to achieve the vision. This responsibility, more than any other, is the defining characteristic of leadership.[18] Without a compelling vision, without clearly articulated values, goals and objectives become mundane, and the tenacity, passion, and drive to achieve the vision is lost; long-term success is jeopardized. Once defined and articulated, the leader must champion the vision and communicate it to *all* levels of the organization. It is the main duty of the leader. Once this is accomplished, the leader ensures that everyone has the opportunity to participate in making the vision a reality. Ultimately, the success of the organization is dependent on the vision and its articulation, commitment by all levels of the organization, and the leader's ability to ensure that the resulting vision is the correct one for the organization.

> The vision is a framework or a lens through which everything that goes on in the organization can be viewed, evaluated, and interpreted.

A vision is the focal point of the organization, the "fountain of youth" where everything else revolves around it. It gives all organizational members a common point of reference, a source of energy for the journey of change ahead. It makes it easier to communicate performance expectations and outcomes, and to measure performance against those clearly defined expectations. The vision is a framework or a lens through which everything that goes on in the organization can be viewed, evaluated, and interpreted. Given that an organization's resources are limited, the focus must be on activities that embody, incorporate, and aid in the execution of the vision.

A leader adds value to the organization. A leader is a visionary of sorts and sees people, events, issues, and the "right path" within the context of the vision. Many, if not the vast majority of, organizations are functional in design and are run by specialists in their fields. As a result, leaders must be able to cross boundaries with ease to enable these "specialists" to see the vision for the organization, which they might not otherwise see. Leaders are generalists in this sense and have the uncanny ability of foresight—to connect ideas, activities, thoughts, systems, processes, and people at all levels of the organization. The leader adds value by providing context, making the leap across to join organizational boundaries, and remaining fixated on the vision and ensuring others are committed and focused on the same vision. Leaders also add value when they remove barriers that inhibit followers from committing to and seeing the full and powerful impact of the vision. These barriers may take many forms and include, but are not limited to, procedural, physical, perceptual, and political.

> The leader adds value by providing context, making the leap across to join organizational boundaries, and remaining fixated on the vision and ensuring others are committed and focused on the same vision.

A leader inspires and motivates. The leader leads by example, the imperative to inspire and motivate. It is the responsibility of the leader to communicate the vision developed in such an inspiring and convincing way that people want to follow and help make the vision reality. People in general, and employees in particular,

> The key is to inspire and motivate all to the extent that the overall vision becomes the vision of each individual who chooses to voluntarily and enthusiastically embrace it as their own. Only then will success become reality.

14

are good and committed, and they want to do a good job. They want to cling to a vision that makes an organization stronger, more open, and responsive to their needs. Leaders unite the people and gain their commitment to this vision by motivating them to act. Leaders are instrumental in helping to facilitate and coach the employees' interpretation and understanding of what goes on in an organization. The more they understand, and the clearer the vision is to them, the better able they are to contribute and commit to it. Leaders are able to inspire confidence where there is doubt, commitment where it is lacking, and motivation where there is none, to unlock the creative potential from followers. The key is to inspire and motivate all to the extent that the overall vision becomes the vision of each individual who chooses to voluntarily and enthusiastically embrace it as their own. Only then will success become reality.

> Leaders are instrumental in helping to facilitate and coach the employees' interpretation and understanding of what goes on in an organization. The more they understand, and the clearer the vision is to them, the better able they are to contribute and commit to it.

Effective leaders display a well-developed ability to inspire and motivate people at all levels of the organization. They have the ability to uncover individual creativity and make it collective and contagious. They develop and voluntarily get follower loyalty and ownership. They empower people to experiment and develop new ideas. And they even let people fail, as long as they learn from the process and their mistakes. Good leaders know that lessons learned from mistakes can be as powerful, if not more so, than lessons learned from successes. They are also acutely aware that the lessons learned from both successes and failures contribute to the vision, the culture, and organizational learning, which are imperative for long-term success.

> Leaders have the ability to uncover individual creativity and make it collective and contagious; they develop and voluntarily get follower loyalty and ownership; they empower people to experiment and develop new ideas; and, they even let people fail as long as they learn from the process and their mistakes. Good leaders know that lessons learned from mistakes can be as powerful if not more so than lessons learned from successes. They are also acutely aware that the lessons learned from both successes and failures contribute to the vision, the culture, and organizational learning which are imperative for long-term success.

Skills, Qualities, Characteristics, and Attributes of Leaders

Although there is no singular pattern of characteristics for leaders, researchers, and students of leadership, leaders themselves have identified common skills, qualities, characteristics, and attributes that emerge repeatedly and are generally accepted as necessary for leaders to be successful and effective. Arguably the most important and crucial of these is credibility—the ability to trust the leader's word, trust that the leader is personally committed to the direction in which that person is leading the organization, and trust that the leader has the knowledge, skills, integrity, and competence to lead.[19] Handy[20] and others suggest that a leader must possess three inherent attributes: a belief in oneself, a passion for the job, and a love for people. I would submit that a good leader needs all of these, which is why so few people are actually good leaders.

Leaders believe in themselves. Leaders have self-confidence and believe in themselves, their capabilities, and their abilities.[21] If leaders do not have confidence in themselves, how can they have confidence in others? This self-confidence is strong enough to persuade others to act and follow the leader and should be coupled with humility to recognize and admit that one does not always have all the answers. Leaders are capable of self-assessment and self-analysis, and they never let their ego get in the way of their willingness to listen intently and sincerely to others, or to accept and embrace the contribution of others. Humility allows leaders to admit that they do not have all the answers.

> Humility allows leaders to admit that they do not have all the answers.

> Being a leader means being really busy and well connected in a plethora of social settings, both formal and informal.

A leader is willing to continually learn, admit mistakes, and make necessary adjustments to improve leadership skills. Leaders will make mistakes, and what makes them leaders and distinguishes them from others is how they deal with failure. Making mistakes does not make leaders question their ability; it makes them work harder to achieve, and it motivates them to do better.

Failure is not really an option a leader accepts easily or readily. When they do fail, leaders learn from their mistakes.

Leaders will make mistakes, and what makes them leaders and distinguishes them from others is how they deal with failure. Making mistakes does not make leaders question their ability; it makes them work harder to achieve, and it motivates them to do better.

Leaders have a genuine passion for the job. This passion provides both the energy and focus that drives the organization, serves as a catalyst for change, and is a source of endless enthusiasm and motivation throughout the organization. At the same time, leaders tend to be social and increase their awareness by being involved in activities outside the organization and their sphere of influence. Leaders are able to capitalize on unanticipated day-to-day events. They need a broad network of relationships, which let them, through spontaneous, formal, and informal encounters, persuade others far beyond their chain of command to support their vision. Leaders read, challenge, help, train, educate, mentor, socialize, and draw ideas from a broad spectrum of sources in order to garner the experiences and perspectives necessary to cope with the demands of leadership and to keep the passion for the job alive. Being a leader means being really busy and well connected in a plethora of social settings, both formal and informal.

Good leaders also operate on the premise that people are inherently good, that they mean well, and that their intentions are noble. They believe in people, and they believe that if given the appropriate information and a chance, people will do the right thing.

Leaders have a love for people. Leadership is about people. Leaders lead people; managers manage things. There cannot be a leader without followers. Leaders have a genuine love for people, and they believe in their inherent goodness and capabilities, they want to understand and motivate them, and they sincerely desire to grow people

---

A strong, effective leader is constantly focused on the vision, rarely confuses activity with results, has the ability to effectively delegate, and can lead teams to success.

---

to achieve their full potential. A leader sees as his main purpose cultivating people and developing leadership throughout the organization. Leaders who do not believe in people, may be respected and even feared and in the short-term; they may be coerced into following, however, long-term, that leader will have no followers. This is a critical point, because leadership is about people, and convincing people to follow on an unknown path toward an unknown future is no easy task. People need leaders and want to be motivated, successful, and heard, and they need to positively contribute to a cause. Good leaders understand and demand this from their followers. Good leaders also operate on the premise that people are inherently good, that they mean well, and that their intentions are noble. They believe in people, and they believe that if given the appropriate information and a chance, people will do the right thing.

According to Bennis, it does not matter how wise, shrewd, or visionary a leader is; a corporation is a collective endeavor, and it needs the collective wisdom, canniness, and vision of all its employees to function at the optimum level.[22] This is the fundamental tenet of leadership.

It is somewhat paradoxical that at the same time the leader must be social and be involved in outside activities, a leader must also have a capacity for aloneness. By the very nature of the position, leadership is sometimes very lonely, and the leader cannot always share concerns and fears with others. The expression "It is lonely at the top" comes to mind. Handy summarized that great leaders have to walk alone from time to time. They also have to live vicariously, deriving their satisfaction from the successes of others and giving those others the recognition that they themselves are often denied.[23]

Successful leaders, no matter their personal style, tend to have certain characteristics, core traits, and skills that contribute to their success and often differentiate them from non-leaders. Many of the characteristics commonly found in good leaders suggest that they tend to have drive, a desire to lead, honesty and integrity, self-confidence, and cognitive ability to make good decisions; and they know their business.[24] An important characteristic of a successful leader's cognitive agility is the ability to see relationships amongst, and cause and

> The real challenge of the leader is to unlock the potential of the workers and unleash the human productive spirit to achieve extraordinary results.

effect between, seemingly unrelated or disparate issues, and the ability to make better decisions because of this characteristic. This is part and parcel of the value that a leader brings to an organization and cannot be underestimated. A strong, effective leader is constantly focused on the vision, rarely confuses activity with results, has the ability to effectively delegate, and can lead teams to success. A good leader demonstrates commitment, tolerance, maturity, and wisdom.

After decades of focusing on process improvement and organizational strategies, organizations have often failed to recognize the most important factor in success: the power and productive potential of people. To the leader, people are an organization's most valuable asset; this is unequivocal. According to Krames, Jack Welch, the CEO of General Electric for over two decades, believes strongly in removing shackles and releasing the competitive spirit of the workers.[25] The real challenge of the leader is to unlock the potential of the workers and unleash the human productive spirit to achieve extraordinary results.

Willingham claimed that a good leader is one who can achieve results through other people, and he identified twelve characteristics often noticed in effective leaders: vision, charisma, character, responsibility, planning, social skills, achievement drive, emotional stability, tolerance for ambiguity, decisiveness, delegation, and a positive outlook.[26] The list of characteristics identified by Willingham summarizes most of the key characteristics that many researchers and practitioners of leadership have identified.

Leaders are people of integrity. They keep their word even if it means personal risk and sacrifice. They walk the talk (many *run* the talk) and practice what they preach. They always do what they say, and they expect the same from their followers. They must earn the trust of those they lead, and trust cannot be built where there is no integrity. Behaving with integrity means being honest, ethical, and consistent in one's actions, attitudes, and choices. By definition, and by the very nature of leadership, a leader is only a leader if that person has followers. Although a leader may hold a formal leadership position and have the legitimate authority to lead, people will willingly follow when they respect and trust the leader.

> To the leader, people are an organization's most valuable asset; this is unequivocal.

Credibility is one of the most important traits any leader can possess. Credibility breeds trust and respect, and it is this respect that enables a leader to lead.

Covey suggested three character traits that are essential to what he refers to as "primary greatness": (1) integrity, (2) maturity, and (3) an abundance

> Credibility is one of the most important traits any leader can possess. Credibility breeds trust and respect, and it is this respect that enables a leader to lead.

mentality. He stated that a character rich in integrity, maturity, and the abundance mentality has a genuineness that goes far beyond technique.[27] Also, he suggested that these characteristics are necessary to align "public performance" with "private performance," thus developing trust and openness in others.

Leaders are effective communicators and listeners. Leaders make every effort to be in front of their people as often as possible, listening intently and seeking to understand. They communicate

> Leaders clearly define expectations and help people to exceed them, whether they believe they can or not.

effectively, providing context and perspective, sharing the broader spectrum and the realities within which the organization operates, and communicating the vision. They often encourage and demand input, spirited debate, and diversity of opinion in making decisions, and they genuinely respect the contribution of others. Leaders align people when a decision is made and expect all participants to enthusiastically embrace the decision and move forward as a team to make the chosen vision a reality. Leaders clearly define expectations and help people to exceed them, whether they believe they can or not.

Leaders embrace and lead change. Leaders embrace change and thrive on chaos. They can see through it all and understand that it is a necessary ingredient for continuous improvement and a higher level of success. Leaders must be willing to continually evaluate every product, service, process, distribution channel, and customer in an effort to seek new opportunities and abandon efforts that are no longer producing the desired results.[28] Dynamic environments require dynamic leaders, people with a constant willingness to evaluate, change, learn, and improve.

Leadership requires incredible energy. Jack Welch defines leaders as people who have energy and are able to energize others. Out of the four E's of leadership, two refer to energy. In looking for a successor, Jack Welch set as key criteria somebody "with incredible energy who can excite others, who can define their vision, who finds change fun and doesn't get paralyzed by it."[29] A leader leads by example, with enthusiasm and persistent energy on constant display. This energy is born of passion for the job and strong personal convictions, and it manifests itself in a consistent and relentless quest for excellence, change, improvement, and achievement. A leader's energy breathes life into an organization, sets the example and pace for the entire organization, and is contagious. Leadership is not easy; it is tough work. It requires long days and nights; travel; and a constant onslaught of disparate, complex, and challenging issues. It requires mental agility, alertness, perspective, and empathy—to understand and feel the needs of others, and to know what to say, when to say it, and how to say it. A leader's energy is replenished by facing challenges, helping others, and continually improving.

Leaders lead by example. Leaders work hard, work smart, and lead by example. They abhor mediocrity and expect and demand excellence—of themselves and of their followers. They arrive at work early, stay late, and achieve many tasks during a typical day. Although long hours are certainly not a key measurement of leadership, leading by example often requires that followers see the leader's energy, stamina, and willingness to do "whatever it takes to get the job done." They work smart, thinking things through, quickly evaluating all possibilities, and exploring the implications of the various alternatives. They question assumptions and leave nothing to chance—no stone unturned. They understand that a sound plan will hold up under scrutiny.

> Leadership is not easy, and because of the attributes and activities required to be a good leader, many people may tend to shy away from its challenges and the personal sacrifices required to "make it" as a leader.

Because leadership requires incredible energy, a wise leader also sets an example by eating right, exercising, getting plenty of rest, avoiding self-destructive behaviors, finding time for self-reflection, learning, teaching, and serving others. These activities bring self-renewal, more energy, a fresh perspective when needed, and, of course, a passion for leading. Leadership is not easy, and because of the attributes and activities required to be a good leader, many people may tend to shy away from its challenges and the personal sacrifices required to "make it" as a leader.

Leaders develop other leaders. Leaders help other people learn to lead and see this as a primary goal. This is perhaps my deepest concurrence with what good leaders generally believe and do. They want people to work more efficiently, generate more ideas, and exercise more creativity and initiative. True leaders know this strategy is a true source of power and pro-

> As leaders develop other leaders, leadership is dispersed across the organization, which increases energy levels in the organization and compounds its effects. That is what true leaders do—they provide tremendous energy themselves and release it from others for the compound effect.

ductivity. Leaders put time and effort into, and believe in, succession planning. They are always on the lookout for new talent they can use in helping them achieve their goals and visions. True leaders know that real power comes from people, their commitment and energy, and the release or unleashing of the human spirit. Leaders also know that people are an organization's most valuable asset, and their learning and knowledge are the sources of competitive advantage for organizations of the future. It is no surprise then that they strive to develop other leaders at *all* levels in the organization. Leaders are deeply concerned with hiring the right people. Leaders know people want to do what they are built to do, which is to positively contribute. Leaders understand that most people really want to do a good job. They have the ability to offer people intrinsic rewards, the tremendous lift that comes from doing a good job, being recognized for it, and having someone believe in their abilities. Good leaders are masters of this type of motivating. Leaders develop others to help them lead while adding value to the organization. They are able to get people to coalesce around organizational goals, but not at the expense or exclusion of individual goals while at the same time, constantly reinforcing the organization's vision and values. When an organization performs well, a good leader ensures employees do well. As leaders develop other leaders, leadership is dispersed across the organization, which increases energy levels in the organization and compounds its effects. That is what true leaders do—they provide tremendous energy themselves and release it from others for the compound effect.

Leadership is building confidence. Leadership is about building confidence and trusting others. Leaders have it and instill it in others. Leaders know that by building confidence, developing others, and creating trust, they are unleashing the competitiveness and productivity of the human spirit, which is the tool whereby ordinary people achieve extraordinary results. Leadership is an art, and in order to better perform this art, a leader must master the self first. Ultimately, leadership development is a process of learning and self-development. Kouzes and Posner perhaps said it best when they said, "The quest for leadership is first an inner quest to discover who you are. Through self-development comes the confidence to lead. Self-confidence is really awareness of and faith in your own powers."[30]

> Self-confidence allows the leader to have confidence in, and support for, the advancement of others. Self-confidence leads to sharing of power, or empowering others, which unleashes human potential and results in extraordinary results from ordinary people.

Self-confidence enables the leader to undertake the difficult ventures necessary to meet his or her goals.[31] Self-confidence allows the leader to have confidence in, and support for, the advancement of others. Self-confidence leads to sharing of power, or empowering others, which unleashes human potential and results in extraordinary results from ordinary people.

Leadership is creating, articulating, and executing a vision. Vision is the first important characteristic of leadership. Leaders who can ignite passion and spark imagination with an accurate and compelling vision of a desired end state that moves us beyond our static boundaries, and who can translate that into clear objectives, are the ones we readily follow. Successful leaders develop goals and people to achieve their vision. Their commitment to goals and the success of others, and thus to the vision, is transparent and blatantly obvious by their actions, focus, intensity, and repeated communication of what must be done and why. Good leaders communicate constantly and are always in front of their followers, influencing, encouraging, critiquing, and listening. Leaders convey an understanding that communication is a two-way process in which leaders listen, hunger for feedback and new ideas, and are driven by a need to compel and to influence, not to command and control.[32] Bennis based his ideas about leadership "on the assumption that leaders are people who are able to express themselves fully. They also know what they want, why they want it, and how to communicate what they want to others, in order to gain their cooperation and support."[33]

Leadership is about results. Leadership is primarily about coping with and embracing change while delivering results. Leaders seem to have the uncanny ability to distinguish between the seemingly impossible and the genuinely impossible. Effective leaders are able to harness the creative power of the human spirit and lead organizations to achieve great things. The most effective change processes are incremental; they happen everywhere consistently and build over time as commitment levels increase. So too do extraordinary results. Leaders strive for commitment, buy-in, and action from the entire organization, and at the same time, they focus on small wins to build employees' commitment to the vision they have created. Small wins form the basis for a consistent pattern of winning that attracts people and increases energy, which, in turn, increases productivity. Leaders know that most people want to be on a winning team. Leaders deliberately cultivate a strategy of small wins to achieve their long-term strategy of making their vision for the organization reality. Leaders achieve this by mobilizing for fast action, sustaining commitment, and experimenting continuously.

> Leaders seem to have the uncanny ability to distinguish between the seemingly impossible and the genuinely impossible.

Leaders achieve results. They strive for personal growth—top-line, bottom-line, sustainable, rapid growth. They measure results by their commitment from their followers. True leaders want to achieve extraordinary results from their followers and know that, in order to do this, they must promote a strong, open, trusting culture where employees are valued, are treated with respect, and have fun as they achieve their goals. Leaders know they have been successful when there is leadership at *all* levels of the organization, and the sum of the whole is much greater than the sum of the parts.

Leaders have emotional intelligence. Goleman, perhaps the foremost authority on emotional intelligence (EI), refers to "the capacity for recognizing our own feelings and those of others, for motivating ourselves, and for managing emotions well in ourselves and in our relationships."[34] A leader has to have the emotional capacity to tolerate uncertainty, frustration, and social pain. Leaders, simply, bring out the best in people. A leader's emotional maturity is exemplified by such capabilities as self-awareness, social skills, empathy, and a strong relationship to performance. According to Goleman, Boyatzis, and McKee, "the leader's mood and its attendant behaviors affect the bottom line by driving the moods and behaviors of everyone else."[35] A leader's emotional intelligence creates a certain culture or work environment. A high level of emotional intelligence possessed by the leader creates a climate in which information sharing, trust, healthy risk-taking, and learning flourish. A low level of emotional intelligence creates a climate rife with fear and anxiety. According to Goleman and others, "a leader needs to make sure that not only is he regularly optimistic, authentic, has a high-energy mood, but also that, through his chosen actions, his followers feel and act that way too."[36] Leaders must make emotional contact with their followers. They have to help people find meaning in the face of chaos and uncertainty. Leaders are attuned to, exude, and express the shared emotional reality of the given situation. Understanding the feelings of others, caring, and building a strong network both inside and outside the organization are crucial to long-term success.

> Leaders know they have been successful when there is leadership at *all* levels of the organization, and the sum of the whole is much greater than the sum of the parts.

Leaders have courage. Leaders are, or appear to be, unflappable during periods of crisis. Leaders have to be capable of dealing with danger—maybe not actual physical danger, but problems and issues that demand real courage. Leaders possess courage to change the status quo, act alone, be unpopular, and stand up for what they believe in yet, at the same time, show energy and passion and release it to others while achieving the organization's goals.

> Leaders have to be decisive, set clear directions, and keep everything moving while being calm in the face of danger. Leaders have to continually show they are not immobilized by crisis.

Leaders have to be decisive, set clear directions, and keep everything moving while being calm in the face of danger. Leaders have to continually show they are not immobilized by crisis.

Failure plays a true role in success. Learning from mistakes is true learning, and courage is the tenet of risk-taking. Leaders have the courage to take risks. Leaders have a strong willingness to stand up for one's beliefs, challenge others, openly admit mistakes, and change one's behavior when necessary. For most, admitting being wrong is one of the hardest things a person can do, yet a good leader is not afraid to do this, even in public. Leaders know that this will only make them stronger as they grow and learn from mistakes.

> For most, admitting being wrong is one of the hardest things a person can do, yet a good leader is not afraid to do this, even in public. Leaders know that this will only make them stronger as they grow and learn from mistakes.

> Consistent practice of high moral standards, a high regard for the needs of people, and a proven track record are what build credibility. Leaders who are consistent and epitomize credibility live out their values every day, for all to see. They do not make commitments unless they are going to keep them.

> Promoting trust is an essential component of any and all leadership regardless of context, style, industry, organization, culture, or country. Without a high level of trust, a leader will probably falter and ultimately fail.

Leadership is consistency and credibility. Trust is the foundation of leadership. Without trust, people cannot and will not follow for long. To build trust, a leader must exemplify a high level of competence and character. And character makes trust possible. Trust may just be a leader's most precious and valuable asset. Leaders with inner strength or character communicate consistency. Consistent practice of high moral standards, a high regard for the needs of people, and a proven track record are what build credibility. Leaders who are consistent and epitomize credibility live out their values every day, for all to see. They do not make commitments unless they are going to keep them. Good leaders go out of their way to be credible and to personify integrity. Without these traits and daily behaviors, leaders cannot remain leaders

> True leaders replenish their energy through their passion for work and their giving to others and the greater good. A leader with great passion ignites the hearts of others, and a leader with great skill and no passion, rarely remains a leader for long. Passion is the fountain of youth, driver of dreams, and creator of continuous energy needed for success long term.

for long, because people will not follow them. And, as you know, leaders who do not have followers are not, by definition, leaders. So by now you can begin to see how simple this seemingly complex topic is becoming.

Leaders consistently promote trust to build their credibility.[37] Promoting trust is an essential component of any and all leadership regardless of context, style, industry, organization, culture, or country. Without a high level of trust, a leader will probably falter and ultimately fail.

Leadership is passion. Effective leaders are passionate about their work, the cause of the organization they are promoting, their commitment to developing other leaders, and the public greater good. A good leader has a passion for giving others what they themselves have been given and have learned over their careers. Leaders make commitments beyond "self," both inside and outside the organization. Passion requires honesty and self-confidence in *who* you are as a person. Effective leaders have to be themselves. Leadership requires great focus and intensity, as well as extraordinary energy levels. True leaders replenish their energy through their passion for work and their giving to others and the greater good. A leader with great passion ignites the hearts of others, and a leader with great skill and no passion, rarely remains a leader for long. Another bit of advice here: if you do not have a passion for the job, mission, company, and industry, get out of the position or company, and find what you care about, because you will not end up being as successful here as you will there. Passion is the fountain of youth, driver of dreams, and creator of continuous energy needed for success long term.

Leadership is great focus and intensity. The sharper the focus, the sharper the leader (well, that's the theory—or the academic in me coming out anyway). Leaders are experts at prioritizing and concentrating on the challenges and barriers that need to be solved in order to move forward. According to Maxwell, "a leader who knows his priorities but lacks concentration knows what to do but never gets it done. If he has concentration but no priorities, he has excellence without progress. But when he harnesses both, he has the potential to achieve great things."[38] Leaders focus on developing their strengths, but they also continue to doggedly work on their weaknesses.

Leaders spend lots of time working on their weaknesses to make them better leaders overall. The weaknesses may never become strengths, but they will become minimal, and the strengths will become points of excellence. They also focus on new things, because growth equals change. And leaders embrace change, they view change as a friend. Focus and intensity drive results. Leaders know this. They focus on creating and articulating their vision, building trust and credibility, developing others, leading by setting the example, and doing, and this is all practiced with an intensity that is boundless—that is, constantly replenished.

Leadership is giving power away. Exemplary leaders make other people feel strong, welcome, valued, and important. They understand that when they do, the chance of achieving their vision is improved. Leaders enable others to take ownership of and responsibility for the organization's success. External control tends to inhibit or erode intrinsic motivation. True leaders understand this and empower others to achieve results and give them credit for doing so. This is one of the things I have struggled with the most in my years as a leader, because I always assume people are self-motivated, and have a difficulty understanding why more people don't get it, want it, need it. I guess I have

> External control tends to inhibit or erode intrinsic motivation. True leaders understand this and empower others to achieve results and give them credit for doing so.

been very fortunate in that I have never suffered from a lack of intrinsic motivation to do the best job possible and learn as much as I can from others along the way. Leaders are instrumental in creating organizational climates where employees are involved and told they are the organization's most important assets. Leaders mean this when they say it. To create this climate and maintain its operation, leaders use power in the service of others, not in service of their own personal interests. Though given the issues cropping up daily on Wall Street/Bay Street with many well-known leaders and companies (WorldCom and Bernie Saunders, Anderson Consulting, SNC Lavalin, bribery, etc.,), one could easily beg to differ. Credible leaders give power away and act as a conduit to others, knowing that it is for a purpose larger and more important than themselves. Leaders act as power generators from which their followers can draw energy, motivation, and similar power.

There are five leadership *essentials* for sharing power (what they consider imperative for strengthening others): ensuring self-leadership, providing choice, developing competence, assigning critical tasks, and offering visible support. "Credible leaders accept and act on the paradox of power: becoming most powerful when we give power away."[39]

> Leaders live the daily values they espouse. They believe them to the core of their being and cannot live any other way. Leaders take every opportunity to show others by their own hand that they are firmly and deeply committed to their vision. Only by walking—no, running—the talk will leaders be judged credible to lead.

A leader is as a leader does. Leaders set the example they want others to emulate. Leaders always do what they say they will do. They do things with the utmost consistency and reliability. True leaders know that this is the only way to build credibility and wholly convince followers, without question, that they believe in their cause. Only then will followers willingly follow. Followers expect leaders to be active participants, to show up, to pay attention, to do, and to participate directly in the process of getting extraordinary things done. Leaders live the daily values they espouse. They believe them to the core of their being and cannot live any other way. Leaders take every opportunity to show others by their own hand that they are firmly and deeply committed to their vision. Leading by living the example is how leaders make visions and values tangible. It is how they provide concrete evidence of their personal commitment and passion for what they believe. Only by walking—no, running—the talk will leaders be judged credible to lead.

Leadership is about the individual and the group. It is a combination of both competence and character. Perhaps the best leaders are those who see their role as developing others and serving their followers. They are those who feel their leadership responsibility is to assure that followers are not only achieving the desired organizational results but are learning and serving, and reaching their individual potential.[40]

Management Too Is About People

Drucker defines management as "the ability to make human strength productive under new and challenging conditions." Drucker believes in human strengths to counter human weaknesses, and the "science of discovering those strengths, of fitting them into a productive framework"[41] is what he calls management. In essence, management is about making people productive. Drucker sees managerial effectiveness as focused operational decisions.[42] On leadership, Drucker believes it is responsibility, accountability, and doing, which is very similar to what many researchers term management. He also believes that management cannot be separated from leadership. These concepts are different "but only as different as the right hand from the left or the nose from the mouth. They belong to the same body."[43]

Managers have to bring people together for joint performance. They have to make human strengths productive in performance and human weaknesses irrelevant. They have to think through organizational results that are required and define appropriate objectives to achieve them (what Drucker refers to as "Management By Objectives"). A manager should "spend hours placing people in the job to match their strengths, helping them to define their objectives, finding the resources they need to work effectively."[44] Management is largely about people—not so much about their feelings as their effectiveness and job performance. Managing is seeing and seizing opportunities in new situations, hiring the right employees, and mobilizing and organizing people to meet them effectively and efficiently.

> Management is largely about people—not so much about their feelings as their effectiveness and job performance. Managing is seeing and seizing opportunities in new situations, hiring the right employees, and mobilizing and organizing people to meet them effectively and efficiently.

Drucker, the management guru, has been fond of saying, "So much of what we call management consists of making it difficult for people to work."[45]

In the future, managers will be challenged to raise productivity levels of knowledgeable professionals, and all groups will focus on working smarter. Both managers and leaders alike will spend inordinate amounts of time on this and similar endeavors to try to keep their organizations high performers.

The Corporate Structure with Leaders and Managers

Contemporary or traditional corporate structure is, in most cases, an accidental design that emerges out of perceived need and chance rather

> What seems to be clear today though is that successful managers and leaders spend time building strong teams around them that can handle the stressful situations that fast-paced and discontinuous change can have on organizations. In this sense, management and leadership are very similar concepts.

than planned choice, and it is usually only as good as its parts. The principal parts of the corporate entity are people, and people come with their own ideals, needs, wants, and sensitivities—in essence, they are all different. Usually, the higher the person rises in the corporate hierarchy, the more closely scrutinized and exposed his or her weaknesses are. According to Bennis, "nowhere are these strengths and weaknesses more exposed and more tested than in the relationship between a CEO and his COO." Bennis submits that the differences on paper between the two roles are very clear, yet sometimes they overlap. However, the distinctions that he makes are supported in the literature by other well-known management gurus, such as Kotter, Nanus, Covey, Maxwell, and Kets de Vries, among others. According to Bennis, "the CEO is the leader, the COO is the manager."[46] The leader has the vision; is concerned with the long view; concentrates on the *what* and *why*; is charged with doing the right thing; thinks in terms of innovation, development, and the future; and sets the tone and direction both inside and outside the company. Juxtaposed to this role is that of the COO, who has hands-on control; takes a shorter view; focuses on *how*; is busy with administration, maintenance, and the present; and sets the pace for the organization.[47] Bennis also argues that despite the differences on paper, in practice the seemingly clear division of responsibilities is "invisible, inextricably interwoven."[48] To make matters more confusing, Bennis argues that every top manager has qualities of the leader; otherwise they probably would not have made it to the top. Thus, at times, the CEO wears both leadership and managerial hats, and the COO sometimes strives for a CEO perspective by wearing a leadership hat—taking a longer view and doing the right thing.

Others, such as Gardner, take a slightly different approach and submit that managers exhibit some leadership skills, and most leaders on occasion find themselves managing. He also argues that while leadership and management are not the same thing, they overlap. "It makes sense to include managing in the list of tasks leaders perform."[49] He also describes aspects of leadership that others describe as managing, such as "planning and priority setting, organizing and institution building, keeping the system functioning, agenda setting and decision making, and exercising political judgment."[50] From this stated position, it is apparent that Gardner sees management as a necessary subset of leadership; it is something leaders do—it is similar yet different. A further distinction he makes is concerning the word "leader," which he refers to as the "leadership team." Gardner argues that "no individual has all the skills and time to carry out all the complex tasks of contemporary leadership."[51] He also argues that the team must be chosen for excellence in performance, and when a whole team shares the trade secret of expecting high performance of their subordinates, they dramatically increase the likelihood of high performance. This is certainly not rocket science but merely something that leaders and managers alike can use to increase performance of their respective teams. What seems to be clear today though is that successful managers and leaders spend time building strong teams around them that can handle the stressful situations that fast-paced and discontinuous change can have on organizations. In this sense, management and leadership are very similar concepts.

A Synthesis of the Major Differences Between Leadership and Management

The following section is a synthesis of the major differences between leadership and management, or leaders and managers, based on a review of the literature over the past three decades. Some of the differences are quite apparent, while others are subtle; however, it is apparent that leadership, or leading, is not the same as management, or managing. Leadership has been the more elusive, inspiring, and debated concept.

Table 1: Elements of Leadership and Management Compared and Contrasted

Definition	Leadership	Management
Primary Tasks	Development of vision and strategies	Keeping current systems operating through planning, organizing, staffing, controlling, budgeting and problem-solving
	Alignment of people	
	Empowerment of individuals	
	Achieving results through intended change	Setting and achieving goals
Key Question	Why?	How?
Fundamental Differences	Develops leaders and followers	Develop processes and subordinates
	Strategist	Tactician
Main Elements Function	Culture and people relationships	Systems and hierarchy
Type of Learning	Innovative	Conventional
Communication	Informal, varied, networks, complex	Formal, structured, simple

Definition	Leadership	Management
Address Change	Leading, embracing, proactive	Managing, accepting, reactive
Tolerance (Change)	High	Low
Major Tasks	Internal and external customers, communicating vision, pulling people	Internal customers, following processes, pushing people
Necessary Traits	Integrity, vision, risk-taking, trust, perseverance, honesty, dedication, self-knowledge, strong sense of purpose, passion, bias toward action, predisposition for life-long learning	Expertise, efficient, risk-averse, focus on preservation, task
Risk Tolerance	High	Low
Style	Ideas, information, interaction	Control, compliance, compartmentalization
Decision Making	Intuition	Logic
Time Orientation	Longer view (wider)	Shorter view (narrower)
Jurisdiction	Beyond job scope (inside and outside organization	Within job function
Emphasis	Vision, intangibles, renewal	Execution, tangibles, status quo
Key Words	Soft and hot	Hard and cooler
Body Parts	Heart and spirit	Mind and hands

Source: A synthesis of many of the elements of the works of Bass (1990), Bennis (1989), Gardner (1990), Kets de Vries (1990), Kotter (1999), and Kouzes and Posner (1995), Maxwell (1999), plus over 20 years experience as both a manager and leader.

Differences Between Management and Leadership in Time Spent on Core Activities

There has been a plethora of research conducted in the area of time spent on core activities among various levels of executives in organizations. While I was searching for information for this book, one set of results seemed particularly interesting. It showed the amount of time spent on three core activities: manager of execution, team and consensus builder, and visionary evangelist. Since a fairly significant portion of this book is devoted to the notion that a core characteristic of being a leader revolves around being visionary, it was important to include and synthesize this information. According to Hagberg Consulting Group,[52] successful leaders spend a large portion of their time thinking at a higher level, while those in trouble tend to spend too much time managing tasks and details. According to Hagberg Consulting Group, successful leaders spend 25 percent of their time on execution, 34 percent on team and consensus building, and 41 percent on vision. Bear in mind that the context or situation may affect the numbers postulated here. In terms of executives in trouble or, for this book, managers struggling to be leaders, 53 percent of their time is spent on execution, 18 percent on team and consensus building, and 29 percent on vision. It is important to note that having a vision or spending a large portion of available time on visioning activities while developing and building teams are fundamental differences between leaders and managers. Also, it appears that leaders do not need to spend as much time on execution since through visioning and related activities and building teams and consensus, should mean employee buy-in and support of corporate and organizational objectives. Therefore, execution of strategy is easier and requires much less time.

The Pillars of Leadership and Management

Leadership and management are both necessary for companies to be successful long term. Sometimes more or better leadership is required, and sometimes more or better management is required. The literature acknowledges that while both leadership and management are different concepts, they do overlap, and in practice, the differences are difficult to explain. This section tries to synthesize the major functions of both roles and to rank the function in order of importance while distinguishing between these vital organizational concepts. While analyzing this section, it might be a good idea to think of both leadership and management as beautiful palaces with wonderful people living in them, being supported on high cliffs by the functions (pillars) that define them. If any one of the pillars is missing or weakened, the palaces fall from the cliffs into the ocean, and lives are destroyed—the organization collapses. This happens in everyday life to many organizations, and in many cases, the failure is the result of poor management or leadership or, quite often, both.

The table below ranks the functions of both leadership and management in order of perceived importance and synthesizes the definition of each using one fundamental word.

Table 2: Fundamental Elements Ranked in Order of Importance

Leadership (Answers *Why?*)	Management (Answers *How?*)
Envisioning: Establish direction, purpose, vision Agenda-driven Results-oriented	Planning: Assess opportunities and threats Establish guidelines for channeling effort and decision making to create efficiency/unity
Establishing Trust: Predictable, reliable, accountable Drive and reinforce future vision with a clear and consistent style	Motivating: Provide incentives to achieve results/goals

Leadership (Answers *Why?*)	Management (Answers *How?*)
Communicating: Provide focus for new attention Often challenge conventional wisdom Need constant change Exercise influence and organize meaning for all members	Organizing: Match people with tasks Delegate authority Allocate resources according to task importance
Empowering: Display a shared vision Demonstrate a mutual sense of trust Exhibit a high commitment to organization	Controlling: Set standards for performance Measure accomplishments Compare results to goals, and reward accordingly

While the above table is not conclusive by any means, it highlights the core differences between leadership and management. By reviewing the most interesting and popular literature on leadership and management over the last three decades, and trying to uncover the fundamental differences between the topics, a small ray of clarity is beginning to emerge. The table above reflects what now appear to be the *core* differences between leadership and management even though, at times, in organizational life, both functions overlap and are almost indistinguishable. Taking this point further and continuing with the pillar analogy, the following diagrams will attempt to illustrate this point more clearly. The figure below contains the main points synthesized in this book and highlights the main differences between management and leadership discussed earlier. The key point here is that both elements are crucial for organizations to be successful. Too much of one or the other will tilt the pillars and make them weak so that over time (and sometimes a very short time), they fall and crumble. While this model may not last as long as Stonehenge, which has been standing for over five thousand years, it may be useful to consider since management and leadership are required for organizational success over the long term.

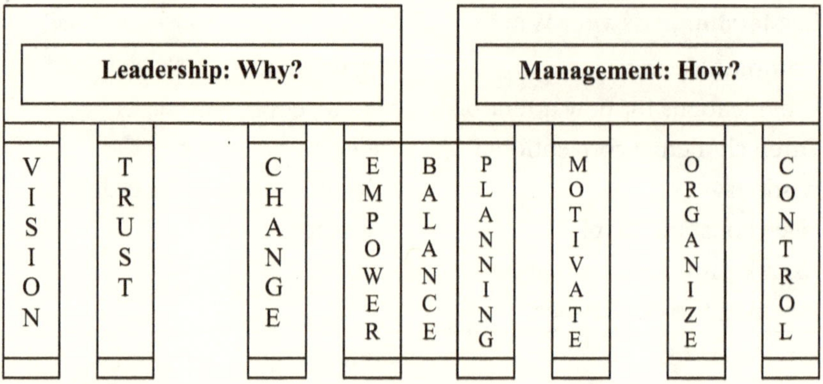

Figure 1: Pillars of Leadership and Management with Key Functions in Order of Importance (from left to right)

Leadership, Management, and Cultural Change

Culture is usually created and maintained by the founder/leader of any organization, and it begins to change as the founder/leader relinquishes control to others, especially if they came from outside the organization. Also, over time the assumptions regarding the culture change, as the external environment and its elements influence the organization in different, ongoing, and even unforeseen ways. The type of leadership required to change a culture, and the methodology used, will be different depending on the stage of the organization life cycle and the magnitude of the change necessary for survival. As an organization matures and becomes more stable, it builds a track record, a long history of successes, and leaders will find that changing deeply embedded assumptions will require much effort and time if those changes are to last and be more than just superficial.

According to Schein[53], there are three stages of organization: founding and early growth, midlife, and maturity and decline. Change to the culture will occur at a more rapid pace when the organization has grown to the point where the number of nonfamily managers outweighs the family members.

From a cultural and leadership perspective, the organization is now facing a very different situation than it has faced in the past. It is established and must maintain itself through some kind of continued growth and renewal process. It must decide how it wants to pursue such growth—through new products or services, mergers or acquisitions, geographic expansions, or new markets. It probably will utilize a combination of all of the above strategies as it rapidly expands. Again, this will pose problems for managers and leaders. It is not easy to add new products, buy companies, expand to new markets, maintain quality, and introduce new technologies, while at the same time growing per annum and changing the organization's culture. According to Schein,[54] the strength of this stage of organization lies in the diversity of its subcultures. Managers and leaders will tend to promote people from their favored subculture. This could tend to weaken the organization over time as the pool of talent shrinks and the organization becomes disproportionately weighted at the executive level by leaders from only a few subcultures. The range of experience will be a narrowed perspective that is less insightful than necessary to face the increased challenges of the organization. The policy of promoting from within will tend to exacerbate this problem. The implications for leadership are multiple. Leadership has to manage the culture change. It will begin by unfreezing the current culture through provision of information that challenges current assumptions. This will cause anxiety, stress, and guilt, which will ultimately motivate change.

Leaders also will have to provide enough safety during this process to keep employees committed to the cultural change; otherwise the traumatic learning process could fail. Leaders will have to provide some vision and insight into the process and the end result. They will have to provide a path, a map, and a process of learning to assure members of the organization that constructive, lasting, and positive change is possible.

Leaders of the future will have to be perpetual learners. This will require: "1) new levels of perception; 2) extraordinary levels of motivation; 3) emotional strength to manage change; 4) new skills in analyzing cultural assumptions; 5) the willingness and ability to involve others, and 6) the ability to learn a whole new organizational culture."[55] Leaders will have to be able to embrace change and ensure they stay focused on the right vision for the organization regardless of the challenges faced and the changes they must institute and endure. In order to accomplish this, leaders must be extremely focused and intense as they take the organization to new heights of learning, productivity, and success. This will require enormous amounts of energy, emotional intelligence, and motivation. Given the magnitude of the changes and challenges that future leaders will face, all levels of the organization must be enthusiastically committed to achieving the vision articulated by the leader. This will be the fundamental factor in achieving success in organizations of the future. The culture of an organization is one of its most irreplaceable assets, and the knowledge it contains could be its best source of competitive advantage. Therefore, leaders will absolutely have to possess the ability to lead change, to learn new organizational cultures, and to understand evolving processes that enlarge and strengthen the culture by building on its strengths and functional elements. Schein states that "leadership will then increasingly be an emergent function rather than a property of people appointed to formal roles."[56] In this sense, leadership is definitely different from management, and there is no reason for this to change anytime soon.

Companies need good management, great leaders, efficient functioning, and energizing relationships. Some organizations are bureaucratic and overmanaged (underled), while others, such as start-ups, are overled (undermanaged), and there are systemic problems associated with both scenarios. The task for the leaders and managers is to find the right balance as a team of dedicated, productive employees—something that is easier said than done. On the subject of leadership and change, "the single most visible factor that distinguishes major cultural changes that succeed from those that fail is competent leadership at the top."[57]

In order to ensure organizations reach their full potential and bring the most valuable asset of any organization with them, leaders of the future must unleash the collective potential of *all* people in the organization, including their managers. By doing so, and achieving this fundamental tenet of leadership, ordinary people will achieve extraordinary results.

> In order to ensure organizations reach their full potential and bring the most valuable asset of any organization with them, leaders of the future must unleash the collective potential of all people in the organization, including their managers. By doing so, and achieving this fundamental tenet of leadership, ordinary people will achieve extraordinary results.

This book on leadership, culture, and change was written with an example of a learning organization in mind, specifically a for-profit university. Universities are under immense pressure to change and must adapt quickly or suffer the consequences. Leadership, organizational culture, and change are major elements of any organization and directly or indirectly affect organizational performance. Any of these elements alone can have a very dramatic impact, either positively or negatively, on organizational performance. These elements together may be the difference between extraordinary results or dismal failure in any organization—public, private, for-profit, not-for-profit, and anything in between. Visionary leadership, strong organizational culture, and resistance to change are very difficult concepts to define, compare, and measure. Despite this, they are precisely the focus of this book. The impact of these elements on future performance will be reported as they relate to and affect the change process at one university.

Organizational Culture Defined

In the last decade or so, organizational culture has been used by some managers to indicate the internal climate and practices that organizations develop around their handling of people, or refer to the espoused values and credo of an organization. In this context, managers and leaders speak of developing "our company culture," the right culture, or a quality culture, suggesting that there are stronger or weaker cultures and better or worse cultures. This also suggests that managers have an idea of the values they are trying to inculcate in their organizations.

A recurring issue in the literature reviewed over the years (and some in this book) is the lack of a common or universally accepted definition of organizational culture. What is the nature of the concept *culture,* and how can it be operationally defined? Hofstede argues, "Organizational/corporate culture has become as fashionable a topic as organizational structure, strategy and control." He also argues that despite this popularity, there is "no standard definition of company culture."[58] A number of authors have defined culture in similar terms and describe it in a similar way.[59] According to Langan-Fox and Tan,

> there appear to be four core issues underlying the many definitions of organizational culture: a) that it is stable and resistant to change; b) that it is taken for granted and less consciously held; c) that it derives its meaning from the organization's members; and d) that it incorporates sets of shared understandings.[60]

Barney defines culture as "a complex set of values, beliefs, assumptions, and symbols that define the way in which a firm conducts its business."[61] Denison defines organizational culture as "the underlying values, beliefs, and principles that serve as a foundation for an organization's management systems, as well as the set of management practices and behaviors that both exemplify and redefine those basic principles."[62] Kets de Vries defines organizational culture as "a mosaic of basic assumptions espoused as beliefs, values, and characteristic patterns of behavior that are adopted by the organization's members in an effort to cope with both internal and external processes."[63]

Based on the literature reviewed with respect to defining organizational culture and comparing the commonalities and their appropriateness, the definition of organizational culture I created can be described as follows: It is a complex system of historical beliefs, values, attitudes, behaviors, assumptions, symbols, and norms that describe how the organization should act, conduct its business, and convey its vision to stakeholders inside and outside the organization. It is stable, deeply held, fundamental, difficult to change, rare, and almost impossible to imitate. In conjunction with strong leadership and a core ideology that embraces change, it can be a source of competitive advantage for learning organizations.

Culture is a difficult term to define, and doing so successfully requires a deep understanding of the hidden and complex aspects of organizational life. Some of what is found in organizations is difficult to explain in easy-to-understand terms. People seem to act irrationally and incomprehensibly while at the same time frustrating us. Organizations seem to be bureaucratic, political, or just plain complex and not understandable. According to Schein, culture is

> a pattern of shared basic assumptions that the group learned as it solved its problems of external adaptation and internal integration, that has worked well enough to be considered valid, and therefore, to be taught to new members as the correct way to perceive, think, and feel in relation to those problems.[64]

The word "culture" frequently conjures up images of things very different from what we are familiar with. According to Schermerhorn, Hunt, and Osborn, "culture is the learned and shared way of thinking and action among a group of people or society."[65]

Hofstede refers to culture as the "software of the mind." He believes that the "hardware" is universal among human beings, but the software of culture takes many different forms. Since we are not born with a culture, but are born into cultures and learn them as we grow, boundaries are developed (learned) between different groups and how they interact with and relate to each other.[66]

Schneider defines organizational culture as "the shared beliefs, expectations, and core values of people in an organization."[67] Robbins and Langton define culture in yet another slightly different way. They state culture is "a system of shared meaning and common perception held by members of an organization, which distinguishes it from other organizations."[68]

As was highlighted earlier, there is no one definition that has been accepted for "culture" even though many have similar threads and elements. See Table 3 for a synthesis of some of the varied definitions of culture.

Table 3: Hancott Synthesis of the Various Definitions of Culture

Key Words	Contributor
Pattern of shared basic assumptions	Schein (1992)
Learned shared way of thinking	Schermerhorn, Hunt, and Osborn (2000)
Shared beliefs, core values	Schneider (1990)
System of shared meaning	Robbins and Langton (2001)
Software of the mind	Hofstede (1997)

Culture is difficult to define, and there are many elements of culture that are common traits in organizations, as well. They are complex and diverse, and they are populated by people with different values, attitudes, beliefs, experiences, and personalities. In short, it is possible that an organization may have many subcultures inside its main culture. Universities are a good example of this. A university—especially a large public one with a varied and colorful history, many departments, and hundreds, if not thousands of employees practicing academic freedom—may have more than one culture. According to Schein, large organizations have subgroups with substantial variations, and it may not be appropriate to talk of *the* culture.[69]

If a university has certain assumptions shared across all its units, it may be appropriate to refer to a common organizational culture, even though various subunits have discrete subcultures. Over time, no matter the integrity of the subunit, it will produce subcultures as a normal process of social evolution. Some of these subcultures will be similar to the main culture, while others will be in conflict, as is often the case with academic affairs (faculty) and administration (management) at traditional institutions. Yet, in spite of ongoing conflict, traditional universities continue to grow and educate students, while at the same time maintaining some semblance of their original founding culture.

An important point to note is that even though traditional public universities in Canada are facing rising costs, funding cuts, rising student enrollments, and decreasing faculty numbers, they are still able to maintain substantial elements of their past culture. With the only constant being change, how is this possible? Is it something that can continue? Will the culture now begin to change? How? Why does it take so long to change the culture of a traditional university? Answers to the questions posed above lie embedded in the words "leadership" and "culture." Culture and leadership are interrelated and integrated elements of life in any organization. These elements, along with the groups of individuals that form the organization, are the essence of its being. Without groups, culture, and leadership, an organization is a name, a thing, and a lifeless entity that cannot continue to exist or grow. Effective leaders must understand the meaning and elements of culture if they are to be successful in executing their visions for the organization. They have to understand culture simply because they are the ones who contribute much to culture (e.g., Hofstede, Schein).

According to Schein,

> culture and leadership are two sides of the same coin in that leaders first create cultures when they create groups and organizations. Once cultures exist, they determine the criteria for leadership and thus determine who will or will not be a leader. But if cultures become dysfunctional, it is the unique function of leadership to perceive the functional and dysfunctional elements of the existing

45

culture and to manage cultural evolution and change in such a way that the group can survive in a changing environment. The bottom line for leaders is that if they do not become conscious of the cultures in which they are embedded, those cultures will manage them. Cultural understanding is desirable for all of us, but it is essential to leaders if they are to lead. [70]

In order for the public universities to maintain their current performance levels, they will need to create a culture that embraces change. They will have to recognize that culture and leadership go hand in hand, that leaders are the creators or changers of culture, and that this attribute is a valuable tenet of effective leadership. Among other things, leaders are charged with creating culture when they lead, create, or merge groups or organizations.

Once a culture is created, it then may determine the criteria and requirements for leadership. If a culture becomes complacent and unable to change, the only way to re-culture is to bring in leadership that understands what needs to be done in order to save the group or organization in its changing environment. The presidents and deans of the public universities need to understand this quickly, or the current culture of their institutions could end up managing them. Just research the last year or so of cultural issues at the University of British Columbia (2015 and 2016) with respect to reporting of sexual assaults, departure of the President under curious circumstances, resignation of the Chair of the Board of Governors and a host of other cultural issues for some interesting reading. In summary, Hofstede makes the point that "the values of founders and key leaders undoubtedly shape organizational cultures, but the way these matters affect ordinary members is through shared practices. Founders-leaders' values become member's practices."[71] Schein sums this up well when he states, "Cultural understanding is desirable for all of us, but it is essential to leaders if they are to lead."[72]

Main Components of Culture

Social structure. This refers to the basic social element of an organization. Two dimensions that stand out as being of particular importance are: (1) the degree to which the basic unit of social organization is the individual, as opposed to the group; and (2) the degree to which a society is stratified into classes or castes. According to Hill, "some societies are characterized by a relatively high degree of social stratification and relatively low mobility between strata (e.g., Indian), while other societies are characterized by a low degree of social stratification and a high mobility between strata (e.g., American)."[73] For a better and more detailed discussion, please refer to Hofstede.[74] The main components of culture are such integrated elements that changing it becomes extremely difficult, and sometimes only a strong leader can change an organization's culture. These elements, even segregated, would tend to slow down change, so one can imagine the impact they have as an integrated whole, the impact they could have on change, and how difficult it is for a leader to initiate change in an organization with a strong culture.

Religious and ethical systems. Religion is such a diverse topic that it cannot be adequately discussed in this book; however, it does need to be mentioned. Religion plays an important role in many societies, and many people are influenced daily by their beliefs and rituals. Religion may be defined as "a system of shared beliefs and rituals that are concerned with the realm of the sacred."[75] Ethical systems refer to "a set of moral principles, or values, that are used to guide and shape behavior. Most of the world's ethical systems are the product of religions."[76]

Language. This is perhaps the most important and obvious way that helps to differentiate one culture from another. Language includes both spoken and unspoken means of communication. Languages enable people to communicate with one another and also "structures the way we perceive the world."[77] According to Hill, because language shapes the way people perceive the world, it also helps define culture. In Canada, for example, there are many different cultures; however, the two major ones are English and French. They are the two official languages in the country. There are many other languages that are becoming more prevalent, and Chinese is one of the fastest growing, especially in Vancouver and Toronto.

Education. The role of formal education is an important element of culture. People need education and training to continue with productivity and to effectively compete for investment from other countries. According to Hill, "formal education is the medium through which individuals learn many of the language, conceptual, and mathematical skills that are indispensable in a modern society. Formal education also supplements the family's role in socializing the young into the values and norms of a society."[78]

Time orientation and use of space. While not as prevalent as the elements mentioned earlier, the use of space (personal distance) and time (relative and actual) can influence how a person should behave and how a culture is understood. Some societies have a very close personal space, and touching is considered appropriate, while in others it is not acceptable and may be forbidden. Some societies are not concerned with promptness (e.g., Mexico), while others expect it (e.g., the USA).

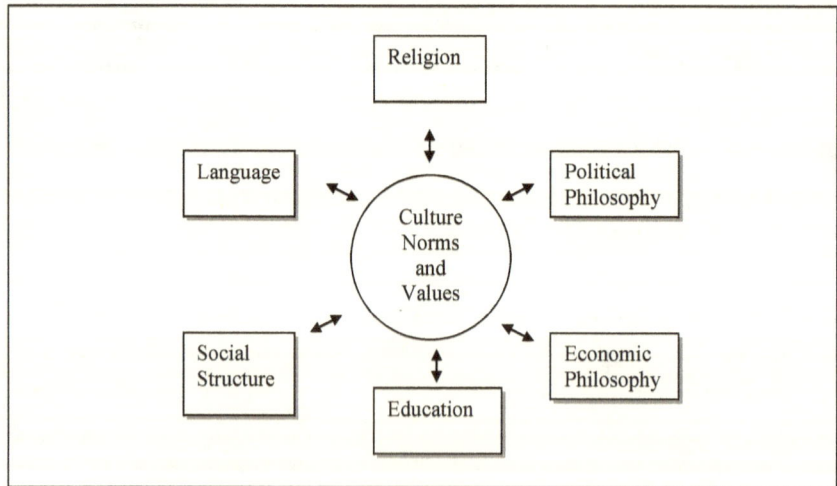

Figure 2: Summary of The Determinants of Culture, as adapted by Hill.[79]

These factors listed above are so embedded in culture that each may play a role in how change is viewed and understood. They also may slow down the change process itself. Educational systems, religious beliefs, and language are thousands of years old, and old systems and processes are difficult to change.

Organizational Culture and Change: Why Are They Important?

As discussed earlier, organizational culture is an important topic in business today, and it is growing in interest within management circles as many organizations are "adopting culture-based strategies."[80] The fundamental assumption underlying recommendations for culture-based strategies is that organizational culture enables positive economic consequences, such as increased employee commitment and cooperation, greater efficiency, improved job performance, better decision making,[81] and outstanding organizational results.[82] However, despite some of these successful elements, there are recent failures that should be mentioned, as a result of incompatible organizational cultures. A few that have been in the news over the past decade come to mind: Seagram and Vivendi, Maple Leaf Foods, AOL, Time Warner, Hub Meat Packers, BCE and Teleglobe International, as well as Daimler-Benz and Chrysler. TD Canada Trust was another merger, and, because of cultural differences, it took almost ten years to be properly integrated into one company. Part of the failure of these mergers was the inability of managers and ultimately leaders to successfully integrate the different cultures into a single, strong culture. According to Langan-Fox and Tan, "a net result of unclear culture strategies is lost productivity and difficulties in translating strategy into improved organizational and individual performance."[83]

The Role of Culture in Change and Organizational Performance

It used to be that the largest companies and governments were the only groups that were constantly reorganizing. Now, with globalization, re-engineering, and mergers and acquisitions, all organizations are doing it. Many of them are getting nowhere. In fact, many mergers destroy value, and research shows that 60 to 70 percent of all mergers fail within three years or fail to provide the synergies suggested prior to the merger. The best way to achieve success and maintain it in the face of dynamic change is through cultural transformation.[84] Effective leaders have innate knowledge that this is true and that the hard work of re-culturing is the underlying tenet of real progress. One particular author who explains this point well is Fullan. He states, "It is a particular kind of re-culturing for which we strive: one that activates and deepens moral purpose through collaborative work cultures that respect differences and constantly build and test knowledge against measurable results."[85] This is a good point, because culture is a very good source of performance if the culture is right and is aligned with the organization's mission, goals, objectives, and strategies. Leaders of an organization strive to ensure that this is so. It is one of their primary responsibilities. Fullan goes on to state that leading in a culture of change means creating a culture (not just a structure) of change. In order to achieve success, a culture change takes inordinate amounts of time, energy, and enthusiasm, which is why effective leaders need these attributes. Fullan makes a good point with respect to the nature of change and what needs to be accomplished. He states, "It does not mean adopting innovations, one after another; it does mean producing the capacity to seek, critically assess, and selectively incorporate new ideas and practices – all the time, inside the organization as well as outside it."[85]

Organizations with strong cultures may be able to achieve superior performance and sustainable competitive advantage. One needs to look no further than universities such as DeVry, Laureate, UCLA, and University of Phoenix, and companies such as IBM, Johnson & Johnson, Procter & Gamble, Walmart, and General Electric as good examples.

51

Each has policies of promotion from within where possible; each has a learning organization focus, where employees are empowered to make decisions to solve problems and provide customer service; and each has grown rapidly over the past two decades. With respect to the public universities in British Columbia, it is more difficult to gauge and state this premise; however, based on their growth in student enrollments and private endowments over the last two decades, it is apparent that they must have good cultures somewhat aligned with a mission and strategies. According to Denison, "the soft stuff in organizations – the people, values, and the level of employee involvement – has a huge impact on business performance."[86]

While it is difficult to precisely define, organizational performance and its level of sustainability are crucial to any organization. In this book, the definition will be kept simple, deliberately, to allow focus on what may be important considerations for universities for future sustainable performance. In a traditional business sense, this area would normally cover in-depth the idea of superior financial performance; however, because public universities are not-for-profit, financial performance is a moot point. They generally are not responsible for their revenues and expenses. What is important though is how well they do with respect to dealing with change (i.e., government policy), increasing student enrollments, funding cuts, increased competition, more demanding students, and difficulties attracting top-quality faculty. These points will be addressed in later sections of the book.

For the purpose of this book, there are three characteristics that will be used to define performance. First, an organization's culture must enable it to do things and behave in ways that add economic value and is a prerequisite for generating *normal* performance. If an institution's culture enables it to behave in ways that weaken its competitive situation, then culture cannot be a good source of organizational performance. Second, the culture found in the organization must be rare; it must have attributes and characteristics that are not common to a large number of other organizations of similar size, structure, and scope.[87] Finally, the organizational culture must be hard to imitate; organizations without these cultures cannot readily engage in the activities that will change their cultures to include the required characteristics. If they try to do so, they may find themselves at some sort of disadvantage and experience a weakened competitive position in the applicable marketplace.[88] A firm's culture can be a source of sustainable competitive advantage if that culture is rare, valuable, and difficult to perfectly imitate.[89] Performance of the organization may then be partly attributable to the organizational culture. Organizations with these types of cultures may want to continue to nurture and develop them. Universities whose reputations are taken for granted, that maintain their status quo, and that expect their cultures to sustain performance in the face of globalization and warp-speed changes in the education industry in British Columbia may suffer in terms of performance.

The Role of Leadership in Building Culture and the Change Process

The unique function of leadership that distinguishes it from management and administration is a real concern for culture. "Leaders create culture and must manage and sometimes change culture."[90] Leadership plays an instrumental role in creating culture and embedding it firmly in the behaviors, beliefs, and attitudes of the group. Whether the organization is a small local company, a large multinational conglomerate, or a medium-sized public university, the challenge of the leader is the same. Creating a positive culture that identifies and develops future leaders and teaches others how to value and embrace change is a fundamental element of the leader's role. By doing so, the leader may be creating an organization that can change as its markets change and enable it to perform better over the long term. Leaders can have a profound impact on the development of an organization's culture, from its inception to growth, maturity, and decline phases that inevitably occur at some point in time through the organizational life cycle. Cultures are built on many premises but none so prevalent, at least in the early stages, as the role and values, beliefs, and attitudes of the founder. The founder is usually the "culture creator" of the organization in the early stages of development. As the firm progresses through its various cycles, other employees, especially the top leaders, play a much larger role in setting the cultural tone. In many cases, these leaders come from outside the organization and are not intimately familiar with the current culture. This may be a benefit in the sense that if a radical change is necessary, the only efficient way to create a new culture is to bring in a new leader. According to Schein, "cultures basically spring from three sources; 1) the beliefs, values, and assumptions of founders of organizations; 2) the learning experiences of group members as their organization evolves; and 3) new beliefs, values, and assumptions brought in by new members and leaders."[91]

With respect to traditional public universities, this approach might not work anymore. This may have been how the universities were founded; however, over the decades that have passed, the focus on academic freedom, reliance on government funding, and the bureaucratic, hier-archical, unionized environments that now placate these institutions in British Columbia relegates the university presidents to positions such as "keepers of the peace," "figureheads with no authority," or "directors of the status quo." Stevens,[92] in his article "The Art of Running a Business School in the New Millennium," quotes Sowell: "A college president cannot hire professors and can seldom fire one, except for something that would get the professor imprisoned or executed."[93] He goes on to make the point that an academic chief has nothing of the powers or responsibilities of a CEO in private industry, which may be an overstate-ment. Participative management/leadership may be effective in times of stability, but this style of leadership may not work in times of rapid, discontinuous change, as is happening now. Sowell states,

> Most of the big decisions either are made by the faculty
> or cannot be made over the opposition of the faculty.
> Moreover, the faculty knows that presidents (and deans)
> come and go, while a full professor goes on like Ole Man
> River. Further, collective decision making by hundreds
> of prima donnas, none of whom can be fired or even
> demoted for being wrong, is not a system that any other
> institution has adopted anywhere else in the world.[93]

At the traditional public universities in British Columbia, the out-side of the organization appears to be much different than the internal workings, level of faculty satisfaction, and performance would indicate. The university press releases and publications regularly announce or stress-increasing enrollments, research grants, prominent graduates, and well-respected faculty achievements. Despite this, there continue to be academic rumblings at these institutions with respect to larger class sizes, lower amounts of government funding for research, and less focus on academic quality. Regarding change, Sowell states the following:

> The reactions of a typical college or university president
> have been analogized to that of a captain of a ship that
> has just struck an iceberg - as the ship sinks the captain

55

states that his highest priority is to save the crew. The next priority is to avoid any inconvenience as the ship goes down by continuing all activities - the midnight buffet, the bingo game, and the shuffleboard tournament. The third priority is to repair the ship. And the fourth and final priority, should time permit, is to save the passengers.[94]

The students in this example are the passengers. This is not an acceptable reaction to such a situation, and in order to come out of it with acceptable results, an organization's priorities must change. Despite the fact that university presidents are having a difficult time building or creating new cultures in their respective institutions, they must strive to push forward and not let the challenges of the status quo deter their efforts. Their ability to affect change, create a stronger culture, and drive future institutional performance depends on it. As governments become more involved in educational affairs, public institutions in British Columbia are being held more accountable for performance. This is especially true in enrollment activities, student access, graduation rates, retention efforts, effectiveness of learning, faculty qualifications, and cost-effectiveness with respect to program delivery. The major thrust then of the leader is to ensure a culture of openness, create a willingness to embrace change, and build an attitude of continuous improvement for all activities. Failure of the leader to deliver these charges likely means maintaining a weak status quo where all stakeholders of the institution ultimately lose.

The Change Process and Leadership

There is a link between understanding culture, the change process, and organizational performance. If the right type of leader is chosen and the process is well understood, change will happen and results have a good chance of improving.[95]

Organizations, leaders, managers, and people in general change things to make systems, process, procedures, products, and services more efficient and effective. According to the classic model of Lewin, the change process consists of three stages: (1) unfreezing a present equilibrium state, to create a climate for change; (2) moving from the initial state to a new end state; and (3) refreezing to lock in the end state that has been achieved.[96]

Kotter has a contemporary model for effecting change that involves an eight-stage process for top-down transformation, from "establish a sense of urgency" to "anchor the new approach in the culture."[97]

According to Fullan, "the goal is to develop a greater feel for leading complex change, to develop a mindset and action set that are constantly refined. There are no shortcuts."[98] He proposes the following change process:

- The goal is not to innovate the most.
- It is not enough to have the best ideas.
- Appreciate the implementation dip.
- Redefine resistance.
- Re-culturing is the name of the game.
- Never a checklist, always complexity.[98]

Goleman has identified six leadership styles that show a relationship (good or bad) between organizational climate and financial performance. The six styles are:

1. Coercive: The leader demands compliance. ("Do what I tell you.")
2. Authoritative: The leader mobilizes people toward a vision. ("Come with me.")

3. Affiliative: The leader creates harmony and builds emotional bonds. ("People come first.")
4. Democratic: The leader forges consensus through participation. ("What do you think?")
5. Pacesetting: The leader sets high standards for performance. ("Do as I do now.")
6. Coaching: The leader develops people for the future. ("Try this.")[99]

Two of the six styles negatively affect climate and, in turn, performance. These are the coercive style (people resent and resist) and the pacesetting style (people get overwhelmed and burn out). All other styles have a significant positive impact on climate and performance.[100] Basically, what this means is that a leader practices various leadership styles (situational leadership) in order to successfully influence climate and performance. This relates back to some of the earlier statements regarding the type of leadership necessary for a successful organization. No one style is necessarily better than the other; however, a leader possesses the ability to change as the situation changes and embraces change as a friend.

In addition, leadership is not just about confronting problems and finding solutions quickly in a crisis situation. According to Heijetz, "instead of looking for saviors, we should be calling for leadership that will challenge us to face problems for which there are no simple, painless solutions – problems that require us to learn new ways."[101] Therefore, understanding the change process, leading an organization through a crisis, and solving problems are not enough; leadership also entails confronting recurring problems that have never been solved.

Why Transformation Efforts Fail

According to Kotter, change efforts fail in the initial stages in over 50 percent of companies. His list of reasons for change efforts failure includes: not establishing a great-enough sense of urgency, not creating a powerful-enough guiding coalition, lacking a vision, undercommunicating the vision by a factor of ten, not removing obstacles to the new vision, not systematically planning for and creating short-term wins, declaring victory too soon, and not anchoring changes in the corporation's culture.[102] While Kotter does not discuss the importance of each reason, the literature is apparently starting to focus on the latter, with respect to a major cause of failure in transformation efforts. Maybe the next time Kotter establishes a list, the items should be ranked in order of priority to reflect their importance. This is a fairly important tenet of leadership: focus on priorities. Kotter seems to like writing about why change efforts fail, and there may be some truth to his assertions based on my leadership experiences.

Common Approaches to Organizational Change

There are probably more approaches to change than this book can include in its limited scope. However, according to Jacobs, there are four common approaches: (1) top-down strategies, (2) bottom-up strategies, (3) representative cross-section strategies, and (4) pilot strategies.[103]

The top-down strategy is basically what it says—an organization's leadership team decides which changes need to be made. This change effort usually involves brief large meetings where leaders explain why new ways of doing business are needed and what will be required from people in the organization to successfully bring about this particular set of changes. In top-down organizations, the desired changes are rarely crystal clear to everyone, and if there is not commitment and collaboration for implementation, the top-down approach might not work.[103]

Bottom-up strategies are another approach where individual teams of frontline workers are accountable for making changes in the way they themselves do business. These employees may end up working independently as teams and create innovative solutions to their own most pressing problems. According to Jacobs,

> this approach usually results in a satisfying, short-run experience with major improvements being made and good results achieved by many of the individual teams; however, the gains for one team are often at the expense of another and the long-term headaches for the entire enterprise usually remain. In most cases, either a lack of overall strategic direction and/or adequate system-wide co-ordination between these internally-focused teams overshadows any incremental progress that is achieved. Commitment is much higher with this approach than a top-down strategy.[104]

In the representative cross-section strategy, cross sections of the people affected by the proposed change are recruited to help decide which changes are necessary and how they can most effectively be implemented. These people or groups may be given various names, but they gain "an extensive understanding of the overall context of the change effort, develop a deep and genuine commitment to their cause, and provide a model of collaboration with representatives from other parts of the organization that they have long held in disdain."[105] Jacobs goes on to state that the problem with this approach is that many other people in the organization are "never meaningfully involved in the process, don't understand the changes themselves or why they are needed."[105] With feelings like this in an organization, people will not feel compelled or committed to their organization's proposed change efforts.

The final method discussed by Jacobs is the pilot strategy. This change effort benefits from having "a well-defined task, the attention and support of organization leaders, and the allocation of resources required to ensure success."[105] People are carefully picked from an area of the organization, and their efforts are showcased throughout the entire organization as an example of how change should be carried out. Often the development of a "not invented here" syndrome and, thus, a new level of resistance is created. In extreme cases, sabotage and infighting occurs as sides entrench and do things their own way, with the result being a "less effective change effort overall."[106]

Several other authors on change and leading change discuss related strategies, and the results are very similar. Conner,[107] Fullan,[108] Kotter,[109] and O'Toole[110] all argue that change must come from *all* levels in the organization, it must be supported by the corporate leadership, and the changes must be embedded in the culture of the organization in order to be lasting. Therefore, what is required is a combination of the proposed strategies, depending on the situation, organization, and magnitude of required change—not unlike the various leadership styles necessary to affect change. Change requires effective leadership and management—leadership supporting change at the strategic level, management executing the strategy using tactics, and managers and leaders working together to take the organization through a change process. One element (leadership or management) is probably insufficient for success in leading a substantial, second-order change effort.

Why People Resist Change: The Leader's Real Challenge

Sometimes people resist change simply because they can, and the costs of not changing in the face of change can be enormous. The loss of market share by American car manufacturers in the 1970s and 1980s to foreign competitors is a good example of some of the effects. Given the enormous costs—and potential opportunities—why is there not much literature out there on the subject? Maybe it is because we understand the reasons people and groups resist change! People resist for a multitude of reasons, and the first ten O'Toole listed are: homeostasis (human instinct), stare decisis (status quo), inertia (it takes considerable force to alter a course), satisfaction (comfort with the way things are), lack of ripeness (change happens when certain preconditions have been met), fear (humans' fear of the unknown), self-interest (change is good for others), lack of self-confidence (change threatens our self-esteem), future shock (we are only capable of so much adaptation), and futility (most change is largely superficial, cosmetic, and illusory—power structure will remain largely unchanged).[111]

O'Toole listed and briefly described thirty-three theories of changes or resistance, and many of them seemed to blur; however, he went on to describe two potent sources of resistance to change on a more practical level. These sources are organizational culture and values of Western society. The culture of an organization can be a source of resistance, but it also can be a source of change. Leaders must decide the type of culture they need in order to achieve the organization's goals, objectives, and vision, while at the same time changing to preserve its core ideology. People resist change for the following reasons: "a) Economic uncertainty, b) Fear of the unknown, c) Threats to social relationships, d) Habit, e) Failure to recognize the need for change."[112] Greenberg's list seems to overlap with O'Toole's; however, there seem to be more succinct categories put forth by Greenberg that make the list shorter, more manageable, and easier to utilize.

In 1997, Colins and Porras do a very good job discussing the role of culture, core ideology, drive for change, and progress, as ways to create visionary companies. With respect to change, they had the following to say:

Self-criticism, on the other hand, pushes for self-induced change and improvement *before* the outside world imposes the need for change and improvement; a visionary company thereby becomes its own harshest critic. As such, the drive for progress pushes from within for continual change and forward movement in everything that is not part of the core ideology.[113]

The Five C's of the Individual Change Process

Manfred Kets De Vries uses the following process to highlight the steps of individual change that he calls the five C's: (1) concern: negative emotional effect; (2) confrontation: focal event, an external threat to well-being, and observation of negative consequences to self and others; (3) clarification: preparatory steps, sudden insights, envisioning new alternatives, reappraisal of goals, and public declaration of change; (4) crystallization: inner journey, interpretation of discontent, working through insights, and increased self-knowledge; and (5) change: internalization of new mind-set.[114] This is but one of many individual change models available; however, it highlights a natural, logical process that people may go through when faced with having to change. It is obvious from viewing this process that change comes with some pain, and it is not easy to go from step one to step five.

Change comes with a price, but the price is sometimes less than the cost of *not* changing. Of course, it can be argued that not all change is necessary, and sometimes change is bad or wrong. However, the main point here is that embracing change is something a leader is expected to do. Organizations face choices, and pain in their system (losing market share, rising costs, increasing competitors, and decreasing profits, to name a few) can be seen as the "main lever that sets the change process in motion."[115] In cases of dramatic or strategic, structural or cultural change, organizations may even move through a mourning cycle as they transform. The steps include stages of shock, disbelief, self-examination, and finally acceptance. Based on personal observation, especially in the last three to five years, this has been occurring with some frequency. In this sense, organizations facing strategic change behave like people—people are the organization, so this should not be surprising to anyone.

> A leader pinpoints the challenge, labels it clearly, rallies the organization's resources, and articulates the negative consequences of a failure to act decisively. The leader's role is to define the existing state of discomfort and make it unacceptable, link the past and present through a new vision, and build strong support and systems that allow for strategic change.

Until organizations feel pain, leaders typically remain locked in past behavior patterns. This is normal and not uncommon. A jolt is sometimes needed to start the process. Because the awareness of the source of organization pain is crucial for any successful transformation effort, leaders quickly act to jump-start and lead the change process. A leader pinpoints the challenge, labels it clearly, rallies the organization's resources, and articulates the negative consequences of a failure to act decisively. The leader's role is to define the existing state of discomfort and make it unacceptable, link the past and present through a new vision, and build strong support and systems that allow for strategic change.[116] In order to really transform an organization, several steps are taken, and leaders throughout the organization play the pivotal role in this process. The order is not crucial; however, in order for the change to last, all steps in any change effort need to be successfully implemented. If not, what may happen, and so often does happen, is that change or doing new things is viewed as a "fad of the week," and employees revert (sometimes quickly) to the "old way" of doing things.

Realigning the corporate culture: creating a shared mind-set. Leaders of public and private universities must create a culture of openness, innovation, and sharing of knowledge. The leader has to set the stage by walking the talk; creating a sense of urgency; building a collective vision for the future; fostering excellence, commitment, and motivation; and encouraging out-of-the-box thinking to create real dialogue. Universities are striving to do this; however, their rich traditions tend to hold them back from achieving strategic change or effective cultural change. Everyone involved in the change process needs to take responsibility for part of the process, or the change effort will not succeed.

> Everyone involved in the change process needs to take responsibility for part of the process, or the change effort will not succeed.

Modeling espoused values: changing behavior. Publicly announcing a new set of values will not ensure a change in behavior. Again, leaders articulate the crucial values for mission accomplishment, and they need to practice what they preach. The leaders need to be trusted that what they say *is* what they will do. Walking the talk is a key characteristic needed when it comes to the successful transformation of behavior from what it is to what is has to be for lasting change to occur.

Building attitudes, competencies, and practices. Leaders strive to provide employees with the proper resources to make the change effort successful. Employees need training, education, and development of emotional intelligence to develop core job competencies. This is crucial for sustainable strategic change. Leaders have a crucial role to play in securing fast, small wins in order to build the can-do attitude of employees who are uncomfortable with dramatic change. Human behavior is such that habit and comfort, safety, and security motivate us (see the works of Maslow, Hertzberg, and Vroom) to maintain the status quo. In order to break habits and push our comfort zones, change is needed. Employees are not motivated solely by money, and leaders understand this point well. In 1979, Terpstra wrote about what motivates employees and how they are motivated.[117] Other approaches that have led to an increased understanding of motivations are Maslow's needs hierarchy, Herzberg's two-factor theory, Vroom's expectancy theory, Adams's equity theory, and Skinner's reinforcement theory. There are certainly others, as well; however, the focus of the next section will be to synthesize these theories and to try to link them to how a leader leads change.

Maslow's hierarchy of needs. According to Maslow, employees have five levels of needs: physiological, safety, social, ego, and self-actualizing.[118] Maslow argued that lower-level needs had to be satisfied before the next higher need would motivate employees. Leaders understand this and try to ensure that employees have sufficient income to be able to focus on increasing performance, while at the same time rewarding employees, developing them, and helping them achieve their highest potential.

Herzberg's two-factor theory. Herzberg categorized motivation into two encompassing factors: motivators and hygienes.[119] According to this theory, people work first and foremost in their own self-enlightened interest, for they are truly happy and mentally healthy through work accomplishment. Motivators or intrinsic factors—such as achievement, recognition, responsibility, and advancement—produce job satisfaction. Hygiene or extrinsic factors, such as pay and job security, produce job dissatisfaction. Unsatisfactory hygiene factors can act as de-motivators, but, if satisfactory, their motivational effect is limited. Leaders understand how complex human/employee motivation is and try to balance such factors as hygiene and motivators. Many leaders are instituting changes in organization policies, because they understand human motivation. There is a trend toward increasing benefits, shorter workweeks, sensitivity and human relations training, as well as increased communication and sharing of corporate information. Leaders know that in order for a change effort to be successful and continue for the long term, it must be embedded in the organization's culture. This will not happen unless employees are motivated to make the change, and all aspects of the effort are clearly communicated.

Adams's equity theory. Adam's theory states that employees strive for equity between themselves and other workers. Equity is achieved when the ratio of employee outcomes over inputs is equal to other employee outcomes over inputs.[120] Again, the leader tries to understand how each employee is motivated and, through continuous communication and employee involvement in the change process, lead the change. The equity in this case might be the employee's involvement in the change process, as everyone has an important role to play, and the leader communicates this fact continuously.

Vroom's expectancy theory. Vroom's theory is based on the belief that employee effort will lead to performance, and performance will lead to rewards.[121] Rewards may be either positive or negative. The theory postulates that the more positive the reward for the employee,

> Vroom's expectancy theory goes further and pushes the notion of contingency—the leadership style should be tailored to the particular situation and to the particular group. What the theory does not say is that this might even be necessary for individuals, as opposed to simply situations or groups. In fact, it might be necessary for each employee to be treated a little differently and lead differently, because they are motivated differently.

the more likely the employee will be highly motivated. Conversely, the more negative the reward for the employee, the less likely the employee will be motivated. Leaders who understand this and find the right employees (those who are individually highly motivated) can, through a system of mutual goal setting, coaching, and leading by example, inspire employees and motivate them to achieve goals they may not otherwise achieve. This is really the role of the transformational leader, according to Burns. Vroom's expectancy theory goes further and pushes the notion of contingency—the leadership style should be tailored to the particular situation and to the particular group. What the theory does not say is that this might even be necessary for individuals, as opposed to simply situations or groups. In fact, it might be necessary for each employee to be treated a little differently and lead differently, because they are motivated differently.

Skinner's reinforcement theory. Skinner's theory states that those employee behaviors that lead to positive outcomes will be repeated, and behaviors that lead to negative outcomes will not be repeated.[122] Leaders and managers should positively reinforce employee behaviors they believe will lead to positive outcomes, and negatively reinforce employee behavior that leads to negative outcomes. Through an understanding of motivation and reinforcing the *right* behaviors (which managers and leaders should know), employees can be motivated to achieve results that improve an organization's performance.

On the topic of leading change and employee motivation, Argyris[123] believes that an organization needs to be redesigned for a fuller utilization of the most precious resource, the workers—in particular, their psychological energy. Structures will change, and decisions will be made by groups rather than by a single boss. Satisfaction in work will be more valued than material rewards. In such an organization, work will be redesigned to give employees the chance to develop to their fullest potential, and at the same time, work will become more meaningful and challenging through self-motivation. Whether or not this actually happens is something for discussion and debate; however, leaders who understand motivation and find the right balance between developing, motivating, and recognizing employees for their efforts will likely be able to lead successful change efforts and increase the performance of their organizations through individual and collective efforts.

Improving business performance and customer focus. The leaders of the public universities need to improve performance and reduce their reliance on government funding for operating costs. They seem to realize this and are working on securing funding from private sources to ensure a pipeline of new students from employers and partnerships that provide advice for degree programs needed by businesses in the future. At British Columbia's public universities, the deans of the various business schools have been acting like VPs of sales and are continually publicly announcing university–company partnerships. The public schools are starting to change and need to do more. They are striving to operate on a profit-and-loss model based on government directives and funding shortfalls, and be more responsive to student needs and expectations. They need to concern themselves with the notions of customer service, market share, geographic coverage, and value of program offerings. Without such a focus and the commitment to make strategic change a reality, some will not survive the onslaught of continuous change and the effects of globalization in the twenty-first century. If they do not, John Sperling (founder of the University of Phoenix) may, in fact, be right—if you are not quick as an institution, you could end up dead.

Instilling the importance of continuous improvement and strategic innovation. Long-term, sustainable competitive advantage may come in the form of knowledge development and sharing. Leaders of public universities must begin to invest in their people and develop them to reach their full potential. Hiring the best researchers is simply not enough. Leaders need to tap the creativity and innovation of their people and motivate them to continually improve. They also need to be rewarded well for doing so. According to Kets de Vries, "the real returns come from strategic innovation."[124] In order to maintain sustainable competitive advantage, innovation must occur at a faster rate than changes in the external environment—no small feat in today's speed-of-light markets.

A final note on change: change is here to stay, with or without us.

Types of Organizational Change

Research has shown that organizations change primarily in two ways: through drastic action and through evolutionary adaptation over time.[125] Some would argue that change is part of a continuum, and change has been discussed at the ends of this continuum to make it easy to think about and visualize.[126]

Since change is a constant in today's complex world, and it is rather discontinuous, understanding change is a vital attribute for leaders of the present and the future. Fullan states,

> Remember that a culture of change consists of great rapidity and non-linearity on the one hand and equally great potential for creative breakthroughs on the other. The paradox is that transformation is less about innovation and more about innovativeness. It is less about strategy and more about strategizing. And it *is* rocket science not least because we are inundated with complex, unclear, and often contradictory advice.[127]

Planned change is viewed as an intentional and goal-oriented activity. Unplanned change happens in an unintentional, ad hoc manner. First-order change is linear and continuous. It implies no fundamental shifts in the assumptions that organizational members hold about the world or how the organization can improve its functioning. Second-order change is multidimensional, multilevel, discontinuous, and radical, and it involves the reframing of assumptions about the organization and the world in which it operates.[128]

If an organization is to survive, it must effectively respond to changes in its environment. It may respond differently depending on its leadership, culture, management, competitive position, competitive actions, and so on.

What Organizations Change

Organizations change five aspects that comprise it: culture, technology, physical setting, structure, and people.[129] Since the topic is the impact of culture on change, this section will focus on the profound importance of changing culture, and its difficulty, because it involves changing the underlying, deeply held values and beliefs of an organization. Therefore, an impact is the difficulty in changing the way things are done in an organization, since culture is hard to change.

As described earlier, culture is like glue that holds an organization together—changing the glue can have dramatic impacts on an organization. Culture is a combination of values, beliefs, and attitudes. Schein writes that an organization's culture is grounded in the founders' and senior executives' beliefs, values, and assumptions, and their decisions and practices are observed and over time adopted by others.[130] Morgan states that "since organization ultimately resides in the heads of the people involved, effective organizational changes always implies cultural change."[131]

Achieving Organizational Change with Leadership

People fear change for a multitude of reasons, not the least of which is the "unknown probability of future success."[132] Change is not a simple process—neither is it familiar or comfortable. The unlearning of habitual patterns can be extremely difficult or even anxiety provoking. A natural tendency for people faced with change is to protect a known process or position, to resist with every fiber of their being. Embracing change or the unknown is *not* a common tendency for most.

> Change is not a simple process—neither is it familiar or comfortable. The unlearning of habitual patterns can be extremely difficult or even anxiety provoking. A natural tendency for people faced with change is to protect a known process or position, to resist with every fiber of their being. Embracing change or the unknown is *not* a common tendency for most.
>
> Even people who believe in change and say they welcome it believe it halfheartedly. What they are really saying is that they want *others* to change, but they do not want to really change *themselves*. Many people have the will to change but not the *skill* to change.

People are often inclined to hold on to dysfunctional patterns, and changing a perspective or view takes a great deal of effort. It is difficult to explain why people tend to cling to the status quo, because there are always many obstacles to overcome, both conscious and subconscious, on the path to change. However, cling we do with white knuckles to the tree of status quo.[133]

Change is hard, no matter what it involves. It is often easier to change *people* than to *change* people. In other words, it is easier to replace current employees or faculty with new ones (with new attitudes and mind-sets) than to transform the ones currently in place. This is a sobering thought, and it is much easier said than done. Even people who believe in change and say they welcome it believe it halfheartedly. What they are really saying is that they want *others* to change, but they do not want to really change *themselves*. Many people have the will to change but not the *skill* to change.

The natural human resistance to change has a parallel in the organic view of organizations. With globalization, increased competition, the Internet, and almost daily advances in technology and improvements in communication, many large, successful companies take a wait-and-see attitude or hunker down in the bunker called status quo. In this age of globalization—the information age, the new economy—discontinuity is the norm, and companies that survive will have to be able to respond swiftly and effectively to the changing demands of the environment.

According to Kets de Vries, "by applying the insights derived from individual changes to the domain of organizational transformation, we can induce, facilitate, and even speed up organizational change."[134]

Changing the Culture of the Organization

This task is very difficult to achieve in the short term and, in fact, may take continuous effort, patience, a dedicated focus, and strong leadership.[135]

Culture sets the tone for how employees behave and interact with each other, what things are valued by the organization, and what expectations are in place for managers and employees. Culture often represents the mind-set of the employees and managers.[136]

Changing culture takes effort and must involve people at *all* levels in the organization. It requires employee buy-in, communication, and strong leadership with a respect for followers.[137] While this is not the only way to change culture, since it is at times deeply held and difficult to change, these elements may make the process of change easier. Also, these elements seem to appear quite frequently in the literature on change and specifically literature that discusses the impact of culture on the change effort.

Integration of Change Theories: A New Framework

Lewin's change theory is old and, while still relevant, is somewhat simplistic and not encompassing, nor can it accurately explain change in today's organizations.

Kotter's top-down process seems more like a list of activities that is driven from the top down, whereas systemic, longer-term change must involve all aspects and all levels in the organization. With this in mind, what follows is a new proposed framework that might work better and explain more than the ones proposed by Lewin and Kotter separately. Lewin describes a simplistic process, and Kotter's is basically a list of steps; however, combined, they have a much tighter, elaborate, and synthesized framework that adds value as a change theory:

1. Having a core strategy for dealing with complex change, especially effectively communicating it (communicate, communicate, communicate).
2. Understanding the need for and benefits of change (Individuals must see the discrepancy between current and desired behaviors—clear, consistent communication is key).
3. Unfreezing (Individuals are encouraged to accept responsibility for the change process).
4. Moving (Resistance to change must be overcome. The benefits of change must be clear, along with the importance of new desired behaviors for the individuals' career advancement. Individuals are shown the way and instilled with confidence).
5. Refreezing (The change is practical, and feedback is given on performance, with appropriate rewards).
6. Ensuring that the new change is made a part of the culture of the organization by involving *all* levels in the process.

In the literature there appears to be some consistency in terms of leadership with respect to what a single, charismatic, visionary leader can achieve. While the results can sometimes be extraordinary, they rarely are sustainable over the long term.[138] There needs to be application and integration of both "hard" (strategy, structure, systems) and "soft" (vision, values, behaviors, attitudes) in order to achieve the best, most sustainable results.

According to several studies,[139] there must be a blend of both approaches since charisma alone, or the power of an individual's personality, is not enough to ensure lasting systemic change.

Table 4 presents a summary of change leadership roles, as proposed by Goleman, which represent interpersonal skills and the ability to manage environments.[140] All of these roles are equally important (depending on the change situation) and are necessary for leaders to obtain extraordinary performance.

Table 4: Summary of Change Leadership Roles

Characteristic Role	Qualities and Attributes	Instrumental Role
Change leadership mind-set	Honesty, integrity, trustworthiness	Management mind-set
Strategic focus	Inspiring	Operational/ technical focus
Systemic/big-picture focus	Competent	Business unit focus
Envisaging/ energizing	High degree of emotional intelligence	Planning and control
Concern for shared values, attitudes, motivating staff	Self-confidence/ awareness, strong desire/energy to achieve openness to new ideas/change	Concern for systems, structures, and resource (human and physical) improvement
	Strong interpersonal skills	

(Source: D. Goleman, Emotional Intelligence, 1998, 95)

The Role of Leadership in Change

Leading change and understanding the process are vital tasks that leaders must accomplish in today's fast-paced environment.[141] While different types of leadership may be appropriate in different situations, in industries of dynamic change, two of the styles may not work well—coercive and pacesetting.[142] The four leadership styles that Goleman in 2000 found most effective in influencing culture and performance are: authoritative, affiliative, democratic and coaching. These are also associated with high emotional intelligence.[142]

According to Fullan, the thing that is needed for sustained performance and long-lasting change is "leadership at many levels of the organization."[143] He also states that "leadership in a culture of change will be judged as effective or ineffective not by who you are as a leader, but by *what leadership you produce in others*."[144]

This point is supported by Argyris when he talks about internal commitment for change that "cannot be activated from the top."[145] According to Fullan, "it must be nurtured up close in the dailiness of organizational behavior, and for that to happen there must be many leaders around us."[146]

Strategic Change and Leadership

Change should be the right leaders' friend. Good leaders recognize that to bring out the best performance in people, they need to let go, empower, lead by example, and then let change run as required. Out of the constant state of change comes some sort of calm. Chaos theory tells us that out of chaos comes a state of order. According to Pascall, Millemann, and Gioja, "the world is not chaotic; it is complex."[147] The theory is best summarized in terms of a *living system* based on four principles:

1. *Equilibrium* is a precursor to death. When a living system is in a state of equilibrium, it is less responsive to changes occurring around it. This places it at maximum risk.
2. In the face of threat, or when galvanized by a compelling opportunity, living things move toward the *edge of chaos*. This condition evokes higher levels of mutation and experimentation, and fresh new solutions are more likely to be found.
3. When this excitation takes place, the components of living systems *self-organize* and new forms and repertoires *emerge* from the turmoil.
4. Living systems cannot be *directed* along a linear path. Unforeseen consequences are inevitable. The challenge is to *disturb* them in a manner that approximates the desired outcome.[147]

Universities are considered living systems in a complex, changing environment where strategic leadership is necessary to ensure they continue to effectively deal with dynamic change to survive. Leaders drive change and must ensure it is present at all levels of the organization in order to effect sustaining second-order change.[148]

In 2002, Greenberg talked about organizational change as inevitable, and several approaches should be considered. He explains the following:

- Shape political dynamics: Win the support of the most powerful and influential individuals in the company. Support of top management will facilitate acceptance of change.

- Educate the workforce: One of the key reasons people resist change is that they fear the unknown—the future. Companies must clearly explain the benefits of change in order to get employee buy-in.
- Involve employees in the change effort: People who play a role in the change effort tend to be more committed than those who are not involved. Failure to involve employees is inviting failure of the change effort.
- Reward constructive behaviors: This is common sense, and leaders normally follow such practices. People should be rewarded for exhibiting the behavior required for successful change. This ties in well with motivational theories proposed by Vroom and Skinner, discussed earlier in this book.
- Create a "learning organization": This is an easy thing to say, but in reality it is very difficult to do. However, planning together to effectively deal with change, thinking outside the box, forming a joint vision, and creating a core ideology based on knowledge development will help the process.[149]

Similar approaches have been proposed by authors such as Goleman[150] and Jacobs.[151]

Kotter[152] proposes a different approach that starts at a much more visionary level and ends up at the practical level whereby the change is anchored in the culture in order for it to be sustainable and long-lasting. What might work a little better is a combination of the two approaches, with a major focus on the vision and strategy (including the core ideology) and communication, since many change efforts fail simply because of poor communication efforts and plans. The premise of Mintzberg is "the best way to 'manage' change is to allow for it to happen,"[153] and by incorporating this view, the result is the following synthesized change process:

1. Develop a shared vision and strategy enhanced by a sense of urgency.
2. Communicate the change vision directly, consistently, and often, and help educate all employees on the benefits of the process and effort.

3. Allow change to happen, allow all employees to change by involving them, and reward constructive change behaviors.
4. As a team, create short-term wins, lead the effort, consolidate gains, and produce more change.
5. Create a learning organization and culture of change as its core ideology - status quo is never acceptable.

While there is no one best way to change an organization, by following the proposed steps above and involving employees in the process, hopefully organizations can improve their track records with respect to successful change efforts.

Leading Change, Culture, and Performance: Do Public Universities Have It?

Leaders can create or develop cultures. They do many other things, as well, but perhaps none is more important than the creation of a strong culture. The process of building culture occurs most often if the leader believes in it and wants it to happen. The leader needs a vision for it, a passion for it, and the enthusiasm and energy level to carry it out.

> Leaders can create or develop cultures. They do many other things, as well, but perhaps none is more important than the creation of a strong culture. The process of building culture occurs most often if the leader believes in it and wants it to happen. The leader needs a vision for it, a passion for it, and the enthusiasm and energy level to carry it out.

According to Schein, "it is crucial to recognize at this stage that if the organization is successful and the success is attributed to the leader, the leader's entire personality becomes embedded in the culture of the organization."[154]

Leaders now need to think ahead, be visionary, and be proactive to change—become a high priest of change and culture. They need to be able to learn new things and, at the same time, unlearn things regarding the culture that may not serve the organization well. Leaders also need to clearly understand the elements of cultural dynamics and where the current culture of the organization needs to be for superior performance. Leaders probably cannot arbitrarily change culture

> A strong organizational culture that is rare, constantly improving, and difficult to perfectly imitate is a source of competitive advantage. Having strong leadership with a vision for the future, articulating that vision, and executing it by walking the talk while building trust in followers, are equally competitive advantages for an organization. Combining the two is like receiving the power source of the sun in one battery—simply awesome, extraordinary performance.

completely by force, enthusiasm, or otherwise; however, an effective leader should be able to evolve culture by building on strengths and letting weaknesses atrophy over time.[155]

A strong organizational culture that is rare, constantly improving, and difficult to perfectly imitate is a source of competitive advantage. Having strong leadership with a vision for the future, articulating that vision, and executing it by walking the talk while building trust in followers, are equally competitive advantages for an organization. Combining the two is like receiving the power source of the sun in one battery—simply awesome, extraordinary performance. Perhaps ending with a quote from Heskett and Schlesinger will drive this important point further:

> From time to time, the leadership in competing organizations has seized on one or more observed behaviors and tried to emulate the leaders of these organizations in ways that might well be regarded as manipulative. The results have been predictably disastrous; this provides further confirmation of the possibility that there is a strong linkage between leadership, culture, and performance – in short, that state-of-the-art leadership delivers outstanding organizational results.[156]

The public universities in British Columbia may have this, but then again, maybe not.

Leadership, Change, and Culture in Universities of the Twenty-First Century

The world around us is constantly changing and changing rapidly. So too are organizational and leadership practices. Throughout most of the twentieth century, many organizations survived and did well with structures that were hierarchical in nature (e.g., the Catholic Church, the Canadian Army, and Ford Motor Company). For the most part, attributes that describe such organizations include: pyramidal structure, hierarchical organization, staff departments, top-down decision making, functional and divisional structures, and position power. Now, especially after the failure of several high-profile companies, new prototypes of organizations are emerging that stress empowerment, flexibility, organizational learning, and knowledge creation. The learning organization and its various structures are gaining popularity. The new economy is driving change at such a rapid pace that the only constant is change. These new prototypes, out of necessity, are more in tune than their predecessors with the changes that have occurred because of increased globalization of organizations and the communication and information technology revolution. The Internet has radically changed how organizations operate, and it appears that this trend will continue into the future at an exponential rate. Future leaders will have to be comfortable dealing with change and leading in this type of environment. As discussed earlier, leaders will be challenged to change the culture of the organization since it is deeply held assumptions, patterns of behavior, core values and beliefs, and many of these elements of culture are based on experience, history, and rooted in religion. These entrenched elements are difficult to change in stable times and in turbulent times. Human behavior has a tendency to try to hold on to what it knows best—the status quo.

According to Manfred Kets de Vries, "with discontinuity the new norm, the original prototype of leadership and organizations has become less relevant. Given the increasing irrelevance of the traditional model, the question then becomes, what kind of leadership and organization will be most appropriate in the twenty-first century?"[157]

The traditional universities in British Columbia, Canada, fall into this category and must radically change in terms of culture, organization, and leadership if they are to continue to influence future trends in education in the province. These traditional institutions continue to be dominated by the three C's—control, compliance, and compartmentalization—which have driven their success for the past three decades or so. This may not be sufficient for future success as the speed of education increases dramatically. According to Kets de Vries, traditional organizations dominated by control, compliance, and compartmentalization "are being outpaced by organizations that focus on ideas, information, and interaction (the three I's). In today's business world, people and processes have become the central themes."[157] While this may not be true in all industries, it appears to hold true in the field of education.

We are currently experiencing rapidly changing paradigm shifts that will envelope traditional and nontraditional institutions alike. Which organizations will be better prepared to survive? Organizations focused on and organized around stability, local markets, hierarchy, and lead by autocratic leadership, or alternatively, organizations structured with a new mind-set predicated on both continuous and discontinuous change, global orientation, is customer or student driven, has a "systems" approach, and subscribes to transformational leadership. The latter organizational description will be necessary to survive the dramatic changes that organizations will face. Hierarchy will be much less prominent in all future organizations. The new structures will tend to be flat and organic rather than hierarchical and rigid. Innovative, fluid, and flexible designs will offer some form of competitive advantage as complex decisions are made quickly and easily. Dr. John Sperling, founder and chairman of the University of Phoenix, believes that there will be two types of universities in the twenty-first century: "the quick and the dead."[158]

Leaders of these new economy organizations will necessarily lead in different ways, as well. They need, now more than ever, to find ways to bind their people to the organization. In addition, they have to take on additional responsibilities. According to Kets de Vries, leaders are no longer leaders in "the traditional paternalistic, autocratic sense. Instead, in addition to being CEO's, they're also chief knowledge officers, transmitting knowledge from one part of the organization to the other."[159]

The new leaders will tend to be known for their roles as chief architects of the organizational structure, chief coaching officers, and chief change officers of organizational culture. Add to this the necessity of leaders to lead with a global vision, while at the same time finding smart ways to simplify decision-making processes, and you have the university president of the twenty-first century. The words "miracle workers" may take on new meaning before long.

The new leaders will tend to be known for their roles as chief architects of the organizational structure, chief coaching officers, and chief change officers of organizational culture. Add to this the necessity of leaders to lead with a global vision, while at the same time finding smart ways to simplify decision-making processes, and you have the university president of the twenty-first century. The words "miracle workers" may take on new meaning before long.

Leaders of the Future

Organizations of the future need to change if they are to be successful in delivering their missions and adding value to the traditional models of educational teaching. Areas for development might include creating a learning culture, building new markets, focusing on students as customers, institutionalizing total quality leadership, leading change, winning in the global marketplace, fostering innovation, and leveraging technology.[160]

Creating a learning culture. According to Covey, the leader of the future will be one who "creates a culture or a value system centered upon principles."[161] He goes on to say that leaders who have the vision, courage, and humility to constantly learn and grow will create a culture. In order for organizations like universities to grow and prosper, they must have visionary leadership, embrace change, and have a passion for learning and delivering knowledge. According to Covey,

> those people and organizations who have a passion for learning – learning through listening, seeing emerging trends, sensing and anticipating needs in the marketplace, evaluating past successes and mistakes, and absorbing the lessons that conscience and principles teach us, will have enduring influence. Such learning leaders will not resist change; they will embrace it.[162]

Building new markets. Leaders and the universities they lead will have to adapt to the changing roles and relationships of different sectors of society and build new markets for their educational programs. If the present trend of cutting government support for universities continues, leaders of these institutions will have to reexamine their mission, sources of funding, and relationships to other sectors, including the private sector. There will be a trend toward more public–private partnerships; more private universities; more online, pragmatic degree programs; and more program offerings to international markets. These activities will change the mission of many traditional universities and enable them to continue to prosper as they secure additional operating funds and meet the needs of the changing marketplace.

Focusing on students as customers. This will be an extremely difficult task for traditional universities. They simply are not structured to do this, and their cultures will not allow them to easily do it effectively. In a traditional sense of organizational structure, the CEO, the chairman, and the board of directors of organizations are the power brokers and decision makers. In the future, this will not be as true. The customers will wield more power, and universities will have to meet their needs or fail. The new structure will be upside down, with the customer on top. Who then is at the bottom? Top management is at the bottom. The structure will change the focus from who is *responsible* to who is *responsive*. This change will be dramatic and challenging to many traditional universities in British Columbia. According to Blanchard,

> the leader of the future, realizing that vision and im-plementation are both leadership roles, will learn to care little about defending the traditional hierarchy. As a result, she or he will be willing to turn the pyramid upside-down to implement a vision.[163]

The Role of Leaders and Cultural Change within the Public University

Universities need to learn how to effectively deal with many types of change. The rate at which they learn, how they learn, and the depth to which they learn are dependent on many factors, not the least of which is the culture of the organization and the dissemination and practice of leadership throughout the organization, at all levels. The basic assumption here is that the more open and collaborative the culture, the more information that is shared, and the stronger the leadership practiced throughout all levels of the organization, the greater the rate of organizational change and the more lasting the change becomes. In fact, change (even in chaos) is absolutely necessary for learning to take place. According to Leider,

> we live in an era of organizational reengineering. To become or remain competitive, leaders must realize improvements through radical change, or reengineering. In the context of radical change ... people cannot be reengineered. All reengineering demands major self-leadership choices. All change is self-change. Change requires self-leadership.[164]

While this quote is certainly not a sole explanation for anything, it does highlight some of the current thinking around the relationship between change and leadership. Also, since leaders are responsible for creating or changing culture, there appears to be a relationship among the three variables.

Culture is usually created and maintained by the founder of any organization, and it begins to change as the founder relinquishes control to others, especially if they came from outside the organization.[165] Also, over time the assumptions regarding the culture have to change as the external environment and its elements influence the organization in different, even unforeseen ways. The type of leadership required to change a culture and the methodology used will be different depending on the stage of the organization life cycle and the magnitude of the change necessary for survival.

According to Schein, there are three stages of organization: founding and early growth, midlife, and maturity and decline. More detailed information on the various stages of a company life cycle follows:

Start-Up. The Childhood Years: You have a vision. During this stage, you develop a plan, develop a business idea, and start your business.

Validation. The Teen Years: Establish where you fit in. You develop the company's unique identity and carve out a distinct place in the eyes of customers. Many companies never make it beyond this stage of development, because it is the hardest test. During validation, you will need to develop a unique value proposition and convert key customers.

Expansion. The College Years: This entails rapid growth and development. You expand your business by pursuing new customers and sales and make a significant investment in your company's future. During the growth phase, you focus on sales growth and you pursue opportunities to expand your business.

Maximize Profitability. The Adult Years: This is a period of adjustment and refinement. You continue to add new products and services to grow and expand your business. Each of these new opportunities will create the need to revisit many of the stages of development that you have already experienced. For each new opportunity, your company may revisit the "validation," "growth," and "maximize profit" stages of company development.

Exit. The Senior Years: This includes retirement and moving on. At some point, you will decide to exit your business. You may sell the company or merge it with another organization. If you have planned properly, you will be able to maximize the value that you receive out of your business.[166]

Therefore, the cultural change mechanisms required are as follows: "change through systematic promotion from selected subcultures, planned change through organization development projects and the creation of parallel learning structures, and unfreezing and change through technological seduction."[167]

The implications for leadership are multiple. Leadership has to start and manage the culture change. It will begin by unfreezing the current culture through provision of information that challenges current assumptions, as first proposed by Lewin.[168] This will cause anxiety, stress, and guilt, which will ultimately motivate change. Leaders also will have to provide enough safety during this process to keep employees committed to the cultural change program; otherwise the traumatic learning process could fail. The leaders will have to provide some vision and insight into the process and the end result. This is part of the visioning discussed earlier in the book. They have to provide a path, a map, and a process of learning to assure members of the organization that constructive, lasting, and positive change is possible. This is imperative if the University of Phoenix is going to continue to successfully evolve as *the* university for working adults in North America. Over the past decade it has struggled as competition and regulation has increased, and it has become US centric and insular. Too much focus on processes, and a culture of compliance with little visioning and strategy. The results have been spectacularly bad. And with the passing of founder John Sperling, I suspect the driving vision has been lost completely. According to Schein,

> leaders of the future will have to be perpetual learners. This will require 1) new levels of perception; 2) extraordinary levels of motivation; 3) emotional strength to manage change; 4) new skills in analyzing cultural assumptions; 5) the willingness and ability to involve others, and 6) the ability to learn a whole new organizational culture.[169]

Leaders will have to be able to embrace change and ensure they stay focused on the right vision for the organization regardless of the challenges faced and the changes they must institute and endure. In order to accomplish this, leaders need to be extremely focused and intense as they take the organization to new heights of learning, productivity, and success. This will require enormous amounts of energy, emotional intelligence, and motivation. Given the magnitude of the changes and challenges that future leaders will face, all levels of the organization must be enthusiastically committed to achieving the vision articulated by the leader. This will be the fundamental factor in achieving success in organizations of the future. The culture of an organization is one of its most irreplaceable assets, and the knowledge it contains could be its best source of competitive advantage. Therefore, leaders will absolutely have to possess the ability to lead change, to learn new organizational cultures, and to understand evolving processes that enlarge and strengthen the culture by building on its strengths and functional elements. Schein states, "Leadership will then increasingly be an emergent function rather than a property of people appointed to formal roles."[170]

> Therefore, leaders will absolutely have to possess the ability to lead change, to learn new organizational cultures, and to understand evolving processes that enlarge and strengthen the culture by building on its strengths and functional elements.

In order to ensure organizations reach their full potential and bring the most valuable asset of any organization with them, leaders of the future will unleash the collective potential of all people in the organization. By doing so, and achieving this fundamental tenet of leadership, ordinary people will achieve extraordinary results. Real, sustaining change depends on the motivation and self-leadership of leaders, followers, managers, and employees. A critical element in sustaining any change effort is reigniting everyone's motivation and talents, and providing support in order to use them effectively in the organization. Changing the vision, structure, and culture of any organization takes a tremendous amount of effort, and ensuring the change is "learned" and sustaining is dependent upon the leadership and support of all levels of the organization.

> A critical element in sustaining any change effort is reigniting everyone's motivation and talents, providing support in order to use them effectively in the organization. Changing the vision, structure, and culture of any organization takes a tremendous amount of effort, and ensuring the change is "learned" and sustaining is dependent upon the leadership and support of all levels of the organization.

Most people are now familiar with the axiom "The only real constant is change." Leaders and managers of the future will have to be well versed in the challenges and dynamics of constant, even radical change. Change is all around us, and our natural tendency is to resist it with all our might. Given this first reaction and natural tendency, it is imperative that managers and leaders be able to communicate the vision of the necessity of change, the real benefits of change, and where it will eventually take the organization. What is needed is a look at the big picture and the ability to address the whole of the organization in a system-like, tiered approach to change. In addition to resistance to change, there is a lack of successful implementation of large-scale, system-wide change. One just needs to look at the results of mergers and acquisitions over the last decade to see examples of extreme failures. The high failure rates and lack of synergy are certainly not things to be proud of. Research suggests that 65 to 70 percent fail or fail to realize pre-merger synergy hopes. "Culture is a set of rituals, ceremonies, and signals that communicate or express myths and values to the world inside and outside the organization."[171] Blending two organizations that are different and trying to achieve synergies at the same time dramatic change is transpiring are extremely difficult. Leadership must understand this and ensure that the process for integration is well thought out before the decision to merge is made.

Leaders and managers of change need to possess and market a compelling vision to keep people committed to the desired future of the organization. The process may take several forms and be a top-down/bottom-up process of interaction and mutual influence between the "official" leader, functional managers, and all employees.[172] Leaders need a clear grasp of the nature of the change to be implemented. To ensure change is accepted more easily and is sustainable, leaders may have to help employees develop and maintain a collaborative team-based approach to problem-solving, an open and sharing culture, and employee development and learning opportunities. Rather than directing, telling, pushing, and driving the organization, the leader expects the best possible from each employee, gets commitment, and actually coaches and mentors

Leaders establish the vision and simultaneously nurture the organization to foster additional "pull" leadership. Involving *all* parts of the organization, working toward integration, using push and pull strategies, and making decisions based on high moral values supported by harmony, cohesion, and trust may help ensure the learning organization changes, as required, to survive the challenges of the future.

individuals to ensure their individual contributions tie in directly to the organization's goals and strategy. Bennis and Nanus[173] from their study of corporate exemplary leaders, describe the process by saying that leaders "pull" rather than push. They pull through a compelling vision that creates focus for change for the organization and ensures that the changes are accepted. Leaders establish the vision and simultaneously nurture the organization to foster additional "pull" leadership. Involving *all* parts of the organization, working toward integration, using push and pull strategies, and making decisions based on high moral values supported by harmony, cohesion, and trust may help ensure the learning organization changes, as required, to survive the challenges of the future.

Organizations provide time for reflection and reflective practice in order to learn from actions and improve upon decision-making capabilities at the individual and team levels. Learning takes place in both informal and formal settings, from the copy station to the classroom, on the job or during breaks, or in meetings and conferences designed for this purpose. Most of what people know is learned on the job by talking to other people, trying new things, and doing their work. Formal training and education, though essential for success and learning, cannot serve as a substitution for informal interactions as a powerful means of learning.

What distinguishes a learning organization from others is the way it is structured to legitimize and create space for informal and formal learning through conscious intention. Learning is part of the culture of an organization and is accomplished in many ways. According to Laiken,[174] this is accomplished through a variety of approaches: (1) by helping to establish supportive, mentoring relationships in which the mentor acts as a coach, or peers act as coaches for one another; (2) by encouraging "communities of practice" for both formal and informal learning and dialogue; (3) by providing skill development, either through action learning or classroom training, providing the process-oriented and facilitative skills necessary to support reflective practice; and (4) by developing a shared set of values, which reinforce and make public the organization's commitment to creating an environment for learning.

In the learning organization, there is a dilemma between the necessity of having very strong leadership as opposed to management and the requirement that teams and individuals be carefully nurtured, be enabled rather than controlled, be empowered rather than overpowered, and be coached versus directed (the "leadership" versus "management" conundrum). Change, especially radical change that does not occur under the conditions of strong leadership and empowered teams, is destined to fail. Leaders are encouraged to enlist widespread involvement, ensuring that individuals and teams affected by change decisions play a key role in helping to make them. Thus, participation in decision making at all levels is built into the inner fabric of the organization, providing room for individual voices within the parameters provided by visionary leadership. According to Kotter, "successful transformation is 70 to 90 percent leadership and only 10 to 30 percent management."[175] Therefore, the leader of the organization necessarily supports and sometimes leads the charge of dynamic change.

In a learning organization conscious intention is created: (1) by helping to establish supportive, mentoring relationships in which the mentor acts as a coach, or peers act as coaches for one another; (2) by encouraging "communities of practice" for both formal and informal learning and dialogue; (3) by providing skill development, either through action learning or classroom training, in the process-oriented and facilitative skills necessary to support reflective practice; and (4) by developing a shared set of values, which reinforce and make public the organization's commitment to creating an environment for learning.

In the learning organization, work-related beliefs and values are clearly articulated as outcomes of the visionary process. Although not everyone will agree, one of the beliefs should reflect a valuing of difference and diversity, and there will be some common values to which everyone attempts to adhere. Some of the values that come to mind are: an open, collaborative approach to problem-solving and differing views, as opposed to a "culture of blame"; a belief in the value of employees as the organization's most valuable assets (prized possessions, as opposed to liabilities); and a belief in lifelong learning and education, both formal and informal, in the classroom and elsewhere. The culture of the organization enables and rewards employees at all levels who have the courage to confront gaps and raise concerns, the skills to solve problems, and the desire to learn. The leaders are instrumental in accepting and modeling this behavior. They invite and accept feedback for their actions, positive or negative, good or bad, as they strive to transform the organization and "put theory into practice" and constantly and diligently, without fail, "walk the talk."

In the learning organization, the culture is one that accepts failure as a learning experience, and it learns from mistakes and remembers them so as to not make the same mistake twice. The organization that is intent on learning from experience must prohibit, both culturally and procedurally, the use of threat, punishment, or blame. Instead, mistakes or problems are viewed as opportunities for learning, and issues of concern routinely surface, with a vision to improve future performance by effectively dealing with the dynamics of change.

Some of the values that come to mind are: an open, collaborative approach to problem solving and differing views, as opposed to a "culture of blame"; a belief in the value of employees as the organization's most valuable assets (prized possessions, as opposed to liabilities); and a belief in lifelong learning and education, both formal and informal, in the classroom and elsewhere. The culture of the organization enables and rewards employees at all levels who have the courage to confront gaps and raise concerns, the skills to solve problems, and the desire to learn.

Conclusion

Organizations can learn, and the extent to which they learn depends on the culture of learning created in the organization, as well as the involvement and commitment of employees at *all* levels *in* the organization *to* the learning organization. The learning organization does not evolve overnight; it is a journey, as opposed to a destination. The process is long, ongoing, and developmental in nature. Learning will be the essential factor if the organization is to cope with rapid continuous change and survive in the future.

In the past, organizations could grow, evolve, and survive just by improving production in a totally mechanistic way. However, this is not acceptable as markets and economies become more unstable, are rapidly changing, organizational structures are necessarily flexible and decentralized, and information flows are lateral, not top-down, with ongoing consultation from all levels in the organization. The necessary form then is an organic, learning organization. Given the extremely volatile external environments in which organizations now operate, the impetus to develop more flexible, organic structures operating in team-oriented work patterns has been generated at all levels in industry.

Increased competition and rapid technological development means that a significant competitive advantage for organizations in the future will be their ability to create new knowledge that is disseminated throughout the organization and that will, in turn, lead to continuous learning and innovation. Under changing circumstances it appears that elements of organizations must develop an expanded understanding of their roles, to question the appropriateness of what they are doing and press to modify their actions and processes to account for new situations. Organizational functions become cells of

> A learning organization cannot evolve unless and until such issues are alleviated. What is necessary is the correct structure, culture, and subculture; a focus on the development of the individual; a commitment to lifelong learning; and a strong commitment by employees, managers, and leaders to accept change, develop interpersonal skills, and accept mistakes as a natural part and main element of learning. Embracing change just may be a core tenet of success.

knowledge as they become more boundaryless. Also, individuals discover sources of error and attribute them to the operating norms or theory in use within the organization. They then invent new strategies to keep organizational performance within normative ranges, based on new assumptions to correct errors, after which they must evaluate the results of the action. In this way, error correction and continuous questioning embody a complex learning cycle and become part of the culture or "way of doing things." Argyris argued that there can be no organizational learning without individual learning, but that individual learning is a necessary but insufficient condition for organizational learning.[176] Until individuals embed their discoveries, challenges, and results of their inquiries into the organizational "memory" that encodes the theory in use, their work as learning agents is incomplete. This, however, implies that organizational structures, processes, and cultures are receptive to fundamental challenges to established norms and procedures to facilitate learning. Changing such complex, intertwined elements is no easy task, even for an organization bent on becoming a learning organization. It remains to be seen if the average organization can do this.

If organizations are to increase their capacity to learn, by both individual and organizational means, there must be recognition and removal of the barriers they have created that inhibit the processes. A learning organization cannot evolve unless and until such issues are alleviated. What is necessary is the correct structure, culture, and subculture; a focus on the development of the individual; a commitment to lifelong learning; and a strong commitment by employees, managers, and leaders to accept change, develop interpersonal skills, and accept mistakes as a natural part and main element of learning. Embracing change just may be a core tenet of success.

Endnotes

1   R. D. Mann, "A Review of The Relationship Between Personality and Performance in Small Groups," *Psychological Bulletin* 66(4): 241-70.

R. Stogdill, "Personal Factors Associated With Leadership. A Survey of Literature," *Journal of Psychology* 25 (1948): 35-71.

R. Stogdill, *Handbook of Leadership* (New York: The Free Press, 1974).

2   B. M. Bass, "From Transactional to Transformational Leadership: Learning to Share The Vision," *Organizational Dynamics* (18)3 (1990): 19-36.

J. M. Kouzes and B. Z Posner, *The Leadership Challenge* (San Francisco: Jossey-Bass, 1995).

P. Senge, *The Fifth Discipline,* (New York: Doubleday Currency, 1990).

G. Yukl, *Leadership in Organizations,* (New Jersey: Prentice-Hall, 1981).

3   Bass, *Transactional,* 85.

4   R. Stogdill in G. Yukl, *"Leadership in Organizations"* (New Jersey: Prentice Hall, 1998), 236.

5   S. Bornstein and A. Smith, *The Leader of The Future: New Visions, Strategies, and Practices for The Next Era* (San Francisco: Jossey-Bass, 1996), 283.

6   D. Hartog et al., "Culture Specific and Cross-Culturally Generalizable Implicit Leadership Theories: Are Attributes of Charismatic/Transformational Leadership Universally Endorsed?" *Leadership Quarterly* 10(2) (1999): 219-257.

7   Bornstein and Smith, *Leader,* 291.

8   Bornstein and Smith, *Leader,* 292.

9   W. Bennis and J. Goldsmith, *Learning to Lead: A Workbook on Becoming a Leader,* (New York: Perseus Press, 1997).

10 Bennis and Goldsmith, *Learning.*

11 J. Kotter, *Leading Change,* Harvard Business School Press (Boston: Mass, 1996), 25.

12 B. Bass, *Bass & Stogdill's Handbook of Leadership: Theory, Research, & Managerial Applications* (New York: The Free Press, 1990).

13   W. Bennis, *Why Leaders Can't Lead* (San Francisco: Jossey-Bass, 1989), 77-78.

14   K. Blanchard, *The Leader of The Future: New Visions, Strategies, and Practices For The Next Era* (San Francisco: Jossey-Bass, 1996).

     J. Bolt, *The Leader of The Future: New Visions, Strategies, and Practices For The Next Era* (San Francisco: Jossey-Bass, 1996).

15   A. Zaleznik, "Managers and Leaders: Are They Different?" *Harvard Business Review* (1992).

16   Bass, *Transactional.*

     W. Bennis, *On Becoming a Leader*, Rev 2nd ed. (Addison-Wesley Pub Co, 1995).

     W. Bennis and B. Nanus, *Leaders: The Strategies for Taking Charge*, 2nd ed. (New York: Harperbusiness, 1997).

     M. DePree, *Leadership is an Art* (New York: Dell Publishing, 1989).

     J. M. Kouzes, B. Z. Posner and T. Peters, *Credibility: How Leaders Gain and Lose it, Why People Demand it* (San Francisco: Jossey-Bass, 1995).

     G. Yukl, *Leadership in Organizations* (New Jersey: Prentice Hall, 1998).

     Zaleznik, *Managers.*

17   Bennis, *Becoming.*

18   Bennis, *Why Leaders.*

     Hartog et al., *Culture*, 219-257

     J. M. Kouzes and B. Z. Posner, *The Leadership Challenge: How to Get Extraordinary Things Done in Organizations* (San Francisco, CA. Josssey-Bass, 1990).

     Credibility: How Leaders Gain and Lose it, Why People Demand it, (Reissue Jossey-Bass Simon and Schuster Books, 1993).

19   Kouzes and Posner, *Leadership.*

20   C. Handy, *The Leader of the Future: New Visions, Strategies, and Practices for The Next Era* (San Francisco: Jossey-Bass, 1996).

21   J. Greenberg, *Managing Behavior in Organizations*, 3rd ed. (New Jersey: Upper Saddle River, 2002).

22   Bennis, *Why Leaders*, 72-73.

23   Handy, *Leader*, 9.

24 G. Dessler, *Management: Leading People and Organizations in The 21ˢᵗ Century.* (New Jersey: Prentice Hall, 1998), 335.

25 J. A. Krames, *The Jack Welch Lexicon of Leadership* (New York: McGraw-Hill, 2002), 28.

26 R. Willingham, *The People Principle: A Revolutionary Redefinition of Leadership.* (New York: St. Martin's Press, 1997).

27 H. R. Covey, *Principle-Centered Leadership* (New York: Simon & Schuster, 1990), 62.

28 P. Drucker, *The Effective Executive* (New York: Harper Collins, 1999).

29 Krames, *Jack Welch*,185.

30 Kouzes, Posner and Peters, *Credibility*, 336.

31 A. Decrane in "The Leader of The Future," F. Hesselbein, M. Goldsmith, and R. Beckhard (San Francisco: Jossey-Bass, 1996), 254.

32 Decrane, *Leader*, 254.

33 Bennis, *Why Leaders*, 3.

34 D. Goleman, *Working With Emotional Intelligence* (NY: Bantam Books, 1998), 317.

35 D. Goleman, R. Boyatzis, and A. McKee, *Primal Leadership. The Hidden Driver of Great Performance* (Harvard Business Review Press, 2001), 44.

36 Goleman, Boyatzis, and McKee, *Primal*, 44.

37 Maxwell, J. *The 21 Indispensable Qualities of a Leader. Becoming the Person Others Will Want to Follow* (Nashville, Tenn: Thomas Nelson, Inc., 1999), 58-59.

38 Maxwell, *The 21*, 53-54.

39 Kouzes, Posner and Peters, *Credibility*, 185.

40 M. De Pree, *Leadership is an Art* (New York: Dell, 1989).

41 P. Drucker, in "The Business of The Kingdom," T. Stafford, *Christianity Today* 43(13) (November 15, 1999): 3-8, accessed July 11, 2003 EBSCO host search, www.apollogrouplibrary.com.

42 P. Drucker, in "Peter Drucker on The Profession of Management," T. R. Pressly and P. F. Drucker, *Ohio CPA Journal* 58(2) (April/June, 1999): 1-3.

43 P. Drucker, in "Peter Drucker," P. A.Galagan, *Training and Development* 52(9) (September, 1998): 1-6.

44 Drucker, *Business*, 3-8.

45 P. F. Drucker, *The Profession of Management* (Boston: Harvard Business Press, 1998).

46 Bennis, *Why Leaders*, 77.

47 Bennis, *Why Leaders*, 77-78.

48 Bennis, *Why Leaders*, 70.

49 J. W. Gardner, *On Leadership*. (New York, NY: The Free Press, 1990), 14.

50 Gardner, *Leadership*, 15-16.

51 Gardner, *Leadership*, 10.

52 Hagberg Consulting Group. (1998), accessed January 08, 2003, http://209.157.100.6/p-compare.html.

53 E. Schein, *Organizational Culture and Leadership* (Reprint, San Francisco: Jossey-Bass, 1997), 304.

54 Schein, *Organizational Culture*.

55 Schein, *Organizational Culture*, 391-392.

56 Schein, *Organizational Culture*, 68.

57 P. Kotter in "The Corporate Culture Connection," B. Dumaine, *Fortune* 125(9) (May 4, 1992): 1-2.

58 G. Hofstede, *Cultures and Organizations: Software of The Mind*, 1st ed. (McGraw-Hill: USA, 1997), 179.

59 G. Hofstede, *Cultures*.

60 J. Langan-Fox and P. Tan, "Images of a Culture in Transition: Personal Constructs of Organizational Stability and Change," *Journal of Occupational & Organizational Psychology* 70(3) (1997): 273 – 294.

61 J.Barney, "Organizational Culture: Can it be a Source of Sustained Competitive Advantage," *Academy of Management Review* 11(3) (1986), 657, accessed EBSCOHost, June 13, 2002, www.apollogrouplibrary.com.

62 D. R. Denison, *Corporate Culture and Organizational Effectiveness* (New York. Wiley, 1990), 1.

63 M. K. De Vries, *The Leadership Mystique. A User's Manual for The Human Enterprise*, (London: Prentice Hall, 2001), 205.

64   E. H. Schein, *Organizational Culture and Leadership*, 2nd ed. (San Francisco: Jossey-Bass, 1992), 12.

65   J. Jr. Schermerhorn, J. Hunt and R. Osborn, *Organizational Behavior*, 7th ed. (New York:Wiley & Sons, 2000), 44.

66   Hofstede, *Cultures*, 1997.

67   B. Schneider, "Organizational Climate and Culture," in *The Steal Motive: Managing The Social Determinants of Employee Theft*, J. Greenberg (San Francisco: Jossey-Bass, 1990), 307, in *Antisocial in Organizations*, R. A. Giacalone & J. Greenberg, eds., (Thousand Oaks: Sage Publications, 1997).

68   S. Robbins and N. Langton, *Organizational Behavior: Concepts, Controversies, Applications* (Toronto: Prentice-Hall, 2001), 693.

69   Schein, *Organizational*, 14.

70   Schein, *Organizational*, 1992.

71   Hofstede, *Cultures*, 1997.

72   Schein, *Organizational*, 1992.

73   C. Hill, *International Business: Competing in The Global Marketplace*, 3rd ed. (Toronto: McGraw-Hill, 2000), 82.

74   G. Hofstede, "The Cultural Relativity of Organizational Practices and Theories," *Journal of International Business Studies* 14 (1983): 75- 89.

75   N. Goodman, "An Introduction to Sociology," in *International Business: Competing in The Global Marketplace*, 3rd ed., C. Hill (Toronto: McGraw-Hill, 2000), 86. Originally published (New York: Harper Collins, 1991).

76   Goodman, *Introduction*, 86.

77   C. Hill, *International Business: Competing in The Global Marketplace*, 3rd ed. (Toronto: McGraw-Hill, 2000), 94.

78   Hill, *International*, 96.

79   Hill, *International*, 81.

80   Langan-Fox and Tan, *Images*, 273 – 294.

81   M. Alvesson, *Cultural Perspectives on Organizations* (Cambridge, MA: Harvard University Press), 1993.

      Barney, *Organizational*, 1986.

J. Heskett and L. Schlesinger, *The Leader of the Future. New Visions, Strategies, and Practices for The Next Era* (San Francisco: Jossey-Bass Publishers), 1996.

R. Kopelman, A. Brief and R. Guzzo, "The Role of Climate and Culture in Productivity," in *Organizational Climate and Culture*, B. Schneider (San Francisco: Jossey-Bass, 1990): 282-318.

82   J. Kouzes and B. Posner, *Encouraging the Heart: A Leader's Guide to Rewarding and Recognizing Others* (San Francisco: Jossey-Bass), 1999.

J. Maxwell, *The 21*.

Schein, *Organizational*, 1992.

83   Langan-Fox and Tan, *Images*, 1-2.

84   M. Fullan, "Principals as Leaders in a Culture of Change," *Educational Leadership*, May (2002).

Schein, *Organizational*, 1992.

85   M. Fullan, *Principals*, 44.

86   T. Mercer, "Study Confirms it: Corporate Culture Matters," *Crain's Detroit Business* 12(48) (1996), accessed May 15, 2002, http://ehostvgw2.epnet.com.

87   Barney, *Organizational*, 1986.

Schein, *Organizational*, 1992.

88   Barney, *Organizational*, 658.

89   Barney, *Organizational*.

Schein, *Organizational*, 1992.

90   Schein, *Organizational*, 209.

91   Schein, *Organizational*, 211.

92   G. Stevens, "The Art of Running a Business School in The New Millennium: a Dean's Perspective," *SAM Advanced Management Journal* 65(3) (2000).

93   T. Sowell, "Titan Problems in Academe," *Forbes* 82 (November, 1998): 2.

94   Sowell, *Titan*, 5.

95   D. Goleman, "Leadership That Gets Results," *Harvard Business Review* (March/ April, 2000).

J. Kotter, "Leading Change: Why Transformation Efforts Fail," *Harvard Business Review* (1995).

J. Jr. Badaracco, *Leading Quietly: An Unorthodox Guide to Doing The Right Thing*, (Boston, MA: Harvard Business School Press, 2002).

D. Myerson, "Radical Change, The Quiet Way," *Harvard Business Review* 79(9), (October, 2001): 92.

96 Lewin, K., "Frontiers in Group Dynamics. Concept, Method and Reality in Social Science," *Human Relations* 1(1), (1947): 5-40, accessed October 15, 2002, EBSCOHost from http://www.apollolibrary.com, 34.

97 Kotter, *Leading*, 21.

98 M. Fullan, *Leading in a Culture of Change* (San Francisco: Jossey-Bass, 2001), 34.

99 Goleman, *Leadership*.

100 Fullan, *Leading*, 35.

101 R. Heifetz, *Leadership Without Easy Answers* (Cambridge, MA: Harvard University Press, 1994).

Fullan, *Leading*, 21.

102 Kotter, *Leading*, 2- 8.

103 R. Jacobs, *Real Time Strategic Change: How to Involve an Entire Organization in Fast and Far-Reaching Change* (San Francisco: Berrett-Koehler Publishers, 1997), 7 – 8.

104 Jacobs, *Real*, 8.

105 Jacobs, *Real*, 9.

106 Jacobs, *Real*, 10.

107 D. Conner, *Leading at The Edge of Chaos* (New York: John Wiley), 1998.

108 Fullan, *Leading*.

109 Kotter, *Leading*.

110 J. O'Toole, *Leading Change: The Argument for Values-Based Leadership* (New York: Ballantine Books, 1996).

111 O'Toole, *Leading*, 161 - 162.

112 Greenberg, *Managing*, 377

113 J. Collins and J. Porras, *Built to Last: Successful Habits of Visionary Companies* (New York: Harper Business, 1997), 84.

114 De Vries, *Leadership Mystique*, 186.

115 De Vries, *Leadership Mystique*, 189.

116 R. Beckhard, *The Leader of The Future: New Visions, Strategies, and Practices for The Next Era* (San Francisco: Jossey-Bass Publishers, 1996).

Fullan, *Leading*.

Kotter, *Leading*.

E. H. Schein, "Organizational Culture," *American Psychologist* 45(2) (1990): 109-119.

117 D. E. Terpstra, "Theories of Motivation: Borrowing The Best," *Personnel Journal* 58 (1979): 376.

118 A. H. Maslow, "A Theory of Human Motivation," *Psychological Review* (July, 1943).

119 F. Herzberg, B. Mausner and B. B. Snyderman, *The Motivation to Work* (New York: John Wiley & Sons, 1959).

120 J. S. Adams, *Inequity in Social Exchange. Advances in Experimental Social Psychology* (New York: Academic Press, 1959).

121 V. H. Vroom, *Work and Motivation* (New York: Wiley, 1964).

122 B.F. Skinner, *Science and Human Behavior* (Boston: Houghton Mifflin Company, 1953).

123 C. Argyris, *Overcoming Organizational Defenses: Facilitating Organizational Learning* (Boston: Allyn & Bacon, 1990).

124 De Vries, *Leadership Mystique*, 203.

125 Fullan, *Leading*.

Kotter, *Leading*.

Schein, *Organizational*, 109-119.

126 J. Latham, *Personal Comments in Comprehensive Paper Answers*. Vancouver, BC: Unpublished, 2003.

127 Fullan, *Leading*, 31.

128 Robbins and Langton, *Organizational*, 586.

129 Robbins and Langton, *Organizational*, 587.

130 Schein, *Organizational*, 109-119.

131 G. Morgan, *Images of Organization* (Thousand Oaks, CA: SAGE Publications, Inc., 1997),150.

132 Latham, *Personal*.

133 Fullan, *Leading*.

Jacobs, *Real*.

De Vries, *Leadership Mystique*.

Kotter, *Leading*.

O'Toole, *Leading*.

Schein, *Organizational*, 109-119.

134 De Vries, *Leadership Mystique*, 180.

135 Fullan, *Leading*.

Jacobs, *Real*.

De Vries, *Leadership Mystique*.

Kotter, *Leading*.

O'Toole, *Leading*.

Schein, *Organizational*, 109-119.

136 Schein, *Organizational*, 109-119.

Robbins and Langton, *Organizational*.

137 De Vries, *Leadership Mystique*.

O'Toole, *Leading*.

Schein, *Organizational*, 109-119

138 Fullan, *Leading*.

Goleman, *Working*.

De Vries, *Leadership Mystique*.

Kotter, *Leading*.

Schein, *Organizational*, 109-119.

139 B. Blumenthal and P. Haspeslagh, "Toward a Definition of Corporate Transformation," *Sloan Management Review* (1994).

J. M. Kouzes, B.Z. Posner B.Z. and T. Peters, *Credibility*.

140 Goleman, *Working*, 95.

141 Fullan, *Leading.*

Goleman, *Working.*

Heifetz, *Leadership.*

Kotter, *Leading.*

142 Goleman, *Leadership.*

143 Fullan, *Leading,* 131.

144 Fullan, *Leading,* 137.

145 C. Argyris, *Flawed Advice and The Management Trap* (New York: Oxford University Press, 2000).

146 Fullan, *Leading,* 133.

147 R. Pascale, M. Millemann and L. Gioja, *Surfing The Edge of Chao* (New York: Crown Business Publishing, 2000), 6.

148 Collins and Porras, *Built.*

Fullan, *Leading.*

Jacobs, *Real.*

Kotter, *Leading.*

Schein, *Organizational,* 109-119.

149 Greenberg, *Managing,* 378 - 379.

150 Goleman, *Leadership.*

151 Jacobs, *Real.*

152 Kotter, *Leading.*

153 H. Mintzberg, B. Ahlstrand and J. Lampel, *Strategy Safari: A Guided Tour Through The Wilds of Strategic Management* (New York: Free Press, 1998), 324.

154 E. Schein, in *"The Leader of The Future,"* F. Hesselbein, M. Goldsmith and R. Beckhard (San Francisco: Jossey-Bass, 1996), 61.

155 E. Schein, in *"The Leader of The Future,"* F. Hesselbein, M. Goldsmith and R. Beckhard (San Francisco: Jossey-Bass, 1996), 64.

156 J. Heskett, and L. Schlesinger, in *"The Leader of the Future,"* F. Hesselbein, M. Goldsmith and R. Beckhard (San Francisco: Jossey-Bass, 1996), 119.

157 De Vries, *Leadership Mystique*, 60.

158 University of Phoenix, *Annual Report*, 2001, 1.

159 De Vries, *Leadership Mystique,* 63.

160 J. Bolt, in *The Leader of The Future*, F. Hesselbein, M. Goldsmith and R. Beckhard, R. (San Francisco: Jossey-Bass, 1996), 168.

161 S. Covey, in *The Leader of The Future*, F. Hesselbein, M. Goldsmith and R. Beckhard, R. (San Francisco: Jossey-Bass, 1996), 149.

162 Covey, *Leader*, 149-150.

163 K. Blanchard, in *The Leader of The Future*, F. Hesselbein, M. Goldsmith and R. Beckhard, R. (San Francisco: Jossey-Bass, 1996), 85.

164 R. Leider, in *The Leader of The Future*, F. Hesselbein, M. Goldsmith and R. Beckhard (San Francisco: Jossey-Bass, 1996), 189-190.

165 De Vries, *Leadership Mystique*.

Schein, *Organizational*, 109-119.

166 Accessed August 20, 2002, http://www.thebdc.com/bizstages/.

167 Schein, *Organizational*, 304.

168 Lewin, *Frontiers*, 5-40

169 Schein, *Organizational*, 391-392.

170 Schein, *Organizational*, 68.

171 Schein, *Organizational*, 367.

172 Bennis and Nanus, *Leaders*.

Kotter, *Leading*.

Schein, *Organizational*, 1990.

Sowell, *Titan*, 1998.

173 Bennis and Nanus, *Leaders*, 1997.

174 M. E. Laiken, *Models of Organizational Learning: Paradoxes and Best Practices in The Post-Industrial Workplace*. NALL Working Paper #25, 2001.

175 Kotter, *Leading*, 26.

176 Argyris, *Overcoming*

High Performance: Elusive Ideal or Possible Reality?

What constitutes a high-performance workplace or a high-performance organization has been the subject of many debates over the last three decades, and there seems to be no signs of this slowing down anytime soon. For strategic advantage, many companies have relied on ways of managing people and organizing work. A new vision is beginning to emerge from the experiences of best-practice companies of what constitutes an effective workplace, something that is now called high-performance workplaces.[1] For most companies, no matter their size or how good their performance has been, the goal of sustained performance over time has proven difficult and often elusive.

With increased competition and the prevalence of the "bigger is better" mentality, the 1990s gave way to the "smaller is better" mantra of the early 2000s, with downsizing, restructuring, and reengineering being the norm. Along with past case studies and recent research studies on the subject, the experiences of best-practice companies can help point the way to high performance. Discussions of high-performance workplaces often focus on quality processes, quality control, flatter organizational structures, continuous improvement, flexible technologies, self-managing teams, innovative compensation schemes, and increased training for employees. A variety of approaches using the above elements have been tried and practiced to varying degrees of success to achieve high performance. "Effectively managing people is a key to all of them."[2] According to Gephart,

> companies that exhibit high performance use all their resources—human, material, and technological – to achieve and sustain competitive advantage. A systems approach is key. High performance emerges out of the links among how work is organized, how people are managed, how technology is used, and how all of these are linked to an organization's competitive strategy and culture.[2]

High-performance companies, through their organization of work and their management of people, are achieving results, including innovation, quality, productivity, customer satisfaction, increased profits and market share, and more flexibility. Some of the findings suggest that flexible forms of work can affect quality and productivity; systems of complementary and reinforcing work practices and human resources practices lead to improved performance; a system of high-performance practices is most effective when it is linked with a competitive strategy and culture; and there is no single set of practices that makes up a high-performance work system.[3]

What seems to be clear is that high-performance organizations use systems, processes, and people to achieve their sustained results. The message from some of the later literature regarding high-performance companies is "the quality of the people matters as much as the quality of the numbers,"[4] and even today, executives still struggle with this paradox.

What Does a High-Performance Organization Look Like?

For a more detailed definition, it might be prudent to look at case studies to glean a deeper understanding of what the term "high-performance" actually means. Many researchers and faculty put forth examples like Southwest Airlines, General Electric, Johnson & Johnson, Merck & Company, as well as others that have sustained profits over decades and have best practices that they develop and share. As mentioned earlier, successful high-performance work systems must be designed and embedded in an organization's competitive strategy and business goals. Consistent achievement of superior performance requires clear goals and directions that are intricately linked to an organization's mission and strategy.[5] Individual, team, and organizational performance is aligned, and employees have the organization's goals as their own. There is complete clarity about product requirements and mutually agreed-upon measures of performance.[6] The focus of quality and product must have a consumer orientation and be customer driven.[7] According to Gephart, "high-performance work systems must enable people, working together, to produce and deliver products and services that meet customer requirements in the context of environments that change rapidly."[8]

In a high-performance system, organizational structures support the management of results, with the organization designed around products, services, or process, as opposed to functions (like traditional companies). Size and structure (i.e., small and decentralized) are not the core issues; they are important, but such things as focus, accountability, cycle time, and customer service, are crucial to high-performance. People have access to and share all information required to perform successfully. Teams and work units have a balanced amount of autonomy, responsibility, decision-making authority, and the necessary resources to perform. Workers are empowered and motivated, and there must be

> In a high-performance system, organizational structures support the management of results, with the organization designed around products, services, or process, as opposed to functions (like traditional companies). Small and decentralized are not the core issues, they are important, but, focus, accountability, cycle time, and customer service, are.

collaboration and trust among all levels of management and the workers. Finally, the teams are part of any strategic change process, since change may be a factor in creating high-performance work systems. According to Gephart, "the processes of change that create high-performance work systems in an organization may be as important as the practices and innovations themselves."[8]

Research has not yet devised a clear definition of a high-performance workplace system or organization. While many of the terms may have now changed, and the literature is somewhat different, many of these characteristics that comprise high-performance systems are not rocket science and may even still hold true today. What may be a more pressing problem is the fact that the literature does not provide clear definitions of organizational performance or high-performance organizations. Many studies use terms such as "transactional efficiency," "input efficiency," "output efficiency," and "effectiveness" to indicate performance.[9] Other studies discuss organizational performance mainly in terms of financial numbers, such as growth, profits, financial turnover, employee turnover, and return on total assets.[10] Still other studies focus on financial measures simply from a stockholder perspective and define organizational performance in terms of dividends, cash flow per share, and earnings per share.[11] An interesting perspective that relates economic performance to tangibles and intangibles and stresses that both are important comes from a consultant by the name of Bob Gunn. Gunn, when commenting on America's "Most Admired" companies, submits that intangibles such as innovation, leadership, talent, and quality play an important role in companies' receiving the distinction. However, the point he makes that may be most interesting is "Among the characteristics standing out among leading companies is that leaders emerge wherever they are needed regardless of whether they hold positions of leadership."[12] This is interesting because it seems to suggest that some combination of financial indicators, people, and leadership is the core component that makes up high-performance, most admired, or successful companies. Another study defined "success" as having demonstrated a profit for each of the preceding five consecutive years.[13] Still another study identified successful companies in Singapore on the basis of being customer-oriented, creating new products, having a clear vision and direction, offering career training, and having a disciplined informal professional atmosphere.[14] So, what then is a high-performance or successful organization? It is an organization that pursues and continually refines best practices. They are intentionally designed to bring out the best in people and create an extraordinary organizational capacity that delivers sustainable high-performance results. They are agile and market driven. They demonstrate respect for individuals and stress team involvement. According to Farquhar,

So, what then is a high-performance or successful organization? It is an organization that pursues and continually refines best practices. They are intentionally designed to bring out the best in people and create an extraordinary organizational capacity that delivers sustainable high-performance results. They are agile and market driven. They demonstrate respect for individuals and stress team involvement.

> high performance requires that the organization be willing to invest in people, to provide the tools and opportunities for self-improvement and to recognize people's contributions. In turn, employees must take charge of their own careers, decide what skills they need to acquire and determine where they wish to employ these skills.[15]

Allerton[16] submits a different definition that was put forth by Development Dimensions International in Pittsburgh that discusses the important roles of culture, employees, and meeting customer needs in a timely manner to ensure business success. The culture provides the employees with the accountability and responsibility necessary to meet customer needs in a timely manner.

According to Fleming and Drucker, an important characteristic of high-performance organizations is their focus on continuous innovation. Experts believe that it takes over three thousand bright ideas to come up with one hundred worthwhile projects, which are narrowed down to four development programs for new products.

Experts believe that it takes over three thousand bright ideas to come up with one hundred worthwhile projects, which are narrowed down to four development programs for new products.

"And four such development programmes are the minimum needed to stand any chance of getting one winner."[17] While these characteristics may be common to successful organizations, the question that is begging to be asked is "Are these characteristics of successful companies similar to characteristics of successful leaders?" Also, without leaders with such characteristics leading organizations, can they really become high-performance? These questions will be answered in the last section of the book.

Empower People
Inspire People
Leadership
Lead Change
Shared Vision

Common Characteristics of Successful Companies

As described earlier, there are numerous characteristics of companies that could be discussed here, and many of them would be related to profits, sales growth, Return on Investment (ROI), Return on Equity (ROE), Return on Capital Employed (ROCE), Return on Net Assets (RONA), and a multitude of acceptable ratios used by financial analysts around the globe. However, since this book is written from the perspective of a leader's viewpoint, the assumption is that organizations led by successful leaders tend to develop and exhibit similar characteristics. Some of the more prevalent characteristics of high-performance organizations then are: (1) employees control resources, including systems, methods, work schedules, and working conditions; (2) leaders build an environment of trust by listening to and communicating with employees; (3) vision and values help guide decision making; (4) individuals have the ability and data to measure their own performance and progress; (5) decision making occurs at the lowest level through employee empowerment; (6) leaders champion continuous improvement, facilitate learning, and reinforce effective performance; (7) risk-taking is encouraged; (8) mistakes are treated as learning opportunities; (9) performance feedback comes from peers, customers, and direct reports; (10) systems are aligned with management to reinforce and drive desired behaviors; (11) effective training is provided; and (12) jobs are designed to provide employee ownership and responsibility. One could easily argue that a high-performance organization shares many characteristics with a learning organization. Maybe high-performance organizations have to become learning organizations before they can be considered high-performance. This book does not address this particular question; however, it might be a good idea to study in the future. The question: does a high-performance organization have to become a learning organization on its way to becoming known for high-performance? Perhaps a past student of mine would like to study this as a potential dissertation—I am only suggesting.

Comparative Analysis of Loblaws and Sobeys

The two chosen companies for this section are probably well-known to most readers, simply because the companies are based in Canada and many people buy their products there. They are widely known here and are two of the largest food retailers in the country. In the United States, and given the emergence of WalMart in groceries, a similar comparison may be made with say, Safeway, USA or Krogers for a similar analysis to see if the theory being used holds true.

Loblaw Companies Limited ("Loblaws") is Canada's largest food distributor, with operations across the country. Loblaws strives to provide superior returns to its shareholders through a combination of share price appreciation and dividends. To this end, it follows certain fundamental operating principles. It concentrates on food retailing with the objective of providing consumers with the best one-stop shopping for everyday household needs. It maintains a significant program of reinvestment in and expansion of its existing markets. It is highly selective in acquisitions and continues to invest in products and technology. Loblaws seeks long-term, stable growth, taking managed operating risks from a strong balance sheet position.[18]

Loblaws is one of the largest private employers in Canada, with over 119,000 employees throughout the business, and it has responsibility to provide fair wages and secure employment. Loblaws believes this responsibility can best be met in a stable, low-cost operating environment in which everyone associated with Loblaws accepts the need to continuously improve service to its customers.[18]

Loblaws is visionary because it is constantly growing in a stable way, with concern for its people, its customers, its image, and its overall reputation. In addition, as part of its mission statement, it highlights and delivers on continuous innovation to its customers.

Sobeys was founded in 1907 in Stellarton, Nova Scotia, and has operations in every province from Newfoundland to British Columbia. According to the Sobeys website, as it continues to grow and expand, one thing that doesn't change is their time-tested approach to creating value for customers and shareholders. Their success lies in over ninety years of superior customer service, excellent product variety, and competitive operations.

Framework for Organizational Evaluations

Loblaws and Sobeys will be compared and contrasted using quantitative data related to high performance, as defined in the literature. Because no company can be completely evaluated on quantitative data alone, let alone accurately compared to a different company, the companies will be evaluated on several criteria developed by Collins and Porras in 1997, using qualitative factors such as time telling versus clock building, the profit myth, core ideology, visionary versus comparison, drive for progress, BHAGS, cultlike culture, promoting from within, and organizational alignment.[19]

Collins and Porras distinguish between time telling and clock building and use those terms to differentiate companies as being visionary or simply a comparison company. They define time telling as "having a great idea or being a charismatic or visionary leader," and clock building as "building a company that can prosper far beyond the presence of any single leader and through multiple product life cycles."[20] The point here is that Collins and Porras believe that leaders of visionary companies tend to be clock builders, as opposed to time tellers. These leaders concentrate primarily on building an organization—building a ticking clock, as opposed to a better product, better quality, or timing a market. Collins and Porras submit that leaders of visionary companies concentrate on building the organizational traits that will make the company visionary and that their greatest creation is *the company itself* and what the company stands for.[20] A very interesting point that Collins and Porras highlight is that charisma is not a required characteristic of the leader. This is contrary to many leadership theories and seems to be a new trend in the leadership literature. They state, "A high-profile, charismatic

> A very interesting point that Collins and Porras highlight is that charisma is not a required characteristic of the leader. This is contrary to many leadership theories and seems to be a new trend in the leadership literature. They state, "A high-profile, charismatic style is absolutely not required to successfully shape a visionary company." In fact, they found in their study that some of the most significant CEOs in history did not have the personality traits of the "archetypal, high-profile, charismatic visionary leader."

style is absolutely not required to successfully shape a visionary company."[21] In fact, they found in their study that some of the most significant CEOs in history did not have the personality traits of the "archetypal, high-profile, charismatic visionary leader."[21]

Time Telling

There have been times in its history when Loblaws has just been telling time. However, in the last two decades it has been successfully striving to build a quality clock. It has evolved from telling time to clock building very rapidly.

Sobeys started off as a good idea by an extremely talented, diligent individual in the late 1890s but did not do much until about a generation later, when a son took over the operation and wanted to expand and diversify the business. Since the early 1940s, it has been expanding and growing but remained a regional player until the late 1990s. Many people and analysts still consider Sobeys to be an east coast entity despite its national presence. It just announced a decision to purchase Safeway Canada (June 2013) for almost six billion dollars. This makes it the number two food retailer in Canada with over twenty-five billion dollars in annual revenues. Loblaws, not to be outdone by Sobeys, just announced a blockbuster deal to purchase Canada's largest drugstore chain, Shoppers Drug Mart, with over 1,200 stores and approximately eleven billion dollars in revenue in 2012 for a whopping $12.4 billion. It is apparent that Loblaws is showing no signs of relinquishing its number one position, and if the deal goes through under the guidance of Galen Weston (Sr.), Galen Weston Jr., the executive chairman, is leaving his mark on the Canadian retail landscape with a vision of leading (or continuing to lead) in this space, moving further along the strategic path set many years ago.

Clock Building

Currently Loblaws has reached the stage of clock building. It does not have, require, or want charismatic leaders or visionary strategies. It wants to execute it strategies with precision and continue with stable growth, superior customer service, and exceptional value for customers, employees, and other stakeholders. The organization has been built on a sound foundation and, with its current leadership position, will continue to move forward with the strong traits it is well-known for. The reputation of the company is now greater than the combined traits of any of its leaders or managers.

The Sobey family is still actively involved in the day-to-day operations of the business and is associated with its strategies. While they are not charismatic leaders, there appears to still be a strong association with the family, their ideas, and their "charisma and vision" for the company. While they are attempting to build a visionary company and the "quality clock," they still have a long way to go to achieve this goal.

In the 2009 Loblaws annual report, the company's mission is to be Canada's best food, health, and home retailer by exceeding customer expectations through innovative products at great prices. This fits again with the clock-building mentality more so than time telling, as defined by Collins and Porras.

In the 2008 Sobeys annual report, the primary goal is "to build long-term shareholder value through income and cash flow growth and equity participation in businesses that have the potential for long-term growth and profitability." That seems to fit more with time telling than clock building, yes? Its vision to be recognized as Canada's best food retailer shows something akin to clock building, but food is only part of its offering.

Table 5. Comparison of Loblaws and Sobeys on Industry Measures (2001)[22]

Measure	Loblaws	Sobeys
Sales/Revenue	$21.5 billion	$11.37 billion
Operating Income	$1.1 billion	$264.6 million
Net Earnings per Share	$2.04	$1.50
Number of Stores	606	1,351
2001 Square Feet	28.6 million	20.7 million
Sales per Square Feet	$566	$485
Average Store Size	46,000 square feet	15,320 square feet
Vision	Exceeding consumer expectations, innovation and diversity, and continuous innovation	Customer service, creating value, and building sustainable worth

In 2010, 2011, and 2012, the following statistics are applicable to the companies.

Table 6. Comparison of Loblaws and Sobeys on Industry Measures 2010 to 2012[23]

Measure	Loblaws			Sobeys		
Year	2010	2011	2012	2010	2011	2012
Sales/Revenue (billions)	$30.84	$31.20	$31.60	$15.52	$15.95	$16.25
Operating Income	$1.35	$1.38	$1.12	$.285	$.308	$.476
Net Earnings per Share	$2.43	$2.73	$2.31	$4.04	$4.40	$4.72
Square Feet (millions)	50.7	51.2	51.5		28.7	29

Measure	Loblaws			Sobeys		
Year	2010	2011	2012	2010	2011	2012
Number of Stores			1,000 (across Canada)			1,349
Number of Employees			134,000			47,000
Average Store Size	64,800 square feet (corporate) 29,400 square feet (franchise)			18,625 square feet		
Vision	To be Canada's best food, health, and home retailer by exceeding customer expectations through innovative products at great prices			No vision statement in 2011 and 2012 annual reports		

Sobeys success lies in over ninety years of superior customer service, excellent product variety, and competitive operations. Sobeys states as their vision,

> Our vision is to make Sobeys the most worthwhile shopping experience in the marketplace by accurately identifying customers' preferences and efficiently meeting their needs. It takes skilled and dedicated people to do that, and the kind of motivation that only comes by making Sobeys a company worthy of their commitment.[24]

The Profit Myth

The myth that businesses operate solely to generate profits for share-holders has been shattered. While profits are important for any business, they are not necessarily the raison d'être, and, in fact, Collins and Porras found that most visionary companies are highly effective profit-making enterprises, but they had a core ideology beyond making money. Their analysis showed that "the visionary companies have generally been more ideologically driven and less purely profit driven than the comparison companies."[25]

Even though the Loblaws annual report is full of financial data, and ROI, RONA, EBIT, EBITDA, and a host of other profitability-related data are explained, the first page of the annual report mentions Loblaws's commitment to its 119,000 employees across Canada. It states, "Loblaw is one of the largest private employers in Canada with over 119,000 employees throughout the business, and has a responsibility to provide fair wages and secure employment."[26]

Sobeys is obviously a good company based on the above metrics and analyses and is trying hard to become a visionary; however, it has a ways to go based on the definition of a visionary company, as described by Collins and Porras in 1997. They define visionary companies as "premier institutions—the crown jewels—in their industries, widely admired by their peers and having a long track record of making a significant impact on the world around them."[27] "They are the best of the best in their industries, and have been that way for decades."[28] The first page of its Annual Report does not mention its people. The first page states the financial and operating overview, and the first nine points are *all* related to financials.

Sobeys states that it had record results in fiscal 2009 (Annual Report, p. 16). Sobeys' stated that "it achieved another record performance in 2010" (revenue and operating earnings) p. 2 of the 2010 Annual Report. Usually, there would be mention of the most important assets, the people who deliver the performance early on in the report, at least for visionary companies.

While the companies are close with respect to how they are perform-ing in the food sector, it is clear from the information outlined above that

Loblaws is the visionary company and Sobeys is a strong, improving, and challenging comparison company. Loblaws has the edge in core ideology, drive for progress, and exceeding customer expectations to make stable, sustainable profits.

Core Ideology

According to Collins and Porras, the visionary companies exhibit a pattern; they all have "the existence of a core ideology as a primary element in their historical development."[29] They define core ideology in a visionary company as "a set of basic precepts that plant a fixed stake in the ground: This is who we are; this is what we stand for; this is what we are all about."[29]

In Loblaws's 2001 annual report, the company states, "Loblaw strives to exceed our customer's expectation with *every* product and service offered."[30]

The second page of the 2001 Sobeys annual report states its vision as "to be the most worthwhile experience in the marketplace ... period."[31] The second sentence is much less vague and is related to people. It states, "Delivering that experience takes motivated people with real commitment to customer service."[31] On page 8 of the 2001 annual report, the company thanks its thirty-two thousand employees and franchises across the country, which is a good sign of a changing ideology. Despite this, page 8 of the report may reflect the importance it places on its employees.

Visionary versus Comparison

The Loblaws 2009 annual report is peppered with examples of how employees are engaged and continue to move up the corporate ladder. Their stories add value and show both the visionary nature of the organization and its promotion-from-within strategy where possible.

In 2009, Loblaws took major steps to embed corporate social responsibility (CSR) into everyday business practices and "making it part of the way we do business." In addition, it lists several key areas of responsibility: respect the environment, source with integrity, make a positive difference in the community, reflect the nation's diversity, and be a great place to work. In addition, the board of directors and management "are committed to *sound* corporate governance practices" (italics added by the author for emphasis).

Drive for Progress

A visionary company preserves a core ideology, and this must be coupled with a relentless drive for progress that impels change in all that is not part of the core ideology. The drive for progress arises from a deep human urge—to explore, to create, to discover, to achieve, to change, and to improve.[32]

On page 10 of Loblaws's 2001 annual report, the company states, "Our fundamental operating principle is to ensure an ever-improving food offering, while providing our customers in each community with the best in one-stop shopping for everyday household needs." The annual report also states, "Efforts are underway to expand the organic product line to 300 key items (from 80) by the end of 2002, to satisfy our customers' needs for variety."[33]

Not much is mentioned in the Sobeys annual report with respect to driving for progress; however, they do mention building sustainable worth. "It requires a clear understanding that creating shareholder worth—while the ultimate measure of success for any public company—can only be the result, not the sole purpose, of our strategy."[34]

Loblaws is Canada's largest retailer and one of Canada's largest employers (134,000 full- and part-time employees). It was named among the Top 100 Employers, Top Employers for Young People, Best Employer for New Canadians, and Best Diversity Employers.[35]

Based on the above analysis, and in an attempt to integrate the theory of Collins and Porras, Big Hairy Audacious Goals, are defined by key points outlined below:

BHAG (Big Hairy Audacious Goal)
Key Points:

- Falls in the gray area where reason and prudence say (*unreasonable yet we will do it*)!
- A BHAG only helps an organization as long as it *has not yet been achieved*

- The goal itself becomes the *motivating mechanism*
- BHAGs take a life of their own and thereby act as a stimulus through *multiple generations of leadership*
- Focus tends to be on *organizational design* and *development of people*
- Continually reinventing with *bold* goals
- A true BHAG is *outside core ideology yet is consistent with it and fully supports it*
- A BHAG should be so clear and compelling that it requires little or no explanation
- A BHAG should *fall well outside the comfort zone* AND *requires belief and heroic effort to pull it off* [36] (Italics added).

To summarize the differences between Loblaws and Sobeys, their respective BHAGs were to be presented below:

Loblaws's BHAG.

Stimulates forward progress.
Creates momentum.
Fits with the core ideology.

The three points outlined above were going to be the comparison elements for each of the companies with respect to their BHAGs. However, there was not enough information available to make a determination as to whether or not the companies even had a BHAG. So, the comparison falls a little short due to lack of available information for this purpose.

Sobeys, Inc BHAG.

Stimulates forward progress.
Creates momentum.
Fits with the core ideology.

Same comments as above with respect to Loblaws.

Cultlike Culture, Trying Something New, and Learning from Mistakes

Elements of a cultlike culture, as portrayed by Collins and Porras, do not seem to be present in either of the organizations to the extent described by the authors. Some of the most common practices that build a strong culture are:

- orientation and ongoing training programs that have ideological, as well as practical, content;
- on-the-job socialization by peers and immediate supervisors;
- rigorous up-through-the-ranks policies—hiring young, promoting from within, and shaping the employee's mind-set from a young age;
- tight screening processes, either during hiring or within the first few years; and
- incentive and advancement criteria explicitly linked to fit with the corporate ideology.[37]

Loblaws: No evidence of this culture in the 2008 and 2009 Annual Report or elsewhere.
Sobeys: No evidence of this culture in the 2008 and 2010 Annual reports or elsewhere.

While it is not certain from the literature and investor relations material available from both Sobeys and Loblaws that they practice all of the items listed, it appears that Loblaws is much further ahead than Sobeys with respect to the above elements. The rationale is that they have so many up-through-the-ranks executives, which underscores the point that they follow the "promote from within" and cultlike culture, as presented by Collins and Porras in *Built to Last*. While this is certainly not conclusive, the nod does go to Loblaws here.

Promoting from Within: How Do They Do It?

Loblaws's annual report shows that on average, the twenty-three senior executives have a total of 430 years of experience. This works out to nineteen years each. Sobeys, on the other hand, have a total of nine executives, and while there is not sufficient information from the annual report to determine average years of service, it is apparent that six of the nine are from outside the company and were recently appointed to executive positions (including the president). The other three executives have held various positions within the company, and the years of service range from two to nineteen years. While not conclusive, it is apparent that Loblaws is following a policy of promoting from within, especially within the executive ranks.

Galen Weston Jr., as executive chairman, continues the trend of senior promotions from within the organization (and family). In 2009, the annual report was ripe with examples of successful immigrants and average Canadians rising through the ranks and being promoted as they built careers with the company.

Paul Sobey is president and CEO of Empire Company Limited, and on page 7 of the 2008 annual report, he gives credit to his people. He states, "It is our people across the company, however, who build this company with consistent focus on superior execution as they work together day-to-day with enthusiasm and commitment."

There was evidence of a focus on people in the 2009 annual report, with pictures and titles, but I could find little evidence to support promoting from within in the annual reports. Having two employees receive Canada's Top 40 under 40 award two years in a row is great news, so the employees are being recognized by peers and Sobeys in the 2008 and 2009 annual reports.

Better Off Tomorrow than Today, and Organizational Alignment

According to Collins and Porras, visionary companies should always work on protecting the core and driving for progress. "Visionary companies do not rely on any one program, strategy, tactic, mechanism, cultural moral, symbolic gesture, or CEO speech to preserve the core and stimulate progress."[38]

Paint the whole picture. Loblaws seems to act in a more comprehensive and consistent manner over time, and it continually expands product offerings, brands, and food choices, as well as growing earnings and dividends. Sobeys has struggled with this over the last decade or so and appears to be more of a small regional player with larger ambitions. In any case, its strategy does not appear to be aligned with its vision.

Sweat the small stuff. There is insufficient evidence to compare and contrast the companies on this element. However, it is evident that Loblaws uses a crafted approach to expansion, store offerings, store size, and consistent growth, backed up with strong (promote-from-within) management, strong (created-over-time) culture, and a focus on continuous improvement—hence, its national presence and its envious industry track record.

Cluster; don't shotgun. Loblaws seems to cluster in the major centers, with larger stores, more offerings, and standard national brands, as well as their own top brands (e.g., President's Choice). Sobeys has more stores (older and smaller) that sometimes overlap in major centers because of its acquisition in 1998. It has to spend more money on refurbishing stores just to maintain its image. It seems to be operating with a shotgun approach.

Swim in your own current, even if you swim against the tide. Loblaws continually develops new, leading brands. Sobeys has grown mostly since 1998 through a large acquisition. In 2013, it announced the purchase of Safeway Canada for some six to seven billion dollars, continuing a trend.

Obliterate misalignments. Loblaws is focused on its core operating principle, which is "to ensure an ever-improving food offering."[39] Sobeys's vision is to be the "most worthwhile experience in the marketplace."[40] This rather vague statement could lead to many misalignments.

Keep the universal requirements while inventing new methods. This element listed by Collins and Porras does not really apply to either company at the moment because of their national presence.

In the 2010 annual report, Loblaws listed eleven key accomplishments and eight new opportunities, including "optimizing its customer offering and shopping experience by re-aligning around a new organizational structure." The new organizational structure introduced in 2010 was the realignment of its retail business into a two-division structure—conventional and discount—in order to better serve the distinct needs of its customers.

In 2008, with the privatization of Sobeys and the acquisition of Thrifty Foods in British Columbia, a case could be made that Sobeys was striving to become a national retailer, which relates to its mission of being widely recognized as the leading food retailer in Canada.

On page 8 of the annual report, there is a brief discussion of the food-focused strategy and regional and local management structures that deploy market-tailored offerings to satisfy the unique occasion-based needs of their customers. There are five distinct store formats based on the uniqueness of each diverse market: full-service, fresh fill-in, community service, convenience, and price discount food stores.

For several years, Sobeys has been focused on three businesses: food retailing; real estate and corporate investments; and a go-national, act-local with an "out-fresh," "out-compete" strategy. It appears that structure and resources are aligned to propel the company's growth and financial performance since Sobeys's records another record performance in fiscal 2010, after achieving the same in 2009.

According to Collins and Porras, "a well-conceived vision consists of two major components –*core ideology* and an *envisioned future*."[41]

Core ideology defines the enduring character of an organization, "its self-identity that remains consistent through time and transcends products/market cycles, technological breakthroughs, management fads, and individual leaders."[41] Core ideology acts as a glue to hold an organization together while it grows, diversifies, decentralizes, and expands. In a great company, it endures as a source of guidance and inspiration. Core values are "a small set of timeless guiding principles that require no external justification; they have *intrinsic* value and importance to those inside the organization."[42] A core purpose "is the organization's fundamental reason for being."[43] An envisioned future "consists of two parts: a ten-to-thirty year big hairy audacious goal and vivid descriptions of what it will be like when the organization achieves the BHAG."[44]

Loblaws mentions in their 2001 annual report that their priorities are to strive to exceed customer expectations with every product and service offered. They intend to selectively focus on expanding products and services through innovation, diversity, and choice to build a shopping experience beyond food.

Sobeys mentions in their 2001 annual report that their vision is to be the most worthwhile experience for all constituents—customers, people, franchisees, suppliers, and shareholders—by operating the best retail food and food service businesses in Canada. Sobeys is focused on superior execution. Given this vision, one must question the sale of SERCA (food service division) in 2005. The company appears noncommittal to its vision, or its vision and strategy are misaligned.

On page 4 of the 2008 annual report, they say the mission will be achieved by transforming into a centralized, marketing-led organization with an unrelenting focus on customers, stores, and products, while leveraging scale and developing capacity for consistent execution to drive profitable growth. In the 2010 annual report, Galen states that by continuing "to focus on strengthening our core businesses, we now have an eye on Loblaws's next evolution – new opportunities to build out from the core."

Sobeys is making great strides in this area, highlighted by the following points: On page 4 of the 2008 annual report, it is stated that one of its key imperatives is the continued improvement in operational execution through the engagement and development of the employees; the other imperatives are reducing the cost base and improving productivity through the organization, and innovation in the products and services offered to customers.

A similar comment was made in the 2009 annual report, in the letter to the shareholders, in which they thank the more than ninety thousand employees at Empire and related companies for their contributions. Also, one of its competitive strengths is touted to be "our passionate 'best in food' focus supported by our fresh food expertise."

The comment on page 6 "While our presence as a national grocer continues to grow, an approach remains distinctly local" reminds me of the adage that going global while acting local can be a competitive strategy. Perhaps that core ideology with the focus on "out-competing" others with local strategies, while building a growing national presence, will work. Certainly the purchase of Safeway Canada assets for approximately six billion dollars will add relevance to that strategy.

In concluding the comparative case analysis, it is perhaps best just to state the obvious—the Weston brothers, Garfield and Galen have created serious achievements and have transformed a family bakery into mighty Loblaws, an evolving supermarket powerhouse. They show no signs of slowing down anytime soon, and their core ideology is not changing. In 2012, Loblaws was still double the size of Sobeys, and with its announcement that it would purchase the Canadian icon Shoppers Drug Mart in July 2013 for $12.4 billion, it would leapfrog to the front again with very strong brands and a national presence. It would be interesting to do this comparison in another decade to see where each company is with respect to the Collins and Porras theory and key business measures.

A Comparison of the Characteristics of Successful Companies

After a comprehensive review of the leadership literature, there appear to be certain characteristics that are crucial to successful leaders and that successful or high-performance organizations possess, even though having these characteristics is no guarantee of success. The following list includes some of the most common and widely discussed characteristics of successful leaders: ability to create, develop, and articulate a vision; ability to align vision with corporate strategy, culture, and people; focus on hiring and retaining the best people through coaching and mentoring; ability to effectively communicate; ability to effectively problem solve; ability to build teams and consensus; ability to manage resources (overlap with management); ability to acquire knowledge through lifelong learning; and ability to inspire others to follow, through integrity and trust. There are many others that could have been placed on this list; however, because of the limited scope of this section, this is the list that will be discussed. The items are ranked in order of importance; however, there may not be complete agreement on the list itself or the ranking. The literature itself is not clear on the major necessary characteristics of effective leaders, managers, or organizations. The discussion below is a result of reading the works of Kotter, Kets de Vries, Maxwell, DePree, Covey, Gardner, Bennis, Kouzes and Posner; Collins and Porras; Blanchard, Schein, Senge, Drucker; Hesselbein, Goldsmith and Beckhard; among others. The next sections will attempt to synthesize the works of these authors into a list of characteristics identified above and attempt to answer the following question: are the characteristics of successful leaders the same as the characteristics of successful companies?

Ability to create, develop, and articulate a vision. Perhaps no other element of leadership is as discussed, debated, and dialogued about than this one. Also, it appears that there is some consensus in the literature regarding the importance of such a characteristic. Several of the key researchers of leadership, including Maxwell, Depree, Kotter, Bennis, Harper, and

Gardner, have all discussed to varying degrees the importance of creating and articulating a vision.

Ability to align corporate strategy, vision, culture, and people. Again, this point is stressed in the literature of leadership and seems to apply directly to, and affect the success of, companies, particularly over the long term. Two of the most prolific authors on this subject over the last two decades or so are Schein (especially for his work on organizational culture) and Senge (for alignment of vision and strategy).

Ability to communicate effectively. This area is of paramount importance to the leader, but it also applies to all other employees as well, so it is not ranked as high as the first two elements. Effective communication allows leaders to share their vision for the organization and put it in terms that all levels understand and can rally toward. Sometimes it is not as much what you say but how you communicate it. It is essential for the successful completion of goals and objectives.

Ability to effectively problem solve. Leaders are able to make decisions in times of dramatic and discontinuous change that will not be popular but will have a positive impact on their organization during times of chaos. The ability to clearly see the problem and rally the employees around the cause to look for the best solutions to it is extremely important.

Ability to inspire others to follow through with integrity and trust. The decision to make this key characteristic a little lower on the scale was a difficult one, but because of the current scandals on Wall Street and even with Hilary Clinton's email scandal and she is running for President and apparently doing well), many of the leaders of these organizations and in politics around the world, have had followers even though they lack integrity or trust. It is possible that this element is vital over the longer term but not as important in the short term. The real question may be how long people will follow such leaders or how long before they get caught doing something wrong. Then what happens to the organization? Enron, WorldCom, Legato, Andersen, and SNC Lavalin are examples of companies whose leaders and executive management followers have been caught in activities that have caused people to severely question their integrity and that have broken the sacred trust they had with stakeholders. Despite the ranking here, it is nonetheless a very important characteristic of successful leaders, and writers such as Gardner, Maxwell, DePree, and Hesselbein make this point in much of their work, though not exclusively.

Ability to build teams and consensus. Successful leaders tend to build strong teams around them and make decisions using consensus, unless, of course, that is not possible and a top-down decision is required. Generally, successful leaders coach and mentor others to develop their skills. A core requirement of doing so is the appreciation of service, followers, and citizenship in the organization. An effective leader values the strength of the team and uses diversity as a tool to better the organization and achieve its goals.

Ability to manage resources. This is essentially an overlapping function with management, but leadership includes some management, and hiring/developing of an organization's greatest asset (its people) is a core task of a successful leader. A leader must constantly and accurately analyze information and systems, properly identify all resources, and then determine how to utilize them efficiently to achieve the goals of the organization.

Ability to acquire knowledge through lifelong learning. Successful leaders believe in and practice acquiring knowledge through lifelong learning activities. They have a continual thirst for seeking, acquiring, and retaining knowledge. Effective leaders have an excellent understanding of self and their environment. This environment is internal and external and includes all aspects of their responsibilities. Successful leaders also use the knowledge they acquire to benefit those they are serving.

Based on this discussion, can the above characteristics now be applied to successful organizations? Do the characteristics that make many leaders successful apply to successful organizations? Both Sobeys and Loblaws will now be analyzed using the above characteristics to determine which ones they possess and which ones are similar/different, and the comparison used to develop a model of performance that may explain how they are inter-related to affect performance. This sounds a bit complicated but let's proceed and see where we end up.

Table 7: Sobeys versus Loblaws

	Sobeys	Loblaws
Vision	Basically regional	National with international focus
Aligns strategy, vision, and people	Yes, but not effective, and slow at execution	Yes, definitely, especially with consistent performance and above-average growth
Communicates effectively	Seems to do so with employees, media, stakeholders, and government	Seems to be able to make any situation positive and is on top of all changing situations
Problem solves	Effective but backtracks on issues that seem complicated and makes mistakes when executing	Excellent at mergers and making them work, even when time is not opportune; executives make few mistakes when executing
Manages resources	Does this well and seems cautious, especially with expansion plans	Excellent and cautious, yet growth-oriented, and masters growing margins and top line
Lifelong learning	Seems to do this well; owners are still actively involved despite the large number of public shareholders	Promotes from within, and the family runs the business despite the large number of public shareholders

As can be ascertained from Table 7, there are significant and not-so-significant differences between the two companies used in the case study. What does appear to be noteworthy are the differences in the financial performance of the two companies over the last two years and then how that performance is similar or different using the characteristics of many companies (based on the assertion that successful companies possess similar characteristics by virtue of their leaders). It is quite obvious that Loblaws has grown faster, is more profitable more consistently, and has a vision for its business that is not only national but also international. Some of these characteristics are also discussed by Collins and Porras[44] as they compared their findings between leading and comparison companies. It appears that from this simple analysis, combined with financial considerations, the companies are different. Loblaws is the leader, and Sobeys is the comparison. While this case is not conclusive by any means, it does pose some fundamental questions that warrant further analysis. The first is: can successful companies possess the characteristics of successful leaders? The second is: can the characteristics listed above, in that order, be used to predict whether or not a company will be more successful than another before the financial performance indicators are analyzed? This is some interesting food for thought, especially for leaders of supposed higher-performance companies.

Culture and Characteristics of Learning Organizations and Relationship to Transformational Leadership

The purpose of this section of the book is to explore the culture and characteristics of learning organizations and their relationship to transformational leadership. It also will focus on how corporate coaching and mentoring can play a role in corporate learning and organizational behavior, since this is something transformational leaders use throughout their careers. Transformational leadership has two key characteristics that are, by definition, tied to coaching and mentoring: intellectually stimulating and intellectually considerate. These characteristics will be discussed later in the chapter. A review of the literature was performed, and the information gathered came from a number of sources, including Chowdhury;[45] Goleman;[46] Hesselbein, Goldsmith, and Beckhard;[47] Pietersen;[48] and Reed.[49] The research found that one of the keys to coping with being competitive in a knowledge-based economy is the ability to learn; this seems to be supported and practiced by transformational leaders, and that lifelong learning, from both an individual and organizational perspective, is considered essential to continued survival in the new marketplace—the knowledge economy. There is a trend for organizations to strive to become learning organizations, and building knowledge partnered with transformational leadership may be the right combination to enhance performance and create lasting competitive advantage. This section concludes that the necessary conditions for learning don't exist in most organizations because the culture is unsuitable; however, most organizations are learning to become learning organizations. Further research must be done on the subject of the effectiveness of transformational leadership with coaching as a strategy to increase learning in learning organizations and development of competitive advantage to improve performance.

Learning, Knowledge, and Competitive Advantage

The concept of the learning organization started to gain momentum when Nonaka published his article "The Knowledge-Creating Company" in the *Harvard Business Review*. He simply declared, "In an economy where the only certainty is uncertainty, the one sure source of lasting competitive advantage is knowledge."[50] Jack Welch of General Electric echoed similar sentiments during his tenure as president and CEO. Some other researchers who agree with innovation and knowledge as future sources of competitive advantage are Drucker,[51] Keller,[52] and Pressly.[53]

Today, most characteristics of organizational design are being greatly affected by the new rules of the knowledge economy, and these new rules are challenging the current styles of leadership and organizational designs. Leaders are developing new leadership approaches and skills in order to succeed in a world where wealth is built on relationships and experiences, not products or technology.[54] Society is entering the new economy, which is knowledge-based and no longer industrial-based. Intellectual capital is the new productive asset. The major implication of managing and leading in the new economy is that leadership is becoming increasingly important, because managers are dealing with humans and not the traditional forms of production, such as land and machinery. Consequently, the traditional organizational structures and management practices employed over the last fifty years are no longer valid in today's knowledge-based economy and must be changed.

> The major implication of managing and leading in the new economy is that leadership is becoming increasingly important, because managers are dealing with humans and not the traditional forms of production, such as land and machinery. Consequently, the traditional organizational structures and management practices employed over the last fifty years are no longer valid in today's knowledge-based economy and must be changed.

De Vries[55] believes that we are in an era of human capital, which is now a critical element in the effectiveness of organizations. The growth of knowledge continues to accelerate; it has changed the very nature of what organizations need to do, the type of products they produce, and how they produce them. Because of the growth of knowledge and the ways it is used by organizations, the nature of individual work is changed as well. There is a huge increase in knowledge work, in which people manage information, deal with abstract concepts, and are valued for their ability to think, analyze, and problem solve.[56]

One of the keys to coping with being competitive in a knowledge-based economy is the ability to learn as individuals and as organizations. The question organizations must answer is: given the rapid changes that are taking place, is learning taking place as fast as the world is changing? Lifelong learning, from both an individual and organizational perspective, is considered essential to continued survival in the new marketplace.[57] Knowledge workers are replacing the industrial-age workers at a phenomenal rate. Most organizations are being forced to embrace continual learning as one of the key ingredients to becoming successful learning organizations.

This section focuses on the need for organizations to become learning organizations. "The leadership challenges in building learning organizations represent a microcosm of the leadership issue of our times: how human communities, be they multinational corporations or societies, productively confront complex, systemic issues where hierarchical authority is inadequate for change."[58] There are several effective strategies being used to become learning organizations. This portion will focus on the use of corporate coaching, mentoring, developing leaders, and creating knowledge as accepted strategies to enhance learning in organizations. The above strategies are employed and practiced by transformational leaders and may be important in developing competitive advantage and improving performance in organizations.

Differences between Knowledge and Learning

Knowledge is an age-old subject that has been the focus of many scholars, from Plato and Aristotle to, more recently, Thomas Kuhn. Knowledge has many definitions in the English language. It can mean information, awareness, knowing, cognition, cognizance, science, experience, skill, insight, competence, know-how, practical ability, capability, learning, wisdom, and certainty.[59] It also can be defined as the full utilization of information and data, coupled with the potential of people's skills, competencies, ideas, intuitions, commitments, and motivations.[60] Knowledge is information that can be transformed into capabilities for effective and immediate action. Knowledge is stored in the individual brain, and much of this is tacit or informal, or encoded in organizational processes, documents, products, services, facilities, and systems, which are mostly explicit.[61] Davenport defined knowledge as

> a fluid mix of framed experience, values, contextual information and expert insight that provides a framework for evaluating and incorporating new experiences and information. It originates and is applied in the minds of knowers. In organizations, it often becomes embedded not only in documents or repositories but also in organizational routines, processes, practices, and norms.[62]

Prahalad and Hamel[63] have brought the resource-based view of the firm to the forefront of academic literature. These theories are particularly important to this book, because the main premise is that the firm's intellectual assets, in the form of tacit knowledge, are the major component of the firm's core competencies. The resource-based view of the firm supports the concept that a firm's competitive advantage is tied to its unique bundle of resources and capabilities. The firm's intangible assets and creative capital, which are largely tacit, are a major part of those resources and capabilities. This is becoming increasingly more relevant as we move from an information-based economy to a knowledge-based economy. Several key CEOs of the last decade have begun to refer to knowledge development as the only real source of competitive advantage. Jack Welch, the former CEO of General Electric, is once such executive who comes to mind.

Development of knowledge that may be a source of competitive advantage is the result of learning, so there is a need to determine how learning takes place in firms. There are several models and processes that try to explain how learning takes place and how knowledge is managed in organizations. Some notable examples are the knowledge space models described by Nonaka,[64] Boisot,[65] and Hall.[66] In addition, Senge[67] describes metanoia, a process of achieving new insight. Argyris and Schon[68] have described three types of learning: single-loop learning, double-loop learning, and Deutero-learning. Hartog[69] discusses a form of learning he calls triple-loop learning. Many of these models, processes, and theories have been theoretical and lack empirical testing.

Learning, on the other hand, means the ability to innovate to generate new ideas and leverage knowledge. Learning is the ability of organizations to generate and generalize ideas with impact.[70] Organizations differentiate themselves from others using learning to generate innovative new ideas. Learning also means "that ideas originating in one part of the organization are codified and shared throughout the other parts, thus avoiding repetition of mistakes and guaranteeing repetition of successes."[71]

Kim defined learning as "the acquiring of knowledge or skill."[72] Knowledge is the "know-why," conceptual part of learning—knowing why something works or happens. Skill is the know-how, application part—having the ability to use the "know-why" to make something happen. Basically, for true learning to occur, the requirement is for both know-why and know-how to be present in the organization.[73] Pietersen believes that learning alone doesn't produce a positive organizational outcome. It is only when learning is specifically targeted toward the goals of the strategic plan that corporate learning produces real value.[74] Leaders must

> It is only when learning is specifically targeted toward the goals of the strategic plan that corporate learning produces real value. Leaders must understand this and incorporate this understanding into real activities that develop employees so they can be more productive.

understand this and incorporate this understanding into real activities that develop employees so they can be more productive. Leaders must be able to 'see' what is coming, and do what is necessary to prepare. This is where 'know-how' and 'know-why' come in to the picture. Leaders knowing, and leaders doing prepares the organization for unknown future events.

Both individuals and organizations learn, but organizational knowledge is the sum of what individuals learn. The critical factor is not just what and how much individuals in organizations learn, but how effectively they transfer what they know to the organization as a whole.

Importance of Organizational Learning

There has been much written in the area of organizational learning, a topic brought to the academic forefront by Argyris and Schon (in the 1980s) and Senge (since 1990). Since then there have been several attempts to suggest some theoretical structure and obtain empirical evidence to better explain the concept of organizational learning and the role that knowledge plays in that domain. Organizational learning is more than the sum of the parts of individual learning.[75] Consequently, there has been some shift in academic research in the last few years from individual learning to organizational learning. However, while learning is important in the context of the organization, it is still important to understand the dynamics of individual learning and how that learning can be transformed into organizational learning. Nonaka[76] proposed the theory of organizational knowledge creation. He argued that while the central theme of organizational learning is that organizational knowledge is created at the individual level, it is then moved into the organizational realm. It is at the organizational level that knowledge is amplified and disseminated into a process that promotes innovation, creativity, and sustained competitive advantage.

There are a number of definitions proposed by various authors. Chowdury stated that "learning organizations are ones that seem to have the capacity to reinvent themselves, to manage knowledge, and to adjust to changing competitive conditions."[77] They have the capacity to both generate and generalize ideas with impact. Merely having new ideas is not enough to be a full learning organization. The idea must be generated or shared with others. Pietersen contended that "the learning organization is one with an enhanced ability to generate, capture, and share knowledge."[78] Clearly, there is a strong linkage between learning organizations and knowledge management. Reed[79] suggested that organizations that can learn fast will be well equipped for the period of rapid change in which society has found itself at the start of the new millennium. He believed that a learning organization is one that builds and shares a common body of learning and knowledge.

The central competitive dimension of what firms know how to do is to create and transfer knowledge efficiently within an organizational context.[80] However, in its attempt to quickly amplify and disseminate that knowledge, there is a danger of an organization losing its competitive edge through the simplification and codification of information, which can be easily imitated. Hall[81] argued that a firm's sustainable distinctive capability is usually comprised of undiffused (or uncodified) tacit knowledge. However, the use of tacit knowledge is frequently overlooked by organizations in the quest to become a learning organization. There is a need to create an "environment" where tacit knowledge can be shared so that novices can become experts. Given that the sharing of tacit knowledge is a socialization process,[82] and that this implies some "doing," the environment must be one where experiential learning can take place.

Nonaka and Konno[83] further explain that this environment, where learning can take place, has been coined by Japanese philosopher Kitaro Nishida, as the concept of *Ba*. *Ba* (equivalent to "place" in English) is a shared space for emerging relationships. It can be a physical, virtual, or mental space. Knowledge, in contrast to information, cannot be separated from the context—it is embedded in *Ba*. To support the process of knowledge creation, a foundation in *Ba* is required.[83] Deming[84] proposed that management's vital role is to make decisions based on predictions, to make predictions based on theory, and to utilize theory based on knowledge. He called knowledge profound, and core knowledge consisted of four parts: knowledge of systems, knowledge of variation, theory of knowledge, and knowledge of psychology.[85] It should be noted that knowledge is occasionally confused with data and information, although they are not interchangeable concepts. Data is a set of discrete, objective facts about events. Information is a message, usually in the form of a document or an audible or visible communication. Data becomes information when its receiver adds meaning. Data is transformed into information when value is added.[86] Paradoxically, information is knowledge that can be transmitted without loss of integrity.[87]

Importance of Individual and Organizational Learning and Leadership

One of the most important competencies for successful leadership of the next century is likely to be self-learning or learning how to learn.[88] According to Arie de Geus, "the ability to learn faster than competitors may be the only sustainable competitive advantage."[89] This appears to be a weak argument, since competitors can easily copy products and services as a result of that learning in a matter of weeks. Fulmer and Goldsmith concur by continually repeating that leadership, leadership investment, and learning are the only sources of sustainable competitive advantage.[90] Again, this is a bit simplistic and does not go far enough to enable a sufficient understanding of what it takes to develop a sustainable competitive advantage.

A firm's knowledge base is derived through a firm's organizational learning, of either tacit or explicit knowledge. Organizational learning is the composite of individual learning within an organization. While individual learning is important to the organization, it is no longer enough to have one person learning for the organization. "It's just not possible any longer to figure it out from the top and have everyone else following the orders of the grand strategist."[91] The organizations that will really excel in the future will be those that determine how to capitalize on people's commitment and capacity to learn at all levels in an organization.[92] What Senge does not discuss here is that what might be even more crucial is the type of leadership necessary to develop learning and knowledge or to allow it to be developed by nurturing and coaching it. This may be the role of the transformational leader.

Realistically, however, learning organizations do not spend all their time developing new knowledge. They recognize there is no reason to reinvent the wheel if the knowledge they need already exists. Learning organizations develop knowledge networks so they can access critical information.[92] Transformational leaders also have great networks, and this is how relationships are classified by such leaders.

Organizational and individual learning is germane to this book in several ways. It is tied to knowledge, knowledge management, corporate memory, leadership, and corporate coaching. Organizational learning is tied to coaching, because coaching can be viewed as contributing to an organization's overall learning, and coaching is something that transformational leaders do a lot of. While coaching focuses largely on individual behavioral changes or individual performance, its foundation is based on the individual continually learning. This is a central tenet of the learning organization—hence, the relevance. As Yukl points out, "learning is another potential outcome from coaching and is at least as important as performance because, taking a longer-term view, it is what the future performance of the organization is dependent upon."[93]

> Consequently, organizational learning is being used as a strategy to create sustainable competitive advantage. Continuous learning could then lead to knowledge development, which may be the only source of sustainable competitive advantage.

Organizational learning is tied to the management of knowledge, because knowledge management is viewed as contributing to an organization's overall learning.[94] Learning, as described by Fiol and Lyles,[95] is the process of improving actions through better knowledge and understanding. Dodgson[96] describes it as the way firms build, supplement, and organize knowledge and routines around their activities and within their cultures, and adapt and develop organizational efficiency by improving the use of broad skills of their workforces. Consequently, organizational learning is being used as a strategy to create sustainable competitive advantage. Continuous learning could then lead to knowledge development, which may be the only source of sustainable competitive advantage. Organizations learn in order to improve their adaptability and efficiency during times of change, and, as such, organizational learning is essential for innovation.[97] For most organizations, ongoing innovation is the key to success. Hall[98] described innovation as the use of knowledge (new or existing) in a new application (product, process, or service package).

Organizational learning also contributes to organizational memory, because learning systems influence not only immediate members but also future members because of the accumulation of histories, experiences, norms, and stories.[99] Organizational memory can be made of both hard data, such as facts, figures, and rules, as well as soft information, such as tacit knowledge, expertise, experiences, anecdotes, critical incidents, stories, artifacts, and details about strategic decisions.[100] In the transition from an industrial- to a knowledge-based economy, firms are compelled to rely more on intellectual capital to maintain competitive advantage. By creating an inclusive, easily accessible organizational memory, knowledge management is being used to help meet those goals.

Brown and Duguid[101] contend that much of learning and innovation takes place in informal "communities of practice." Very often, learning in an organization takes place by members sharing stories and anecdotes of actual work practice, as opposed to what is mentioned in formal job descriptions or manuals.[102] Nonaka and Konno support these arguments with their concept of *Ba*. Given that much of this transfer of knowledge occurs at the tacit level, it is important to create and maintain an environment where this learning can continue to contribute to a firm's organizational memory. An organization's memory can accumulate faster in an environment where sharing is encouraged.

Much of a firm's organizational memory is of a tacit nature, remaining in the minds of the individuals in the form of histories, experiences, norms, and stories. This informal (tacit) knowledge practice[103] is the key to organizational learning. Brown and Duguid[103] assert that new collaborative technologies should be designed based on these communities of practice rather than on formal descriptions of work. The resulting knowledge base can be treated as "group memory" or organizational memory. Quinn, Anderson, and Finklestein[104] suggested that technology has created new opportunity and rules for organizational change that can enhance organizational intellect and organizational memory.

Developing a Learning Organization

Creating a learning organization has been a popular strategy for the past few years; however, the key to successful leadership is building a teaching organization. A teaching organization is "one that teaches people the importance of facing the realities of their current situation, searching everywhere for the best possible response, and mobilizing the resources to get it done - and then teaches them how to carry on these essential tasks."[105]

Developing a learning organization is not a trivial task, because changing the corporate culture is required. Hargrove states, "In reality, this kind of learning organization cannot be formed without personal transformation on the part of a critical mass of people."[106] A learning organization, therefore, is only as good as its people, and creating this type of organization requires personal transformational learning on the part of its people.

This learning is based on the principle that the problems that need to be solved in organizations are inseparable from who people are and the way they think and interact. It involves questioning assumptions, not the least of which is the tendency to draw self-esteem from having the answers. It also involves a long-term commitment to continuous learning and improvement.[107]

In order for organizations to become learning-oriented, employees need to feel empowered to take risks, experiment, and share knowledge. This may be easier to achieve in more organic, flatter-structured organizations than in hierarchically organized firms that practice a command-and-control style of management, with the possible exceptions of perhaps developed militaries. The concept of leadership has changed from a command-and-control style to one where leaders are acting as change agents and servant leaders.[108] The combination of technological advances, intense global and domestic competition, and more demanding employees has altered the role of leaders. "The new job of the leader will be to coach, develop, train, delegate, facilitate, and run interference rather than doing all the planning, organizing, and directing from an authoritative base."[109]

Yukl defined learning organizations as "organizations that encourage learning in their employees, and implement learning on a continuous basis so that the company can remain competitive within its ever changing environment."[110] Since transformational leaders practice some of the things that Yukl states learning organizations are, it is possible that learning organizations are run by transformational leaders. With an emphasis on learning, individuals in learning organizations are encouraged to share and apply new knowledge, challenge assumptions or mental models, and apply new ideas to problem-solving to make changes to their environment and better meet company objectives.[111] Also integral to the culture of a learning organization is the empowerment of all employees to solve problems and encourage flexibility, innovation, and initiative.[112] Again, this is essentially what transformational leaders do, and they exhibit many of the characteristics described above relating to learning organizations.

These concepts are similar to Hock's vision of what a chaordic organization is. He described these organizations simply as a place where individuals are allowed the flexibility to learn based on what is happening in their work environment.[113] This leads to the learning organization that can be self-organizing, self-governing, adaptive, and nonlinear. These are the qualities that are needed in order to be able to adapt to the complexity that exists in today's economic environment. Transformational leaders also must learn on the fly, because they are leading the organizations through these cycles of rapid and often chaotic periods of discontinuous change.

Importance of Creating a Learning Culture

In order to succeed in becoming a learning organization, it is necessary to have the appropriate culture and place that can accommodate learning. Schein defines organizational culture as "the accumulation of prior learning based on prior success."[114] The focus on this topic will be limited here, in favor of focusing on learning, coaching, mentoring, and knowledge development as key elements of a learning culture.

> To develop a learning culture, companies must accept that they make mistakes as part of their decision-making process and believe that people who are learning grow from their mistakes. They appreciate diversity in thought and action, knowing that there isn't one best way of doing things. They also realize the interdependence of various units in the organization and make great efforts to create synergy through the sharing of information and knowledge.
>
> Leaders must be role models in learning; thus, the concept of self-leadership is paramount. One of the most important roles for leaders of today is to develop the self-leadership capabilities of others in the organization. Continual learning is only one of those self-leadership activities that should be developed.

Kim[115] points out that in the early stages of an organization's existence, individual learning and organizational learning are almost synonymous. However, it is important for organizations to share the information on a wider scale—thus, the importance of shared mental models. One of the shared mental models that have been recognized as an effective way to capture and share knowledge is that of communities of practice. Most writers acknowledge that an organization's unrecorded wisdom is more valuable than its captured knowledge. They also find that this unrecorded asset is developed and enhanced by social exchanges in a community atmosphere. People form communities of practice where real learning takes place. Most effective learning is social and active, not individual and passive; therefore, a culture needs to be created where individuals are interacting on the social basis and creating communities of practice. The development of a learning organization will significantly increase the job satisfaction of employees throughout the organization by allowing them to share their creativity and innovation.[116]

To develop a learning culture, companies must accept that they make mistakes as part of their decision-making process and believe that people who are learning grow from their mistakes. They appreciate diversity in thought and action, knowing that there isn't one best way of doing things. They also realize the interdependence of various units in the organization and make great efforts to create synergy through the sharing of information and knowledge.[117]

Senge states "that there are three different types of leaders needed to build learning organizations":[118]

1. Local line leaders, who can undertake meaningful organizational experiments to test whether new learning capabilities lead to improved business results
2. Executive leaders, who provide support for line leaders, develop learning infrastructures, and lead by example in the gradual process of involving the norms and behaviors of a learning culture
3. Internal networkers, or community builders, the seed carriers of the new culture, who can move freely about the organization to find those who are predisposed to bring about change, help out in organizational experiments, and aid in the diffusion of new learning.

Therefore the starting point to building an organizational culture, which is conducive to effective organizational learning, is at the top of the organization with its leaders. Leaders must be role models in learning; thus, the concept of self-leadership is paramount. One of the most important roles for leaders of today is to develop the self-leadership capabilities of others in the organization. Continual learning is only one of those self-leadership activities that should be developed. The process of developing self-leadership in others has been labeled "super leadership."[119] There are a number of self-leadership strategies that can be undertaken by all individuals in an organization. It is paramount that leaders need to be the models of self-management, to set an example for others to follow. In addition, the leaders themselves can coach and mentor their subordinates and peers to be better at self-leadership. In essence,

> In essence, leaders need to practice effective self-leadership, become role models of effective self-leadership, and use coaching techniques in their management practices to teach and encourage others to improve their self-leadership skills and capabilities.

leaders need to practice effective self-leadership, become role models of effective self-leadership, and use coaching techniques in their management practices to teach and encourage others to improve their self-leadership skills and capabilities.

Relationship between Coaching, Learning, Culture, and Transformational Leadership

As the world of the twenty-first century becomes more complex and dynamic, the options for learning continue to expand dramatically. One of the ways to maximize learning is through the use of a coach or a mentor who can help focus the learning activity.[120] Learning is a highly individualized process, and, as such, coaching and mentoring facilitate enhanced learning because of the individualized nature of the coaching and mentoring process. Reed[121] agrees by suggesting that learning organizations represent significant evolution of organizational culture, and, as such, their emergence requires a new set of leadership capabilities. He believes that an organization can increase its learning potential by becoming a coaching organization. Many organizations are trying to do this and failing miserably as outlined earlier but perhaps the best way to achieve success and maintain it in the face of dynamic change is through cultural transformation (see the work of Fullan[122] and also Schein[123]). Effective leaders have an innate knowledge that this is true and that the hard work of re-culturing is the underlying tenet of real progress. According to Fullan, "it is a particular kind of reculturing for which we strive: one that activates and deepens moral purpose through collaborative work cultures that respect differences and constantly build and test knowledge against measurable results."[124] This is a good point, because culture is a very good source of performance if the culture is right and is aligned with the organization's mission, goals, objectives, and strategies. The leaders of the organization spend considerable amounts of time and effort on this to ensure that this is so. It is one of their primary responsibilities. Fullan goes on to state that leading in a culture of change means creating a culture (not just a structure) of change. In order to achieve success, a culture change takes inordinate amounts of time, energy, and enthusiasm, which

> This is a good point, because culture is a very good source of performance if the culture is right and is aligned with the organization's mission, goals, objectives, and strategies. The leaders of the organization spend considerable amounts of time and effort on this to ensure that this is so. It is one of their primary responsibilities.

is why effective leaders need these attributes. Fullan makes this point with respect to the nature of change and what needs to be accomplished. He states, "It does not mean adopting innovations, one after another; it does mean producing the capacity to seek, critically assess, and selectively incorporate new ideas and practices – all the time, inside the organization as well as outside it."[124]

Organizations with a strong learning organizational culture can achieve superior performance and sustainable competitive advantage through learning and, of course, executing a strategy well. One needs to look no further than companies such as Apple, IBM, Facebook, and Under Armour as good recent examples. With respect to the public universities in British Columbia, it is more difficult to gauge and state this premise; however, based on their growth in student enrollments and private endowments over the last two decades, it is apparent that they have good cultures somewhat aligned with a mission and strategies. According to Denison[125] in Mercer, "the soft stuff in organizations – the people, values, and the level of employee involvement – has a huge impact on business performance."[126]

There are many examples of organizations whose culture impacts performance in dramatic ways. Some have been discussed here and many more in the Collins and Porras[127] literature and subsequent book. Others include such companies as General Electric, Motorola, Johnson & Johnson.

A firm's culture can be a source of sustainable competitive advantage if that culture is rare, valuable, and difficult to perfectly imitate (see the work of Barney[128] and also Schein[129]). Performance of the organization may then be partly attributable to the organizational culture. Organizations with these types of cultures should continue to nurture and develop them. Universities cannot take their reputations for granted, maintain the status quo, and expect their cultures to sustain performance in the face of globalization and warp-speed changes occurring in the education industry in Canada. The University of Phoenix and other organizations like it are no exceptions either and have suffered poor results in recent years as a result of complacency in the face of these changes.

Transformational Leadership and Learning Organizations

Leadership and organizational culture are intertwined and are complementary functions within, and of, organizations. These elements are the core fabric that make up organizations and make them successful (or in cases where they are poor or misaligned, are the reason they sometimes fail). According to Schein,[129] leaders create and manage the culture of groups and organizations. Leaders create organizational culture through role modeling, strategic visioning, and policy making. After the initial creation of culture (usually based on the founder's vision), the culture of the organization evolves as group members incorporate and sustain the original norms. As the organization adapts to environmental forces, the organizational culture eventually defines the leadership.[129]

An understanding of the interplay between leadership and organizational culture is an important factor for developing effective learning organizations. Employees in rigid and immobile organizations often find themselves adjusting to environmental uncertainty when they are forced into organizational change by default. A goal of most leadership is to be good at aligning organizational strategy and forecasting environmental uncertainty in order to develop appropriate response mechanisms for maintaining effective organizational culture in changing or dynamic environments.

In today's information economy with a focus on service, many companies have drifted away from traditional models of management, originally developed for industrial-age firms, and now demand a broader range of leadership styles that are adaptive to the dramatic changes in the work environment. Several of the promising paradigms of leadership and organizational culture include components on valuing people: "the value of people,"[130] "human concern,"[131] "people orientation,"[132] "concern for people,"[133] and "individualized consideration."[134]

Cooke and Rosseau,[135] in their definition of constructive organizational cultures, emphasized the importance of people and tasks to meet higher-order needs. Effective leadership balances both transformational leadership and transactional leadership. Transformational leaders motivate followers to work for transcendental goals and to perform beyond the expectations those followers have for themselves. According to Bass,[136] transformational leaders change culture by realigning the original culture with a new vision. Transactional leaders, in contrast, sustain the existing organizational culture (maintain status quo) by relying on traditional exchanges between leaders and followers. The learning organization that is constantly changing and adapting to new environmental challenges needs a leadership and culture that evolves, as well. Transformational leadership seems to be the style that works best. According to Cascio,[137] transformational leadership is required for networked and culturally diverse organizations. Also, since transformational leaders use coaching and mentoring among networks both inside and outside the organization, and since both have been shown to be effective at building effective leadership in organizations, transformational leadership should be an effective style for the emergence of learning organizations.

Leadership, Coaching, Learning, and Performance

Transformational leadership includes coaching, and it could be argued that this type of leader is an effective coach. Coaching has been used extensively, in one form or another, over many generations, to increase the effectiveness and performance of individuals. Lately, coaching has entered the corporate realm whereby internal and external professionals are being used to coach individual managers and leaders. This has led to the increased efficiency of individual managers and executives, as well as to augmenting their capabilities to learn and grow.[138] It should be emphasized that unlike counseling, coaching focuses on the present and future potential and not on a person's past performance or experiences.

Coaching also should be distinguished from mentoring. Mentoring is generally viewed as developmental and as a learning process for people who are moving through either work- or life-related transitions.[139] It is most often used in supporting individuals through their career progress. Also, unlike counseling, which is often concerned with poor performers, mentoring is used with the organization's better performers and the ones who have a higher potential for advancement.[140] According to Mink and others,[141] a mentor facilitates overall career growth of an associate over a long period of time. Coaching, on the other hand, is a more general term that refers to continually developing employees so that they are more effective in their personal and work roles. Coaching takes place over a short or intermediate time frame.[141] It is the process by which employees gain the skills, abilities, and knowledge they need to develop themselves professionally and become more effective in their jobs and personal lives.[142]

Very rarely do individuals or organizations achieve success and sustained performance on their own—there are too many roadblocks and pitfalls along the road to success. Transformational leaders coach as part of their skill set, and many of them have been coached to success themselves. A good example that comes to mind is Jack Welch, the former CEO of General Electric, who was mentored for several years and coached many others throughout his tenure at the helm of GE.

Although there is increased interest in coaching as a personal and corporate tool to facilitate learning, develop leadership, and enhance personal and corporate performance, coaching is not a fad or current trend. Coaching articles and testimonials have increasingly been appearing in training and business publications.[143] Kinlaw insisted that coaching is fad-proof for two reasons: "First, there is never a time in which helping individuals increase their competencies and confidence will not be valued. Secondly, coaching is effective even in environments that are non-supportive or chaotic."[144]

Hargrove[145] believed that our rapidly changing world is the cause of the increasing popularity of coaching as individuals seek to find meaning and direction in their lives on both the personal and work levels. According to Mink and others,[146] coaching is gaining prominence because of the lack of skills and competencies of employees, in part due to technological changes, complexities in the workplace, diverse cultural backgrounds of workers, and a shortage of skilled labor. Increasingly, employees must learn more rapidly and adjust constantly to the changing workplace in order to stay competitive in the marketplace.

Coaching is a process that allows individuals to develop positive attitudes to change, as well as enhances their learning in organizations. "In today's organizations, those who survive and prosper will be those who learn how to learn at the individual, team and organizational level. In today's environment of comparatively rapid change, good coaching provides a foundation for continuous improvement."[147] Given that many organizations in today's changing environment are moving away from the traditional command-and-control style of managing and moving into a more empowering and participative style of management, the use of coaching is taking on more prominence. The coaching concept is one where individuals are encouraged to take on more responsibilities within the organization, although within a supportive structure. According to the definition of transformational leadership developed by Burns,[148] coaching may be the way transformational leaders so effectively receive buy-in to their ideas from followers. There may be a stronger relationship between these two elements, but the relationship is not the focus of this book, so no more time or space will be devoted to it here.

Coaching occurs through supportive and, at times difficult, interactions between a coach and an individual and brings about clarity and a shift in invisible patterns and behaviors within the individual, which can result in transformation, personal growth, and learning.[149] Hence, there appears to be a direct relationship between leadership, coaching, learning, and performance.

> The attitude surrounding how managers view mistakes maybe needs some serious review. Instead of a mistake as a personal failure and a cause for discussion, warnings, and reductions in salary or responsibility, perhaps a more leadership-like approach is to view mistakes as real learning opportunities. "The attitude around mistakes needs to be one where a mistake is a breakdown on the path to accomplishment, rather than something that represents a personal failure."

In order for organizations to become learning-oriented, employees are empowered to take risks, experiment, share knowledge, and be able to admit areas where they are challenged. "If the vast majority of the staff stop learning then the organization will surely collapse."[150] While this is not new or certainly earth shattering, it does make a point. Learning is important to organizational survival. Along the same lines, a good rule to remember is to not make the same mistake twice. Traditionally, people are uncomfortable disclosing what they don't know, and they cover up their mistakes rather than learn from them. Argyris[151] calls these "defensive routines" that are learned early in childhood and reinforced in organizational cultures. "They [defensive routines] overprotect individuals or groups and inhibit them from learning new actions."[152]

The attitude surrounding how managers view mistakes maybe needs some serious review. Instead of viewing a mistake as a personal failure and a cause for discussion, warnings, and reductions in salary or responsibility, perhaps a more leadership-like approach is to view mistakes as real learning opportunities. "The attitude around mistakes needs to be one where a mistake is a breakdown on the path to accomplishment, rather than something that represents a personal failure."[153] Transformational leaders allow mistakes and even coach their employees through mistakes to ensure they learn from them and understand the importance of not making them again. Hargrove calls for the need for a personal transformational shift in individuals from an "attitude of knowing" to the "attitude of learning." Until this transformation happens and they know what to do, individuals are unlikely to disclose ignorance or uncertainties or let down the facade. Thus, change must take place to ensure new and open learning for individuals and organizations. It is within this context that individuals, through coaching, can begin their personal transformation and learn to break defensive routine patterns. In order to change behaviors, Senge advocates the need for individuals to examine their mental models or personal assumptions by looking inward to unearth internal pictures and hold these images up to scrutiny. Senge states, "It also includes the ability to carry on 'learningful' conversations that balance inquiry and advocacy."[154]

Learning within a coaching relationship allows individuals to lower their defenses, discuss personal issues, as well as explore blind spots, attitudes, biases, and weaknesses. According to Tobias, "to achieve lasting and fundamental change, people need to alter their perspectives, to see things in a new light, or to overcome internal resistances that may be unrecognized and habitual."[155] Through artful questioning and challenging individuals to be honest with themselves, those being coached can see patterns of behavior that do not aid in their progress, personal success, and learning. Again, this is what transformational leaders practice and know how to do well.

Additionally, a coach can "offer honest and objective feedback that can be accepted or rejected without job-threatening consequences or public embarrassment."[156] Feedback is one of the elements that is necessary for growth and learning. "Studies show that learning is severely hampered without feedback, and that people's motivation (and subsequent performance) diminishes over time unless they know how they are doing."[157]

While learning can occur at all levels of the organization and under many conditions, an organization that embraces coaching will create an environment where learning is maximized. A working environment in which creativity and innovation, coupled with honest feedback in safe conditions, encourage employees to transform behavior patterns and create continuous learning leads to collective effectiveness and competitive advantage. This is the type of environment that a learning organization tries to develop.

> While learning can occur at all levels of the organization and under many conditions, an organization that embraces coaching will create an environment where learning is maximized.

Learning and Transformational Leadership

Managers and leaders have a need to determine their own learning needs and, thus, feel a strong desire to self-direct their learning, choosing when and how to attain the training they require. This concept is supported by the coaching framework, which maintains the role of coach as facilitator and supporter of adult learning. Coaching sessions are tailored to the needs of the person being coached. The individual sets the agenda, while the coach listens, questions, and guides the individual to discover answers for him/herself. This approach follows adult learning principles whereby the learner is in charge of the learning agenda. The coach helps the individual to develop strengths, manage weaknesses, and build positive relationships in all areas of a person's life. The coach is only the facilitator, or catalyst, in the learning process. Tobias characterized coaching with respect to learning, stating that "coaching allows for ongoing, continuous learning, offering support, encouragement, and feedback as new approaches are tried and new behaviors are practiced."[158] Coaching supports learning and change by constantly focusing on the growth and potential of the individual, which is also a large part of what a transformational leader does. A transformational leader develops other leaders, at all levels of the organization, through coaching and mentoring.

> In summary, it is important that leaders continue to grow and evolve as the environment around them changes. Equally important is the fact that new leaders need to be trained and developed to take on the ever-increasing challenges of today's organizations. Coaching can take a prominent role in helping managers become leaders and in assisting existing leaders to be more effective in their changing roles.

The executive or leadership coaching process involves leadership assessment and an ongoing focus on development.[159] "Coaching enables leaders to further their own learning quickly, while getting a different – and sometimes more accurate – picture of what is happening in the organization, especially with respect to how people experience the leader and the leadership team."[160] Goleman and others[161] found that most of the leaders in a large successful firm had mentors in the early stages of their careers. General Electric and Motorola have leadership development

166

programs where all senior executives have coaching and mentor assignments with other junior leaders, which sometimes last for five years or more. It is commonly known that mentors have been used for centuries to successfully cultivate leaders. If the objective of the relationship between a mentor and a mentee is to develop leadership skills, then the relationship moves to a coaching one. The coach works on the person's specific goals and aspirations. The coaching agenda will ultimately lead to a leader development program.[161]

Learning within a coaching relationship allows individuals to lower their defenses, discuss personal issues, as well as explore blind spots, attitudes, biases, and weaknesses. "To achieve lasting and fundamental change, people need to alter their perspectives, to see things in a new light, or to overcome internal resistances that may be unrecognized and habitual."[162] Through careful questioning and encouraging individuals to be honest with themselves, the person being coached can see patterns of behavior that do not aid their progress, personal success, and learning. They can then plan activities, learning and training to overcome these barriers to progress.

Senge[163] suggests that, in learning organizations, leaders' roles differ dramatically from those of the charismatic decision makers who could not create an organization all on their own. He suggests that "the new role requires skills of designing teaching and stewarding so that a vision of a better future state can provide the incentive that will pull people in the organization through uncertainty and perhaps adversity."[164] This view is endorsed by Haines, who described "an effective leadership triangle where the key roles should be those of a trainer, coach, and the facilitator."[165] This also ties in with the key elements of the transformational leader mentioned earlier—*intellectually stimulating* (helping followers recognize problems and show them ways of solving them) and *interpersonally considerate* (giving followers the support, encouragement, and attention they need to perform their jobs well).[166]

In summary, it is important that leaders continue to grow and evolve as the environment around them changes. Equally important is the fact that new leaders need to be trained and developed to take on the ever-increasing challenges of today's organizations. Coaching can take a prominent role in helping managers become leaders and in assisting existing leaders to be more effective in their changing roles. In keeping with the concept of organizational learning, it is important to recognize that it is no longer enough to just have a handful of people learning for an organization. The organizations that will succeed are those that discover how to co-opt people's commitment and capacity to learn at all levels in an organization.[167] "In reality, this kind of learning organization cannot be formed without personal transformation on the part of a critical mass of people."[168] According to Zaleznick,[169] one-to-one interactions between leader and follower are crucial to transforming followers into leaders. Transformational leaders deal with others as individuals; consider individual needs, abilities, and aspirations; listen attentively; further development; and advise, teach, and coach.[170] A learning organization, therefore, is only as good as its people, and creating this type of organization requires personal transformational learning on the part of all its employees. The role of the transformational leader then fits well in this setting. Transformational leadership may be the best leadership style for the learning organization.

Transformational Leadership and Firm Performance

As discussed in detail earlier in the book, there appears to be a relationship between transformational leadership and firm performance, and several studies have hinted at the link between the two topics.[171] Bass defines transformational leadership as a superior form of leadership that occurs when leaders "broaden and elevate the interests of their employees, when they generate awareness and acceptance of the purposes and the mission of the group and when they stir their employees to look beyond their own self-interest for the good of the group."[172] Keller asserts that transformational leaders strive to achieve results beyond what is normally expected by inspiring a sense of importance about the mission at hand.[173] Can superior leadership deliver superior results, and are the results sustainable? Well, the literature seems to suggest that *transformational* is a popular style of leadership that many CEOs practice, and when they practice it, there is little doubt that the style results in positive organizational outcomes. From my own research in Canada, this certainly holds true. In order for the performance to be sustained, the outcomes must necessarily be related to some element of competitive advantage. The purpose of leadership is to ensure that through coaching and mentoring, knowledge is continually developed by the organization's most valuable assets—its employees—so that the major source of competitive advantage is maintained. This may be the only way to sustain performance since, as Welch has been quoted as saying, "knowledge development may be the only source of real competitive advantage."

By incorporating and synthesizing some of the work of the writers mentioned above, it may be possible to create a paradigm that analyzes the relationship between transformational leadership, performance, and competitive advantage. The elements that will make this paradigm will include parts from the definitions put forth by Burns, Bass, and Keller.[174] Transformational leadership is a style of leadership that inspires others by intellectually stimulating them to perform beyond *normal* expectations and self-interest to achieve challenging organizational goals. A transformational leader inspires a sense of mission through visioning and stimulates new ways of thinking and problem-solving. Often transformational leaders possess a charismatic quality whereby they are seen as those who can lead the group and, therefore, organization to a higher level of achievement than might otherwise be expected. According to Bass transformational leadership is a superior form of leadership that occurs when leaders "broaden and elevate the interests of their employees, when they generate awareness and acceptance of the purposes and the mission of the group and when they stir their employees to look beyond their own self-interest for the good of the group"[175]. What is not discussed in the literature is the amount of time transformational leaders might spend on these core activities. The paradigm below will no doubt be controversial; however, it is something that needs to be addressed, and maybe a good place to start is here.

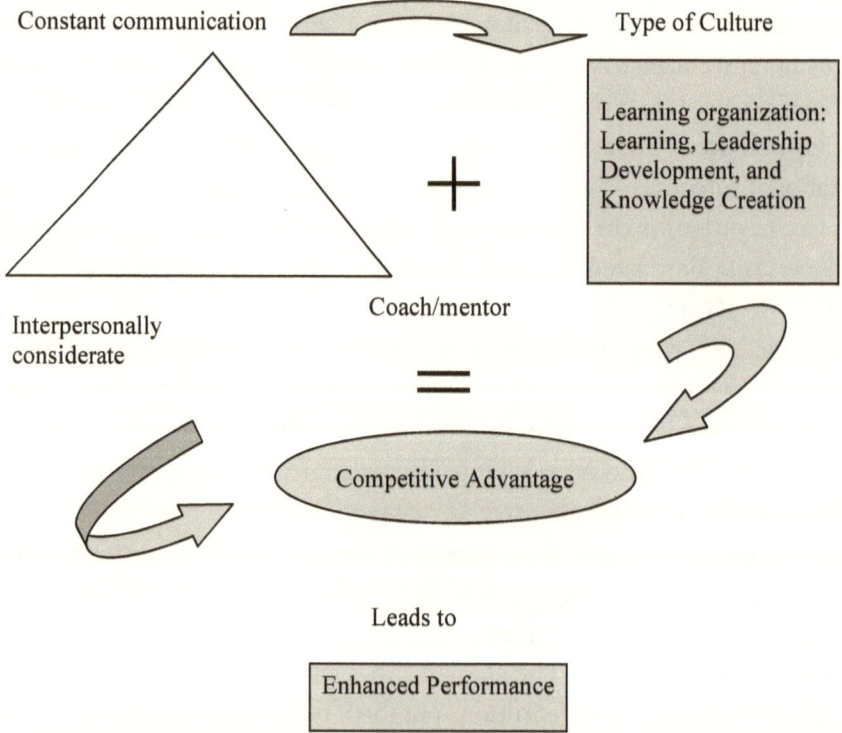

Figure 3: Model of Relationships

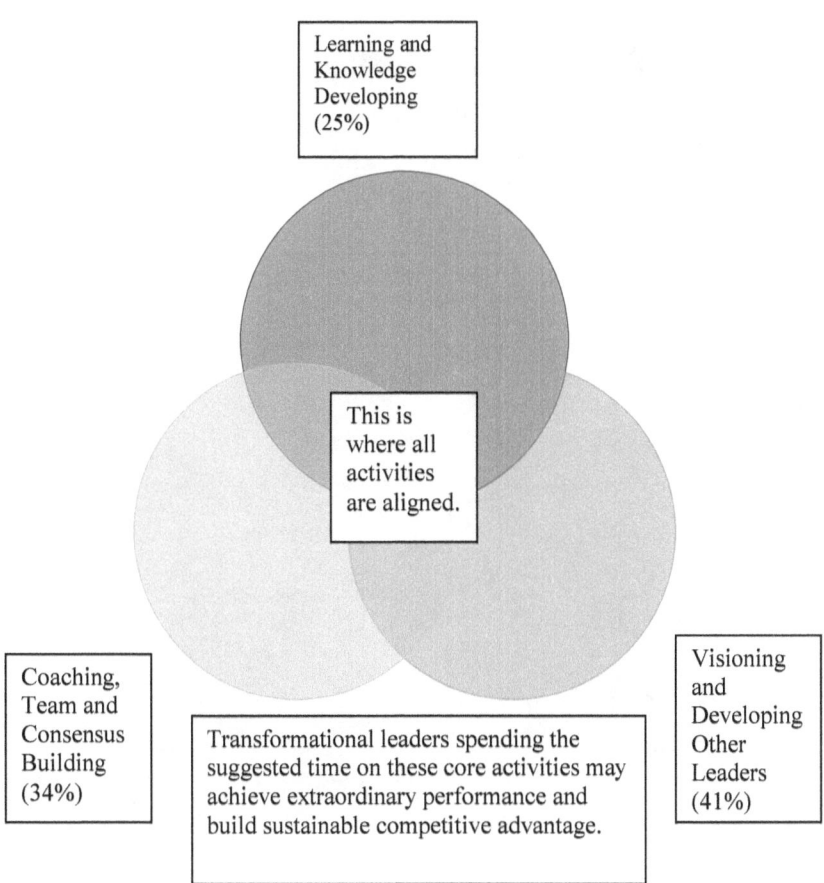

Figure 4: Paradigm for Performance and Competitive Advantage

Some additional research suggests that CEOs should spend one-half to one-third of their time on the leadership development program of their organizations.[176]

Possible Paradigm for Understanding the Relationship between Transformational Leadership, Organizational Culture, Competitive Advantage, and Performance

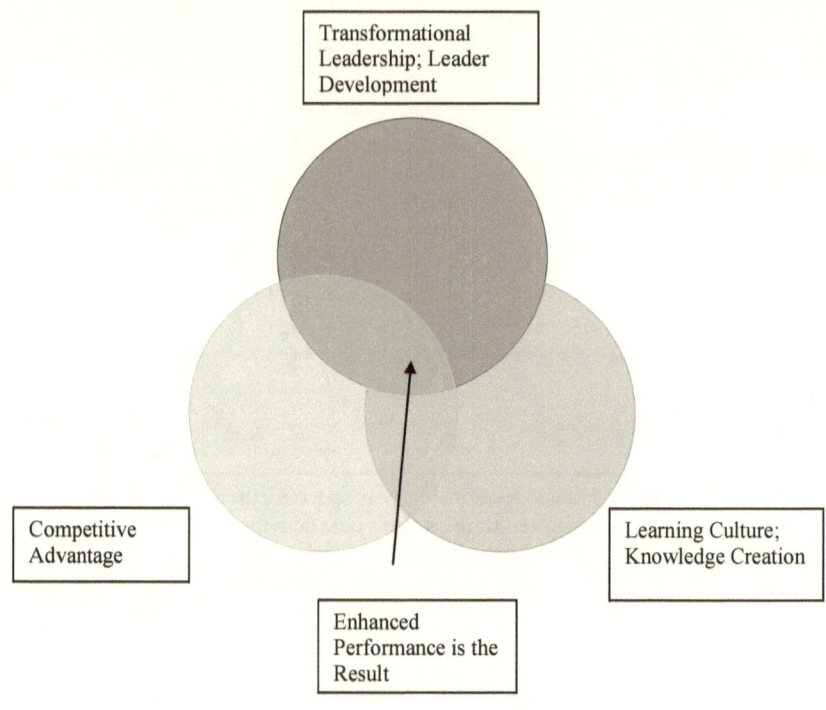

Figure 5: Possible Paradigm

Conclusion

Learning, particularly continuous learning, is important to the individual and to the organization, "because it develops one's capability."[177] However, despite the fact that everyone recognizes that learning is the key to success for most organizations in the future, it is difficult to put these learning principles into practice. By their very nature, organizations don't readily encourage new learning. "In fact, leaders who wish to install widespread change need to first recognize that they're working against a paradox. Organizations thrive on routine and the status quo. The professionals in organizations rely on established systems in order to carry out their jobs with minimal resistance and stress. As a result most people in companies today have to challenge themselves to learn something really different after a long time."[178]

Even though there has been much progress on the learning front, many organizations are still struggling with how to use information to become more intelligent.[179] For example, one of the current dilemmas with respect to learning organizations is "how do organizations become open to learning and at the same time be opaque enough to protect their intellectual property."[180]

"Most learning theorists seem to position learning as an end in itself rather than as a means to an end."[181] Schein agrees by stating, "The necessary conditions for learning don't exist in most organizations because the culture is unsuitable, at least for long-term learning."[182] Despite the comments cited above, most organizational authors agree that most organizations are just now learning to become learning organizations.[183] Organizations have no choice if they are to survive in the ever-changing and increasingly complex and chaotic environment that is the knowledge era. Transformational leaders will play a vital role in this process and will need to ensure that learning becomes a source of knowledge development, since it may be the only source of sustainable competitive advantage.

Endnotes

1   M. A. Gephart, "The Road to High Performance," *Training & Development* 49(6) (June, 1995): 29-39, accessed EBSCOHost, July 4, 2003,www.apollogrouplibrary.com.

2   Gephart, *Road*, 30

3   Gephart, *Road*, 31

4   S. Crainer and D. Dearlove, "Excellence Revisited," *Business Strategy Review* 13(1) (2002), accessed EBSCOhost, July 4, 2003, www.apollogrouplibrary.com, 15.

5   J. P. Kotter, *John P. Kotter on What Leaders Really Do* (Boston: Harvard Business, 1999).

6   *Drucker.* "The Practice of Management Reflections on Peter F. Drucker's Landmark Book Shaker A. Zahra," *The Academy of Management Executive* 17(3) (Aug., 2003): 16-23.

    Kotter, *Leaders.*

7   Gephart, *Road.*

8   Gephart, 33.

9   J. Begin, *Strategic Employment Policy: An Organizational Systems Perspective.* (Englewood Cliffs, NJ: Prentice-Hall, 1991).

    R. E. Boyatzis, *The Competent Manager: A Model for Effective Performance.* (NY: Wiley, 1982).

    M. E. Porter, *Competitive Advantage: Creating and Sustaining Superior Performance.* (NY: Free Press, 1985).

    P. Stannack, "Perspectives on Employee Performance," *Management Research News* 19(4/5) (1996): 38-40.

10 M.M. Heffernan and P.C. Flood, "An Exploration of the Relationships Between The Adoption of Managerial Competencies, Organizational Characteristics, Human Resource Sophistication and Performance in Irish Organizations," *Journal of European Industrial Training* 24(2/3/4) (2000): 128-136.

11 H. T. O'Hara et al., "Financial Indicators of Stock Price Performance," *American Business Review* 18(1) (January, 2000): 90-100, accessed EBSCOHost, July 4, 2003, www.apollogrouplibrary.com.

12 B. Gunn, "The Performance Edge," *Strategic Finance* 81(11) (May, 2000): 14-16, accessed EBSCOHost, July 4, 2003, www.apollogrouplibrary.com,14.

13 R. W. Rowden, "High Performance and Human Resource Characteristics of Successful Small Manufacturing and Processing Companies," *Leadership & Organization Development Journal* 23(1/2) (2002): 79-83, accessed EBSCOHost, July 4, 2003, www.apollogrouplibrary.com.

14 J.B. Cunningham and P. Gerrard, "Characteristics of Well-Performing Organizations in Singapore," *Singapore Management Review* 22(1) (2000): 35-64, accessed EBSCOhost, July 4, 2003, www.apollogrouplibrary.com.

15 C. Fraquhar, "People Power," *Canadian Business Review* 23(1) (Spring, 1996): 42.

16 H. E. Allerton, "High Performance," *Training & Development* 52(7) (July, 1998): 11-13, accessed EBCOHost, July 4, 2003, www.apollogrouplibrary.com.

17 A. Fleming and P. Drucker, "Innovation by Numbers," *Economist* 367(8329), 1-3 (June 21, 2003): 2.

18 Loblaws *Annual Report*, 2001, 1.

19 Collins and Porras, *Built*, 1997.

20 Collins and Porras, *Built*, 23.

21 Collins and Porras, *Built*, 32.

22 www.loblaw.com

    www.sobeys.ca

23 Loblaws, *Annual Report*, 2010, 2011, 2012.

    Sobeys, *Annual Report*, 2010, 2011, 2012.

24 *Corporate structure*, www.sobeys.ca, 6.

25 Collins and Porras, *Built*, 55.

26 Loblaws, *Annual Report*, 2001.

27 Collins and Porras, *Built*, 1.

28 Collins and Porras, *Built*, 3.

29 Collins and Porras, *Built*, 54.

30   Loblaws, *Annual Report*, 2001, 1.

31   Sobeys, *Annual Report*, 2001, 1.

32   Collins and Porras, *Built*, 82.

33   Loblaws, *Annual Report*, 2001, 11.

34   Sobeys, *Annual Report*, 2001, 6.

35   Loblaws, *Annual Report*, 2012, 4.

36   Collins and Porras, *Built*, 1997.

37   Collins and Porras, *Built*, 136.

38   Collins and Porras, *Built*, 212.

39   Loblaws, *Annual Report* 2001, 10.

40   Sobeys, *Annual Report* 2001, 2.

41   Collins and Porras, *Built*, 221.

42   Collins and Porras, *Built*, 222.

43   Collins and Porras, *Built*, 224.

44   Collins and Porras, *Built*, 232.

45   S.D. Chowdhury, "Turnarounds: A Stage Theory Perspective," *Canadian Journal of Administrative Sciences* 19 (2002): 249-266.

46   D. Goleman, *Working With Emotional Intelligence* (NY: Bantam Books, 1998).

47   F. Hesselbein, M. Goldsmith, and R. Beckhard, *The Leader of The Future* (San Francisco: Jossey-Bass, 1996)

48   W. Pietersen, "The Mark Twain Dilemma: The Theory and Practice of Change Leadership," *Journal of Business Strategy* 23(5) (2002).

49   P. Reed, *Extraordinary Leadership - Creating Strategies for Change*. (London, UK: Kogan Page Limited, 2001).

50   I. Nonaka in "Knowledge is Power," J. Grecco, *The Journal of Business Strategy*, (March/April, 1999). Originally published in *The Knowledge Creating Company* 69(6) (Boston: Harvard Business Review, 1991):96-104.

51   P. F. Drucker, "The Discipline of Innovation," *Harvard Business Review* (November – December 1998): 3-8, reprint 98604.

52 R. T. Keller, "Transformational Leaders Make a Difference," *Research Technology Management*, 38(3) (May/June,1995).

53 P. Drucker in "Peter Drucker on The Profession of Management,"T. R. Pressly and P. F. Drucker, *Ohio CPA Journal* 58(2) (April/June, 1999): 1-3.

54 R. Hargrove, *E-leader: Reinventing Leadership in a Connected Economy.* (Perseus Publishing, 2001).

55 De Vries, *Leadership Mystique.*

56 R. Kanter, *Evolve!: Succeeding in The Digital Culture of Tomorrow.* (Boston: Harvard Business School Press, 2001).

57 Bennis, *Becoming.*

    S. Chowdhury, *Management 21C.* (London: Prentice-Hall, 2000).

    Schein, *Organizational.*

58 Hesselbein, Goldsmith and Beckhard, *Leader,* 56.

59 K. Sveiby, *New Organizational Wealth* (San Francisco, CA: Berrett-Koehler, 1997), 29.

60 T. H. Davenport and L. Prusak, *Working Knowledge* (Boston: Harvard Business School Press, 1998).

61 A. Brooking, *Corporate Memories, Strategies For Knowledge Management* (London: Thompson Business Press, 1999).

62 T. H. Davenport, "Putting The Enterprise Into The Enterprise System," *Harvard Business Review* (July – August, 1998): 5, reprint 98401.

63 C. K. Prahalad and G. Hamel, "The Core Competence of The Corporation," *Harvard Business Review* (May-June, 1990): 79-91.

64 I. Nonaka, "A Dynamic Theory of Organization Knowledge Creation," *Organization Science,* 5(1) (1994).

65 M. Boisot, "Is Your Firm a Creative Destroyer? Competitive Learning and Knowledge Flows in The Technological Strategies of Firms," *Research Policy* 24(4) (1995).

66 R. Hall, *Developing Capabilities and Managing Knowledge in Supply Chains* (Durham, England: University of Durham Working Paper, 1996).

67 P. M. Senge, *The Fifth Discipline: The Art and Practice of The Learning Organization* (New York: Doubleday Currency, 1993).

68 C. Argyris and D. A. Schon, *Organizational Learning: A Theory of Action Perspective* (Reading, MA: Addisson Wesley, 1978).

69 Hartog et al., *Culture*, 219-257.

70 D. Ulrich, J. Zenger and N. Smallwood, *Results-Based Leadership* (Boston, Mass: Harvard Business School Press, 1999).

71 Ulrich, Zenger and Smallwood, *Results*, 89.

72 D. Kim in *The Basic Requirements For High Performance*, J. Boyett, and J. Boyett, (1998): 93, accessed September 28, 2002 from www.apollolibrary. com.EBSCOHost.

73 J. Boyett and J. Boyett, *The Guru Guide* (New York, NY: John Wiley & Sons Ltd, 1998).

74 W. Pietersen, *Reinventing Strategy* (New York, NY: John Wiley & Sons Ltd, 2002).

75 M. Dodgson, "Organizational Learning: A Review of Some Literatures," *Organization Studies* (1993): 375–394.

76 I. Nonaka, "A Dynamic Theory of Organization Knowledge Creation," *Organization Science* 5(1) (1994).

77 S. Chowdhury, *Management*, 242.

78 Chowdhury, *Management*, 46.

79 Reed, *Extraordinary*.

80 B. Kogut and U. Zander, "Knowledge of The Firm, Combinative Capabilities, and The Replication of Technology," *Organization Science* 3(3) (1992).

81 R. Hall, *Developing Capabilities and Managing Knowledge in Supply Chains* (Durham, England: University of Durham Working Paper, 1996).

82 I. Nonaka, *Dynamic*.

83 I. Nonaka and Konno, "The Concept of Ba: Building a Foundation For Knowledge Creation," *California Management Review*, Spring (1998).

84 W. E. Deming, *The New Economics for Industry, Government, Education* (Cambridge, MA: MIT, 1993).

85 S. Hilmer and D. Karney, "Towards Understanding The Foundations of Deming's Theory," *Journal of Quality Management* 2(2) (1997): 20.

86 T. H. Davenport and L. Prusak, *Working Knowledge* (Boston: Harvard Business School Press, 1998).

87 B. Kogut and U. Zander. "Knowledge of The Firm, Combinative Capabilities, and The Replication of Technology," *Organization Science* 3(3), 1992).

88 C. Argyris, C. And D. A. Schon, *Organizational Learning: A Theory of Action Perspective* (Reading, MA: Addisson Wesley, 1978).

89 Arie de Gues in "The Professional Development of Principals: Innovations and Opportunities," K. D. Peterson (2002):6. *Educational Administration Quarterly* 38(2) (2002): 213-232.

90 R. M. Fulmer and M. Goldsmith, "The Leadership Investment: How the World's Best Organizations Gain Strategic Advantage Through Leadership Development." New York: *American Management Association*, AMACOM (2001).

91 P. Senge, *The Fifth Discipline: The Art and Practice of The Learning Organization* (New York: Doubleday Currency, 1990), 4.

92 Senge, *Fifth*.

S. Harper, *The Forward Focused Organization* (New York: AMACOM, 2001).

93 Yukl, *Leadership*, 9.

94 Davenport and Prusak, *Working*.

95 C. M. Fiol and M. A. Lyles, "Organizational Learning," *Academy of Management Review* 10(4) (1985).

96 M. Dodgson, "Organizational Learning," *Academy of Management Review* 10(4), 1993.

97 M. Dodgson, *Organizational*.

J. Landry, "Information Characteristics as Constraints to Innovation," (paper from proceedings of the Twenty-Fifth Hawaii International Conference on Systems Sciences, CA: IEEE Press, 1992).

98 R. Hall, *Developing Capabilities and Managing Knowledge in Supply Chains* (Durham, England: University of Durham Working Paper, 1996).

99 V. Balasubramanian, "Organizational Learning and Information Systems," *Rutgers University Working Paper* (1996).

100 M. Morrison, *Leadership and Management Skills for Practical – Vocational.* (Mosby Incorporated, 1993).

101 J. S. Brown and P. Duguid, "Organizational Learning and Communities-of-Practice: Toward a Unified View of Working, Learning and Innovation," *Organization Science* 2(1) (1991).

102 V. Balasubramanian, "Organizational Learning and Information Systems," B.M. Bass, *From Transactional*, 1996.

103 Brown, J.S., & Duguid, P. (1991). "Organizational Learning and Communities-of-Practice: Toward a Unified View of Working, Learning and Innovation." *Organization Science* 2(1) (1991).

104 Quinn, J.B., Anderson, P. & Finklestein, S. "Leveraging Intellect." *Academy of Management Executive* 10(3) (1996).

105 F. Hesselbein, M. Goldsmith and I. Sommerville, *Leading Beyond The Walls*. (San Francisco: Jossey-Bass, 1999, 145).

106 R. Hargrove, *Masterful Coaching* (San Francisco, CA: Jossey-Bass, 1995, 100).

107 R. Hargrove, *Masterful*, 101.

108 C. Bartlett, C. and S. Ghoshal, "Changing The Role of Top Management: Beyond Systems to People," Boston, MA: *Harvard Business Review* 73(2) (1995).

109 S. Stowell and M. Starcevich, M., "The Coach, Creating Partnerships For a Competitive Edge." OK: *Centre for Management and Organization Effectiveness* (1998): 3.

110 Yukl, *Leadership*, 454.

111 Senge, *Fifth*.

112 Yukl, *Leadership*.

113 D. Hock, *The Birth of the Chaordic Organization of Turning Chaos and Order Into Money and Meaning in The New Millenium* (Bantam Doubleday: Dell Publishing Group, 1998).

114 Schein, *Organizational*, 115.

115 J. Boyett and J. Boyett, *Guru*.

116 Reed, *Extraordinary*.

117 De Vries, *Leadership Mystique*.

118 Hesselbein, Goldsmith and Sommerville, *Leading*, 46.

119 H. Sims, H. and C. Manz, *Company of Heroes: Unleashing the Power of Self-Leadership* (NY: Wiley and Sons, 1996).

120 Chowdhury, *Management*.

121 Reed, *Extraordinary*.

122 Fullan, *Principals.*

123 Schein, *Organizational.*

124 Fullan, *Leading*, 44.

125 D. R. Denison, *Corporate Culture and Organizational Effectiveness* (New York, NY: John Wiley & Sons, Inc., 1990).

126 T. Mercer, "Study Confirms It: Corporate Culture Matters," *Crain's Detroit Business* 12(48) (1996), accessed May 15, 2002, http://ehostvgw2.epnet.com,1.

127 J. Collins and J. Porras, *Built to Last: Successful Habits of Visionary Companies.* (New York: Harper Business, 1997).

128 Barney, *Organizational.*

129 Schein, *Organizational.*

130 M. Sashkin, *Pillars of Excellence: Organizational Beliefs Questionnaire* (PA: Bryn Mawr, 1984).

131 379. R. H. Kilmann and M. J. Saxton, *Kilmann-Saxton Culture-Gap Survey* (Tuxedo, NY: Xicom, 1991).

132 R. A. Cooke and J. C. Lafferty, "Organizational Culture Inventory," *Human Synergistics,* (Plymoutth, MI: 1994).

133 R. R. Blake and J. S. Mouton, *The Managerial Grid.* (Houston, TX: Gulf Publishing, 1964).

134 B. M. Bass, *Leadership and Performance Beyond Expectations* (NY: Free Press, 1985).

135 R. A. Cooke and D. M. Rousseau, "Behavioral Norms and Expectations: A Quantitative Approach to the Assessment of Organizational Culture," *Group and Organizational Studies*, 13 (1988).

136 Bass, *Leadership.*

137 W. F. Cascio, *Managing Human Resources: Productivity, Quality of Work Life, Profits* (McGraw-Hill Ryerson, Limited, 1995).

138 Hargrove, *Masterful.*

D. Kinlaw, *Coaching, Winning Strategies For Individuals and Teams* (England: Gower Publishing Ltd, 1997).

O. Mink, K. Owen and B. Mink, *Developing High-Performance People: The Art of Coaching* (Boston, MA: Addison-Wesley, 1993).

J. Whitmore, *Coaching For Performance*. CA: Nicholas Brealey Publishing Ltd, 1998.

139 R. Garvey, "Mentoring in The Marketing Place," (Unpublished doctoral dissertation, Durham University, England, 1998).

140 F. Stone, *Coaching, Counseling and Mentoring* (NY: AMACOM, 1999).

141 Mink, Owen and Mink, *Developing*.

142 Stone, *Coaching*.

143 R. Kilburg, "Forward: Executive Coaching as an Emerging Competency in The Practice of Consultation," *Consulting Psychology Journal*: Practice and Research 48(2) (1996).

Kinlaw, *Coaching*.

Kinlaw, *Coaching*, 4.

144 Kinlaw, *Coaching*, 4.

145 R. Hargrove, *Masterful Coaching* (San Francisco, CA: Jossey-Bass, 1995).

146 Mink, Owen and Mink, *Developing*.

147 Mink, Owen and Mink, *Developing*, 1.

148 M.B. Burns, *Leadership*.

149 Hargrove, *Masterful*.

150 M. Downey, *Effective Coaching* (London: Orion Business Books, 1999), 12.

151 Argyris, *Overcoming*.

152 C. Argyris, *On Organizational Learning* (Cambridge, MA: Blackwell, 1993), 20.

153 Hargrove, *Masterful*,104.

154 Senge, *Fifth*, 8.

155 L. Tobias, "Coaching Executives," *Consulting Psychology Journal* 48(2) (1996): 88.

156 J. H. Katz and F. A. Miller, F. A., "Coaching Leaders Through Culture Change," *Consulting Psychology Journal: Practice & Research* 48(2) (1996): 111.

157 A. Bandura & A. R. Butz, in "The Leadership Challenge," J. M. Kouzes and B. Z. Posner (San Francisco: Jossey-Bass, 1995), 288.

158 Tobias, *Coaching*, 87.

159 Goleman, Boyatzis and McKee, *Primal*.

160 Goleman, Boyatzis and McKee, *Primal*, 229.

161 Goleman, Boyatzis and McKee, *Primal*.

162 Tobias, *Coaching*, 88.

163 Senge, *Fifth*.

164 P. Senge in "Extraordinary Leadership – Creating Strategies For Change," P. Reed (London, UK: Kogan Page Limited, 2001), 131.

165 S. Haines in "Extraordinary Leadership – Creating Strategies For Change," P. Reed (London, UK: Kogan Page Limited, 2001), 131.

166 Greenberg, *Managing*, 285.

167 Senge, *Extraordinary*.

168 Hargrove, *Masterful*, 100.

169 A. Zaleznik, "The human Dilemmas of Leadership," *Harvard Business Review* (1963).

170 B. M. Bass, "Does The Transactional – Transformational Leadership Paradigm Transcend Organizational and National Boundaries?" *American Psychologist* 52(2) (1997).

171 B. Avolio, *Full Leadership Development: Building The Vital Forces in Organization* (Thousand Oaks: Sage Publications, 1999).

Bass, *Leadership*.

Bass, *Transactional*, 19-36.

J. M. Howell and B.J. Avolio, B.J.,"Transformational Leadership, Transactional Leadership, Locus of Control, and Support For Innovation: Key Predictors of Consolidated- Business-Unit Performance." *Journal of Applied Psychology*, 78(6) (1993):891- 902.

Keller, *Transformational*, 41-44

172 Bass, *Transactional*, 2.

173 Keller, *Transformational*, 41

174 Burns, *Leadership*.

Bass, *Leadership*.

Bass, *Transactional*, 19-36.

Keller, *Transformational*, 41-44

175 Bass *Transactional*, 2.

176 S. Harper, "The Forward Focused Organization," in Roger Enrico CEO of PepsiCo (New York: AMACOM, 2001), 30.

177 J. Adair, "Effective Strategic Leadership: An Essential Path to Success Guided by The World's Greatest Leaders," Pan Macmillan Australia Pty Limited, *Business & Economics* (2002):321.

178 Goleman, Boyatzis and McKee, *Primal*, 225.

179 M. J. Wheatley, *Leadership and The New Science,* 2nd ed. (San Francisco: Berrett-Koehler, 1999),110.

180 Hesselbein, Goldsmith and Sommerville, *Leading*, 32.

181 Pietersen, W. *Reinventing Strategy* (New York, NY: John Wiley & Sons Ltd, 2002), 47.

182 E. H. Schein, "Organizational Culture," *American Psychologist* 45(2) (1990): 115.

183 Chowdhury, *Management*.

Goleman, Boyatzis and McKee, *Primal*.

Hesselbein., Goldsmith and Sommerville, *Leading*.

Pietersen, *Reinventing*.

Reed, *Extraordinary*.

Analysis of Leadership Styles

Leadership means many things to many people, and a review of the literature on leadership confirms this position. There are almost as many definitions of leadership as there are books on the subject. Some of the definitions make reference to management, and some make leadership seem so aloof that it is something to be wished for, as opposed to something that can be learned. This section will focus on leadership from the middle 1960s to the late 1990s.

According to Fiedler, leadership is "an interpersonal relation in which power and influence are unevenly distributed so that one person is able to direct and control the actions and behaviors of others to a greater extent than they direct and control his."[1] This early definition seems to have elements of management, especially the directing and controlling portions, which have been discussed in an earlier section as functions of management to distinguish it from leadership. Over the last seven decades or so, various theories of leadership have been developed, proposed, practiced, studied, and dispelled.

Trait Leadership

At the beginning of the twentieth century, successful leaders were seen as people of certain stature who were in positions of leadership simply because of a possession of traits that made them somewhat superior to others. Having these traits could be the result of inheritance through family birthrights or the result of social adventure. This "trait theory" of leadership was popular until the 1940s, when it was decided that this narrow approach was insufficient to fully understand leadership.

Situational Leadership

The next category of leadership theories to emerge considered the situation at hand to be more important than the traits or behaviors of the leader. This type of theory was often also known as the contingency theory of leadership. In this approach, the behavior of the leader depends on the situation surrounding the organization. Researchers at this time discovered that a leader's traits were not static but changed with the situation. They theorized that this probably meant that one style of leadership was not more prevalent or effective than another but that the style was changed to fit the circumstance. The main point to come out of this type of leadership research was that it may not be appropriate or even a good thing to have one leadership style for all situations. In fact, the situation was believed to determine who would emerge as leader. Bass stated, "The emergence of a great leader is a result of time, place, and circumstance."[2] According to this theory, a great leader had no real control over his actions because he was directed by the environment.[3]

According to Bass, "by 1960, the dominant paradigm for the study of leadership had evolved from research on the traits and situations that affect leadership to something more dynamic."[4] This type of leadership to which Bass was referring was transactional leadership, which has as its basic tenet the exchange between leaders and subordinates. In the 1970s and 1980s, a new theory arose in which the leader, through development of followers, and open communication at all levels (as opposed to simple exchange), transformed people to be something more than they thought they could be and obtained better performance for themselves and the organizations. The leaders embodied ideals with which followers identified, and the leaders asked them to transcend their own self-interests. This new paradigm was what Bass termed transformational leadership.[4]

Transactional Leadership

In this type of leadership, employees have clearly defined roles and are punished or rewarded based on their performance. One characteristic of transactional leaders is that they work to clarify roles and task requirements of employees. These leaders recognize the desires and needs of subordinates and make it clear that if they work to fulfill their job requirements, then based on the level of performance, these desires and needs will be met. According to Chen Hsien, a transactional leader sometimes uses what is termed initiating structure or consideration in order to increase employees' expectations that they will be rewarded if their efforts are successful.[5] This leadership is an exchange process in which subordinates' needs are met if their performance is consistent with what was originally contracted with the leader.[6] On a very basic level, this type of leadership could be viewed as leaders asking followers to do something, and if they do it well, they will be rewarded for their level of performance of the tasks at hand. In summary, transactional leadership alone is a high level of oversight over employees with rewards based on performance and alignment of employee outcomes with the organization's goals. This could be termed the managing leader as opposed to the visionary leader (transformational leader). Perhaps an example to illustrate is the current CEO of Apple, Tim Cook. Apparently, he is very focused on efficiency, and improving processes as well as aligning employee outcomes with Apple's goals which is a transactional type leader. Juxtaposed against is the previous CEO of Apple, Steve Jobs who was widely viewed as a visionary leader who was much more focused on the vision, the future of Apple and how to create an industry for itself, hence, he was viewed as a transformational leader. Apple is the same company perhaps, with the same logo, with similar products but its culture is changing and that is the result of the leadership styles of its past two CEOs. I trust that this example helps to illustrate the differences in these leadership styles.

Transformational Leadership

Bass and Avolio define a transformational leader as someone who can "elevate the desires of followers for achievement and self-development, while also promoting the development of groups and organizations."[6] There were five basic characteristics that describe a transformational leader: individualized consideration, idealized influence (charisma), idealized influence (behavior), inspirational motivation, and intellectual stimulation. Individualized consideration involves a leader paying special attention to the needs for achievement and growth of each individual by acting as a mentor. The role of the leader as coach and mentor is described in great detail in the question on learning organizations, so it will not be discussed in further detail here—suffice it to say that it is of paramount importance and should make up a considerable portion of the leader's time. By using this characteristic, leaders develop each employee to successively higher levels of achievement within the organization.

Idealized influence (behavior) involves leaders acting as role models for subordinates. The leader has a vision and a strong sense of mission that is directly shared with subordinates. The leader models behaviors that indicate a high standard of moral and ethical conduct. The leader takes risks but shares them with employees, causing them to feel partly responsible. Bass and Avolio[7] say that subordinates identify with this and try to emulate their leaders.

With the second dimension of idealized influence (charisma), leaders use behaviors that place the needs of others over their own in order to inspire trust, commitment, respect, and admiration in their employees. In this component of transformational leadership, followers interact with the leader and are inspired by the bigger picture, the vision that the leader has for the organization, and the importance of the roles played by employees is made clear. Ohman stated that "interactions with the leader are inspiring, enabling others to see the interrelationships between the current work and the vision—as well as how their work contributes to accomplishing the vision."[8] The leader's vision is consistent with the leader's actions, and that person can be counted on by employees to do the right thing [9] and avoid using power for personal gain.[10]

Inspirational motivation involves behaving in a way to provide meaning and challenge to subordinates' work. When employees are challenged, they usually become more motivated, and this inspires others around them. The leader strives to display enthusiasm and optimism, encouraging teamwork and team spirit. The leader develops and articulates a powerful vision for the future of the organization and gets followers actively involved in this vision. Leaders ensure that they communicate clearly stated expectations and motivate employees to strive to meet these goals.

Intellectual stimulation encourages creativity among employees. Mistakes are allowed as a part of learning and are used as examples of what to do when they happen. The leaders never publicly criticize the mistakes of others, and they encourage employees to try new approaches, even if they're different from the leader's own approach. Subordinates are encouraged to question, probe, develop ideas, reframe problems, and offer unique perspectives and innovative solutions to problems. These types of behaviors are found in learning organizations, as discussed earlier, and if employees continually develop, are personally challenged, and are part of the solution to problems, there may be performance improvements that reverberate throughout the organization, as a result. Employees, as a result of this approach, actually become more effective problem solvers and are challenged to a higher level of potential than would otherwise be the case. I believe the latter two dimensions are the ones associated with Steve Jobs and helped Apple create an industry (the creativity, passion and vision with which Jobs pushed the organization forward), is still felt today even though he is not with us.

What Is a High-Performance Organization?

A review of the literature of the last decade does not provide much clarity regarding the definition of a high-performance organization. However, there appear to be some central themes that emerge as prevalent. Some of the key elements that characterize high-performance organizations include: a team or group approach to production, developed autonomy and control, flat lean structures and advanced human resource practices, and an espoused management philosophy of feedback and open communication.[11]

According to Berry, organizational success is measured by "financial goals, customer satisfaction, employee growth and developments, and innovation."[12] Berry conveys the idea that, in a high-performance organization, people challenge the status quo and the organization to improve. He believes that there is a long-term perspective, and shareholders who make a commitment to the organization are rewarded with value over time. This is not dissimilar to the views of Collins and Porras,[13] who presented the internal workings of several highly successful, visionary companies. They used terms like "preserve the core," "stimulate progress," "articulate big-hairy-audacious goals (bhags)," and "core ideology." The main point of the book was that visionary companies have these elements to varying degrees and strive, at all costs, to ensure they hire the best people at all levels in the organization to preserve and develop these elements.

The literature reviewed for this book seems to solidly support the idea that high-performance organizations have, as integral elements, high-performance work teams (of five to twelve individuals) who undergo training and development in brainstorming, effective interpersonal skills, problem-solving, conflict handling, consensus building, and decision making.[14]

According to Katzenbach and Smith, current business literature indicates an increasing use of teams in the workplace, noting that teams can accomplish more than individuals, and, through teams, employees will be more motivated and energized.[15]

The High Performance Leadership paradigm shown below is

something I developed to help others visualize at glance, what I believe are the main requirements to create a high performance organization over time. Even if an organization does not do all these things well, a focus on them will probably mean above average performance that could be sustained over a long period of time. My personal views and experiences with leadership dwell on the necessity of the focus being transformational leadership for high performance. The next section of the book tries to support and take this viewpoint further.

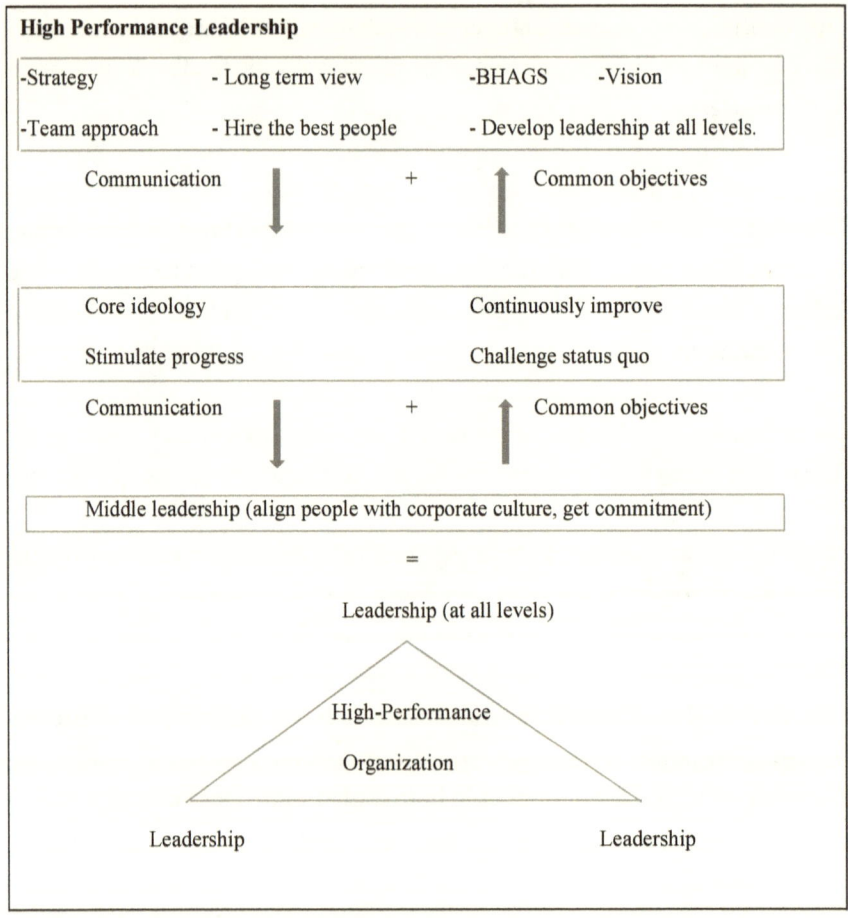

Figure 6: New Paradigm for High-Performance Organizations

Transformational Leadership and Organizational Performance

Transformational leadership has been studied quite frequently over the last two decades and continues to be popular in the business literature of today. Theories of transformational leadership attempt to describe leadership behaviors that are associated with above-average leadership in general when leaders are compared and associated with above average performance by subordinates. Kouzes and Posner's[16] visionary leadership describes five key transformational leadership behaviors, which can be assessed by the Leadership Practices Inventory (LPI). These behaviors are: challenging the process, inspiring a shared vision, modeling the way, enabling others to act, and encouraging the heart. It is argued that through the use of transformational leadership behaviors, subordinates become inspired to transcend their own interests and become committed to achieving the leaders' vision for the organization.[17] In these studies, it is argued that transformational leadership can allow subordinates to achieve well-above-average organizational performance. Harper[18] calls this type of leadership "breakthrough" leadership. Leadership is much more than having followers or allies. According to Harper, "leaders do much more than develop followers: they develop leaders. They know the company cannot rely on one or two leaders to create its future. A company needs leaders at all levels if it is to excel in the marketplace."[19]

According to Berry, the type of leadership found in excellent service companies is "values-driven leadership – a set of endearing ideals, principles, and beliefs that guide decision making and action."[20] Berry also conveyed seven ideals that collectively define values-driven leadership: excellence, innovation, joy, teamwork, respect, integrity, and social profit.[21]

Berry makes an interesting point when he discusses the way companies create sustainable excellence by cultivating other leaders throughout the organization. Instead of a layer of middle management, he sees the need for "middle leadership." He stresses the idea that "cultivating" middle leadership is a key role of values-driven leaders.

A review of literature also described organizational performance in several different ways and includes different elements. Two of the most extensive studies used return on assets (ROA), return on equity (ROE), and return on sales (ROS) as the main indicators of organizational performance.[22] According to Robins and Wiersema,[23] ROA is one of the most widely employed measures of performance because it has been shown to relate to a variety of other indicators of a firm's financial performance.

A firm's success can be characterized in many ways, and studies have shown that stock price alone may not be a good indicator of performance. Thompson and Strickland [24] have identified the types of goals that firms usually establish against which to measure their success. These performance areas are: market share and sales volume, product quality, new and improved product introduction, productivity, ability to improve, annual earnings, profitability, return on investment, improvement in employee skills, and employee flexibility.

Leaders learn how to tailor their leadership behaviors in order to effectively deal with a multitude of complicated, and often, new situations as they strive to increase individual and organizational performance. One of the most studied leadership styles over the last two decades, transformational leadership, may be an effective style for producing exceptional organizational performance.

According to Boehnke and DiStefano, "a transformational leadership style will universally help leaders work more effectively with people to reach their needs and create exceptional performance."[25]

Integration of Change Theories and a New Framework for Performance

Lewin's change theory is old and while still relevant, is somewhat simplistic and not encompassing nor can it accurately explain change in today's organizations.

Kotter's top/down process seems more like a list of activities that are driven from the top/down whereas systemic, longer term change must involve all aspects and all levels in the organization. With this in mind, what follows below is a new proposed framework that might work better and explain more than the ones proposed by Lewin and Kotter separately. Lewin describes a simplistic process and Kotter's is basically a list of steps, however, combined, they have a much tighter, elaborate, and synthesized framework that adds value as a change theory.

1. Having a core strategy for dealing with complex change especially effectively communicating it (communicate, communicate, communicate).
2. Understanding the need for and benefits of change. Individuals must see the discrepancy between current and desired behaviors – clear consistent communication is key.
3. Unfreezing – individuals are encouraged to accept responsibility for the change process.
4. Moving – resistance to change must be overcome. The benefits of change must be clear along with the importance of new desired behaviors for the individuals' career advancement. Individuals are shown the way and instilled with confidence.
5. Refreezing – the change is practical and feedback is given on performance with appropriate rewards.
6. Ensuring that the new change is made a part of the culture of the organization by involving *all* levels in the process.

There appears to be some consistency in the literature of leadership with respect to what a single, charismatic, visionary leader can achieve.

While the results can sometimes be extraordinary, they rarely are sustainable over the long term (see the works of Fullan, Goleman, Kets De Vries, Kotter, Schein[26]). There needs to be application and integration of both "hard" (strategy, structure, systems) and "soft" (vision, values, behaviors, attitudes) in order to achieve the best, sustainable results.

According to several studies (Blumenthal & Haspeslagh; Kouzes & Posner[27]) there must be a blend of both approaches since charisma alone, or the power of an individual's personality, is not enough to ensure lasting systemic change.

Table 8 below presents a summary of change leadership roles as proposed by Goleman[28] which represent interpersonal skills and the ability to manage environments. Both of these roles are equally important (depending on the change situation) and are necessary for leaders to obtain extraordinary performance.

Table 8: Summary of Change Leadership Roles[29]

Characteristic Role	Qualities and Attributes	Instrumental Role
Change leadership mindset.	Honesty/integrity/trustworthy.	Management mindset.
Strategic focus.	Inspiring.	Operational/Technical focus.
Systemic/big picture focus.	Competent.	Business unit focus.
Envisaging/energizing.	High degree of emotional intelligence.	Planning and control.
Concern for shared values, attitudes, motivating staff.	Self-confidence/awareness, strong desire/energy to achieve openness to new ideas/change.	Concern for systems, structures, and resource (human and physical) improvement.
	Strong interpersonal skills.	

The Role of Leadership in Change and Performance

Leading change and understanding the process is a vital role that leaders must play in today's fast-paced environment (see the works of Fullan, Goleman, Heifetz, Kotter[30]). While different types of leadership may be appropriate in different situations, in industries of dynamic change, two of the styles may not work well - coercive and pacesetting.[31] The four leadership styles that Goleman[31] found most effective in influencing culture and performance are: authoritative, affiliative, democratic and coaching. These are also associated with high emotional intelligence.

According to Fullan, the thing that is needed for sustained performance and long lasting change is "leadership at many levels of the organization."[32] He also states that " ... leadership in a culture of change will be judged as effective or ineffective not by who you are as a leader, but by *what leadership you produce in others.*"[33]

This point is supported by Argyris when he talks about internal commitment for change that "cannot be activated from the top."[34] According to Fullan, "It must be nurtured up close in the dailiness of organizational behavior, and for that to happen there must be many leaders around us."[35]

Leadership, Culture, and Performance: Is There a Relationship?

Leaders can and do create or develop cultures. They do many other things as well but perhaps none is more important than the creation of a strong culture. The process of building culture occurs most often if the leader believes in it and wants it to happen. The leader needs a vision for it, a passion for it, and the enthusiasm and energy level to carry it out. According to Schein, "It is crucial to recognize at this stage that if the organization is successful and the success is attributed to the leader, the leader's entire personality becomes embedded in the culture of the organization."[36]

Leaders now have to think ahead, be visionary, and be proactive to change – become a high priest of change and culture. They need to be able to learn new things and at the same time, unlearn things regarding the culture that may not serve the organization well. Leaders also need to clearly understand the elements of cultural dynamics and where the current culture of the organization is and needs to be for superior performance. Leaders probably cannot arbitrarily change culture completely by force, enthusiasm, or otherwise, however, an effective leader should be able to evolve culture by building on strengths and letting weaknesses atrophy over time.[37]

A strong culture, that is rare, constantly improving, and difficult to perfectly imitate is a source of competitive advantage. Strong leadership with a vision for the future that can articulate it and walk the talk while building trust in followers is equally a competitive advantage for an organization. Combining the two is like receiving the power source of the Sun in one battery – simply awesome, extraordinary performance. Perhaps ending with a quote from Heskett and Schlesinger will drive this important point further. They state:

> From time to time, the leadership in competing organizations has seized on one or more observed behaviors and tried to emulate the leaders of these organizations

in ways that might well be regarded as manipulative. The results have been predictably disastrous; this provides further confirmation of the possibility that there is a strong linkage between leadership, culture, and performance – in short, that state-of-the-art leadership delivers outstanding organizational results.[38]

Other researchers have concluded that a relationship exists between leadership, culture, and organizational performance. Kotter and Heskett have reported positive relationships between strong cultures and long-term economic success. Kelloway and Barling[39] report increases in performance levels when transformational leadership trickles down through the organization.

Many companies, at times, seem to have this but then again, maybe not.

High-Performance Companies and Leadership in the Twenty-First Century

The world around us is constantly changing and changing rapidly. So too are organizational and leadership practices. Throughout most of the twentieth century many organizations survived and did well with structures that were hierarchical in nature for example the Catholic Church, the Army, and Ford Motor Company. For the most part, attributes that describe such organizations are as follows: pyramidal structure, hierarchical organization, staff departments, top-down decision making, functional and divisional structures, and position power. Now, especially after the failure of several high profile companies, new prototypes of organizations are emerging that stress empowerment, flexibility, organizational learning and knowledge creation – the learning organization and its various structures are gaining popularity. The New Economy is driving change at such a rapid pace that the only constant is change. These new prototypes, out of necessity are more in tune than their predecessors with the changes that have occurred due to increased globalization of organizations and the communication and information technology revolution. The Internet has radically changed how organizations operate and it appears that this trend will continue into the future at an exponential rate. Future leaders will have to be comfortable dealing with change and leading in this type of environment. According to Kets De Vries, "With discontinuity the new norm, the original prototype of leadership and organizations has become less relevant. Given the increasing irrelevance of the traditional model, the question becomes, what kind of leadership and organization will be most appropriate in the twenty-first century?"[40]

Figure 7 was created to explain the type of leadership and the elements that must be embraced for leading complex change and obtaining extra-ordinary performance. It focuses on the necessary leadership attributes, as well as the actions that need to be taken under the leadership team. Another important point embedded within the framework is that communication must be constant, at all levels and to all stakeholders, while embracing and developing a culture of change (specifically Theory

E and O). And, finally, this must be an ongoing and throughout the organization process, so that all members understand the change process and the benefits (or, the *what's in it for me* question). I hope that this helps to distill the requirements for navigating complex change while maintaining high levels of performance.

New Competency Framework for Leading Complex Change and Obtaining Performance

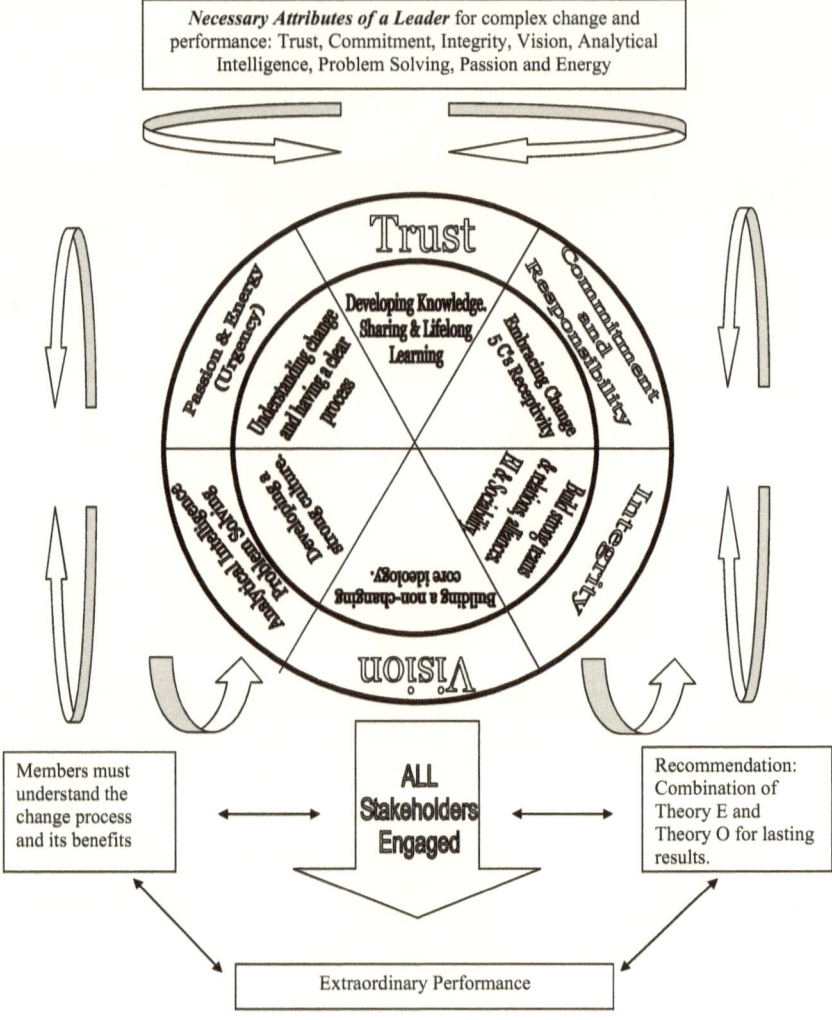

Figure 7: New Contemporary Framework for Leading Complex Change & Obtaining Performance

(Source: A synthesis of frameworks proposed by Fullan, 2001; Kets De Vries, 2001; and Goleman, 2000)

Leadership Characteristics That Work Well in High-Performance Organizations (A Comparison of Angiotech Pharmaceuticals and QLT Therapeutics)

Companies are under immense pressure to change and must adapt quickly or suffer the consequences. Companies are composed of individuals, and the human tendency is to resist change and tend toward the status quo. People and their level of motivation have a substantial impact on the performance of most organizations, and it is the leadership of the organization that is responsible for attracting and hiring high-performance people to the organization. Leadership and development of teams, organizational culture, and change are major elements of any organization and directly or indirectly affect organizational performance. Any of these elements alone can have a very dramatic impact, either positively or negatively on organizational performance. These elements together may be the difference between extraordinary results and dismal failure in any organization—public, private, for-profit, not-for-profit, and anything in between. Visionary leadership, strong organizational culture, and resistance to change are very difficult concepts to define, compare, and measure. There is a compounding effect when high performance is added to the mix. This section will attempt to accurately define high performance and assess the impact of leadership style on future performance, with a focus on two of the leading biotechnology companies in British Columbia, Canada, for comparison purposes. The comparison is longitudinal (over several years) to try to make the comparison more robust and even though the data is dated, it is for illustration purposes only.

Both Angiotech Pharmaceuticals and QLT Therapeutics Ltd. fall into this category and must radically change in terms of culture, organization, and leadership if they are to continue to influence future trends and remain leaders in biotechnology in the province. These two institutions continue to be dominated by the three C's, control, compliance, and compartmentalization that have driven their success for the past decade or so. This may not be sufficient for future success as the speed of change increases dramatically and the tolerance for failure by shareholders is basically nil. According to Kets De Vries, traditional organizations dominated by control, compliance, and compartmentalization "are being outpaced by organizations that focus on ideas, information, and interaction (the three Is). In today's business world, people and processes have become the central themes"[40]. While this may not be true in all industries, it appears to hold true certainly in the biotechnology arena.

The biotechnology industry is currently experiencing rapidly changing paradigm shifts that will envelope traditional and non-traditional institutions alike. Which organizations will be better prepared to survive? Organizations focused and organized around stability, local markets, hierarchical structures, and lead by autocratic leadership, or alternatively, organizations structured with a new mindset predicated on both continuous and discontinuous change, a global orientation, a customer driven focus, a "systems" approach, and a combination of transformational/situational leadership. The latter organizational description will be necessary to survive the dramatic changes that organizations will face. Hierarchy will be much less prominent in all future organizations. The new structures will tend to be flat and organic rather than hierarchical and rigid. Innovative, fluid, and flexible designs will offer some form of competitive advantage as complex decisions are made quickly and easily.

Leaders of these New Economy organizations must necessarily lead in different ways as well. They must, now more than ever, find ways to bind their people to the organization. In addition, they have to take on additional responsibilities. According to Kets De Vries, leaders are no longer leaders in " ... the traditional paternalistic, autocratic sense. Instead, in addition to being CEO's, they're also *chief knowledge officers*, transmitting knowledge from one part of the organization to the other"[41]. The new leaders will tend to be known for their roles as chief architects of the organizational structure, chief coaching officers and chief change officers of organizational culture. Add to this, the necessity of leaders to lead with a global vision while at the same time finding smart ways to simplify decision-making processes and you have the CEO of the twenty-first century. As mentioned earlier and important enough to be reinforced, the words "miracle-workers" may take on new meaning before long.

Leaders of the Future Can Create
High-Performance Organizations

Companies of the future are going to change if they are to be success-ful in delivering their missions. They must add-value to the traditional models of producing products, delivering services, expanding markets and training, and developing employees. Areas for development might include creating a learning culture, building new markets, focusing on customers, institutionalizing total quality leadership, leading change, winning in the global marketplace, and fostering innovation. Several of these factors are discussed briefly in the next section.

Creating a learning culture. According to Covey in Hesselbein et al., the leader of the future will be one who, "creates a culture or a value system cen-tered upon principles."[42]

He asserts that leaders who have the vision, courage, and humility to constantly learn and grow will achieve success creating a learning culture. In order for organizations like Angiotech and QLT to grow and prosper, they must have visionary leadership, embrace change, and have a passion for learning and delivering knowledge.

According to Covey,

> Those people and organizations who have a passion for learning – learning through listening, seeing emerging trends, sensing and anticipating needs in the market-place, evaluating past successes and mistakes, and ab-sorbing the lessons that conscience and principles teach us, will have enduring influence. Such learning leaders will not resist change; they will embrace it.[43]

Building new markets. Leaders and the companies they lead will have to adapt to the changing roles and relationships of different sectors of society and build new markets for their products.

Focusing on customers. This will be an extremely difficult thing for traditional organizations to do. They are simply not structured to do so and their cultures will not allow them to easily do so effectively. In a traditional sense of organizational structure, the CEO, the Chairman, and the Board of Directors of organizations are the power brokers and decision makers. In the future, this will not be as true. The customers will wield more power and universities will have to meet their needs or fail. The new structure will be upside-down with the customer on top. Who then is at the bottom? Top management is at the bottom. The structure will change the focus from who is *responsible* to who is *responsive*. This change will be dramatic and challenging to many biotechnology firms. According to Blanchard, in Hesselbein et al.:

> The leader of the future, realizing that vision and implementation are both leadership roles, will learn to care little about defending the traditional hierarchy. As a result, she or he will be willing to turn the pyramid upside-down to implement a vision.[44]

The Role of Leaders and the Performance of the Organization

Organizations today must learn how to effectively deal with many types of change. The rate at which they learn, how they learn, and the depth to which they learn is dependent on many factors, not the least of which is the culture of the organization and the dissemination and practice of leadership throughout the organization, at *all* levels. The basic assumption here is that the more open and collaborative the culture, the more information that is shared, and the more strong leadership is practiced throughout all levels of the organization, the greater the rate of organizational change and the more lasting the change becomes. If the change is the correct one, it is then logical to assume that the performance of the organization is enhanced, at least in the short term. According to Leider in Hesselbein et al.[45], "We live in an era of organizational reengineering. To become or remain competitive, leaders must realize improvements through radical change, or reengineering."

Culture is usually created and maintained by the founder of any organization and begins to change as the founder relinquishes control to others especially if they came from outside the organization (see the works of Kets De Vries and Schein[46]). Also, over time the assumptions regarding the culture initially created has to change as the external environment and its elements influence the organization in different, even unforeseen ways. The type of leadership required to change a culture (or enhance performance) and the methodology used will be different depending on the stage of the organization life cycle the organization finds itself and the magnitude of the change necessary for survival. As an organization matures and becomes more stable, it has a track record, a long history of successes and leaders will find that to change deeply embedded assumptions will require such effort and time if changes are to last and be more than just superficial. Along the same lines, if performance is suffering and needs to be improved, the leader needs to choose the correct style for the situation at hand.

According to Schein, there are three stages of organization: founding and early growth, midlife, and maturity and decline. Since both

Angiotech and QLT have been operating for only a few decades or so, it will be assumed for the purposes of this illustration that they are in the early growth stage. For more detailed information on the various stages of a company life cycle, please refer to appendix B. Therefore, the cultural change mechanisms required are as follows: "change through systematic promotion from selected subcultures, planned change through organization development projects and the creation of parallel learning structures, and unfreezing and change through technological seduction."[47]

How companies actually move from the founding and early stage dominated by a founder to the midlife stage has many variants and events. The first dramatic change is the promotion of a new CEO and president. This had recently happened at both companies and therefore, for the next few years or so, the culture of Angiotech and QLT should remain relatively unchanged from their current culture. The culture will be maintained because it is clearly identified with the founder. Change will occur to the culture at a more rapid pace when the organization has grown in size to the point where the sheer number of external managers overweighs the founding members (which is now happening at both firms). From a cultural and leadership perspective, the organizations are now facing a very different situation than they faced in the past. They are leaders in their fields, are losing money still, are spending huge sums of capital on research and development activities, and also, must maintain performance through some kind of continued growth and renewal process. These companies must decide how they want to pursue such growth, through new products or programs, mergers or acquisitions, geographic expansions, or new markets. Angiotech and QLT will probably utilize a combination of all of the above strategies as they rapidly expand market share and try to develop new drugs to market. (Please refer to appendix C for a brief synopsis of both companies and their corporate strategies). Again, this will pose problems for managers and leaders since it is not easy to add new drugs, attract new shareholders, buy companies, expand to new markets, maintain quality and introduce new technologies while at the same time growing at over twenty percent per annum and changing the organization's culture. According to Schein[48], the strength of this stage of organization lies in the diversity of its subcultures. Managers and leaders will tend to promote people from their favored subculture.

This could tend to weaken the organization over time as the pool of talent shrinks and the organization becomes disproportionately weighted at the executive level by leaders from only a few subcultures. The range of experience will be a narrowed perspective that is less insightful than necessary to face the increased challenges of the company. The policy of promoting from within will tend to exacerbate this problem. The implications for leadership are multiple. Leadership has to start and manage the culture change. It will begin by unfreezing the current culture through provision of information that challenges current assumptions as first proposed by Lewin[49]. This will cause anxiety, stress, and guilt, which will ultimately motivate change. Leaders will also have to provide enough safety during this process to keep employees committed to the cultural change otherwise the traumatic learning process could fail. The leaders will have to provide some vision and insight into the process and the end result. They have to provide a path, a map, and a process of learning to assure members of the organization that constructive, lasting, and positive change is possible. This is imperative if the company is going to continue to successfully evolve as *the* leader in its respective field of specialization. According to Schein,

> Leaders of the future will have to be perpetual learners. This will require 1) new levels of perception; 2) extraordinary levels of motivation; 3) emotional strength to manage change; 4) new skills in analyzing cultural assumptions; 5) the willingness and ability to involve others, and 6) the ability to learn a whole new organizational culture.[50]

Leaders will have to be able to embrace change, adapt to situations and ensure they stay focused on the right vision for the organization regardless of the challenges faced and the changes they must institute and endure. In order to accomplish this, leaders must be extremely focused and intense as they take the organization to new heights of learning, productivity, and success. This will require enormous amounts of energy, emotional intelligence, and motivation. Given the magnitude of the changes and challenges that future leaders will face, all levels of the organization must be enthusiastically committed to achieving the vision articulated by the leader. This will be the fundamental factor in achieving success in organizations of the future. The culture of an organization is one of its most irreplaceable assets and the knowledge it contains could be its best source of competitive advantage. Therefore, leaders will absolutely have to possess the ability to lead change, to learn new organizational cultures, and to understand evolving processes that enlarge and strengthen the culture by building on its strengths and functional elements. Schein states, "Leadership will then increasingly be an emergent function rather than a property of people appointed to formal roles."[51] Leaders of the future, in order to ensure organizations reach their full potential and bring the most valuable asset of any organization with them, must unleash the collective potential of all people in the organization. By doing so, and achieving this fundamental tenet of leadership, transformational leaders changing to meet any situation will help ordinary people achieve extraordinary results. Is there any other way?

Real, sustaining change depends on the motivation and self-leadership of leaders and followers, managers and employees. In the public universities this group is comprised of the president, vice-presidents, deans, faculty, and staff. A critical element in sustaining any change effort is re-igniting everyone's motivation and talents providing support in using them effectively in the organization. Changing the vision, structure, and culture of any organization takes a tremendous amount of effort and ensuring the change is "learned" and sustaining is dependent upon the leadership and support of all levels of the organization.

Leaders and managers of the future will have to be well versed in the challenges and dynamics of constant, discontinuous, even radical change. Change is all around and the natural human tendency is to resist it sometimes at all costs. Given this first reaction and natural tendency, it is imperative that managers and leaders be able to communicate the vision of the necessity of change, the real benefits of change, and where it will eventually take the organization. What is needed is a look at the "big picture" and the ability to address the whole of the organization in a system like, tiered approach to change. In addition to resistance to change, there is a lack of successful implementation of large scale, system wide change. One just needs to look at the results of mergers and acquisitions over the last decade to see examples of extreme failures. The high failure rates and lack of synergy is certainly not something to be proud of.

Leaders and managers of change must possess and market a compelling vision to keep people committed to the desired future of the organization. The process must be a top-down/bottom-up process of interaction and mutual influence between the "official" leader, functional managers, and all employees (see the works of Bennis & Nanus, Kotter, Schein and Sowell[52]). Leaders need a clear grasp of the nature of the change to be implemented. To ensure change is accepted more easily and is sustainable, leaders must help employees develop and maintain a collaborative team-based approach to problem solving, an open and sharing culture, foster and support employee development and learning, and empower employees to solve problems together more efficiently. Rather than directing, telling, pushing, and driving the organization, the leader expects the highest possible from each employee, gets commitment, and actually coaches and mentors individuals to ensure their individual contributions tie in directly to the organization's goals and strategy. Bennis and Nanus[53], from their study of corporate exemplary leaders describe the process by saying that leaders "pull" rather than push. They pull through a compelling vision that creates focus for change for the organization and ensures that the changes are accepted. Leaders establish the vision in the systems and members and simultaneously nurture the organization to foster additional "pull" leadership. Involving all parts of the organization, working toward integration, using push and pull strategies and making decisions based on high moral values supported by harmony, cohesion, and trust will help to ensure the organization changes as required to survive the challenges of the future. The leader of an organization is comfortable dealing with the constant challenges of dynamic and discontinuous change but this must be embraced and embedded in the culture of the organization which means all stakeholders too.

A high-performance organization provides time for reflection and reflective practice in order to learn from its actions and improve upon its decision-making capabilities at the individual and team level. Learning takes place in both informal and formal settings from the copy station to the classroom, on the job or during breaks, or incorporated in meetings and conferences designed for this purpose. Most of what people know is learned on the job by talking to other people, trying new things, and doing their work. Formal training and education though essential for success and learning, cannot serve as a substitution for informal interactions as a powerful means of learning.

Change, especially radical change that does not occur under the conditions of strong leadership and empowered teams, is destined to fail. Leaders are encouraged to enlist widespread involvement, ensuring that individuals and teams affected by change decisions play a key role in helping to make them. Thus, participation in decision-making at all levels is built into the "inner fabric" of the organization, providing room for individual voice within the parameters provided by visionary leadership. According to Kotter, "Successful transformation is 70 to 90 percent leadership and only 10 to 30 percent management."[54] The leader of the organization leads the charge of dynamic change.

In a learning organization, work related beliefs and values are clearly articulated as outcomes of the visionary process. Although not everyone will agree, and one of the beliefs should reflect a valuing of difference and diversity, there will be some common values to which everyone attempts to adhere. Some of the values that come to mind are: an open, collaborative approach to problem-solving and differing views as opposed to a "culture of blame"; a belief in the value of employees as the organizations' most valuable assets, prized possessions as opposed to liabilities; a belief in lifelong learning and education, both formal and informal, in the classroom and elsewhere. The culture of the organization must enable and reward employees at all levels who have the courage to confront gaps and raise concerns, the skills to solve problems, and the desire to learn. The leaders must be instrumental in accepting and modeling this behavior. They must invite and accept feedback for their actions, positive or negative, good or bad, as they strive to transform the organization and "put theory into practice." In short, the transformational leader must constantly and diligently, without fail, "walk the talk."

In the organization of the future, the culture must be a one that accepts failure as a learning experience and it learns from mistakes and remembers them so as to not make the same mistake twice. The organization that is intent on learning from experience must prohibit, both culturally and procedurally, the use of threat, punishment, or blame.

Instead, mistakes or problems are viewed as opportunities for learning, and issues of concern are routinely surfaced, with a vision to improving future performance by effectively dealing with the dynamics of change. In summary, learning organizations in general (as Angiotech and QLT are striving to be), must thrive on and welcome change as a means for growth and new opportunities. How do they do this? They make incremental, continuous improvements and value innovation at all levels. They welcome change as a source of innovation, creativity, and opportunity for growth. They create a culture (or invent one) that is open, collaborative, and nurturing. They reward and provide learning, have strong leadership and reward employees for courage as they focus on high performance. They practice individual development and employee empowerment. Finally, they form, develop, and optimize teams to effectively deal with change to achieve organizational goals, learning how to learn as they grow. Both Angiotech and QLT are striving to be better performing organizations and due to their short existences, measuring long term performance is difficult. They appear to have made significant advances in performance and may be expected to do well in the future; however, due to the current turmoil in the financial markets, comparisons may not be truly accurate and in fact are difficult. The table below highlights some of the key financial performance indicators found in the literature as discussed earlier and provides a quick comparison of the two companies.

Table 9: Comparison of Performance Indicators from 2006 – 2008

QLT Inc.

	2008 (in millions USD)	2007	2006
Revenue	124.9	127.9	175.1
Net Income (Loss)	134, 891	(109,997)	(101,605)
Total Assets	491.7	548.9	639.1

(Source: www.qltinc.com; www.nasdaq.com)

Table 10: Comparison of Performance Indicators from 1998 – 2002

QLT Inc.

	2002 (in millions USD)	2001	2000	1999	1998
Revenue	110.5	83.4	32.8	17.7	8.3
Net Income (Loss)	13.6	71.5	4.4	(24.6)	(17.9)
Total Assets	345.8	317.9	260.0	222.9	67.3
New Products	4	0	0	0	1

(Source: www.qltinc.com; www.nasdaq.com)

Table 11: Comparison of Performance Indicators from 2006 – 2008

Angiotech Pharmaceuticals, Inc.

	2008 (In millions USD)	2007	2006
Revenue	283.3	287.7	315.1
Net Income (Loss)	(741,176)	(65,940)	10,774
Total Assets	385.2	1,150.1	1,224.6

(Source: www.angiotech.com)

Table 12: Comparison of Performance Indicators from 1998 – 2002

Angiotech Pharmaceuticals, Inc.

	2002 (in millions USD)	2001	2000	1999	1998
Revenue	7.3	1.1	4.8	4.5	2.3
Net Income (Loss)	(20.1)	(8.3)	(1.2)	(9.9)	(6.7)
Total Assets	151.6	162.7	165.9	35.4	25.8
New Products	22*	4	2	4	1

(Source: www.angiotech.com)

* Denotes similar uses for coatings but different medical devices as opposed to completely new products.

Company Comparisons of Key Financial Ratios

Return on Assets (ROA) = Net Income/(Beginning + Ending Total Assets)/2
This key ratio measures the company's ability to utilize its assets to create profits.

Return on Investment (ROI) = Net Income/Long-Term Liabilities + Equity
This key ratio measures the income earned on the invested capital.

Return of Equity (ROE) = Net Earnings/Total Equity (Average)
This key ratio measures the return on the shareholder's equity.

The final ratio, and arguably the most crucial, is the amount of money a company can generate from operations on a consistent basis, which is called cash flow. The formula for calculating cash flow: = net profit + depreciation – increases (or + decreases) in accounts receivable – increases (or + decreases) in inventories + increases (or – decreases) in accounts payable – decreases (or + increases) in notes payable (bank loans).

The table below shows these ratios for both companies for two years, since the losses for the earlier years could tend to distort the figures and make comparisons. The problem with using the numbers generated from only two years of operating results is the inability to place much faith in them and the inherent meaning of the actual calculations. Still, it is a starting point, and unless and until top managers and the leaders are interviewed to add further detail to the numbers, that is all that is available to explain performance, which may be problematic. The next section briefly explains what the numbers could mean going forward for both companies and should be taken lightly and used cautiously.

Table 13: Comparisons Using ROA, ROI, ROE, and Cash Flows

	QLT Inc.		Angiotech Pharmaceuticals	
Ratio	2002	2001	2002	2001
ROA	7.0%	44.0%	−13.2%	−5.1%
ROI	4.3%	24.3%	−14.4%	−5.3%
ROE	4.0%	24.0%	−14.4%	−5.9%
Cash Flow	10,549	99,669	−19,427	−6,831

(Source: www.qltinc.com; www.nasdaq.com, www.angiotech.com)

The revenue growth experienced by QLT Inc. over this period has been quite phenomenal (from $32.8 million in 2000, to $83.4 million in 2001, and $110.5 million in 2002). Angiotech Pharmaceuticals, on the other hand, has shown a much lower revenue growth rate (from $4.77 million in 2000, down to $1.12 million in 2001, and $7.33 million in 2002). It appears from this comparison that Angiotech is struggling to grow revenues, whereas QLT is rapidly selling products and is a much better performer, using sales growth as a main criterion. While the data gathered and the comparison and contrasting of the key performance criteria are not conclusive, it does appear that QLT Inc. is a better performer and may be poised to do better in the future because of its strong financial position and its transformational leadership. However, with only one main product and increasing competition, there is only so much that leadership can account for, and it is important, but it cannot be everything.

Conclusion

Organizations can learn and the extent to which they learn depends on the culture of learning created in the organization as well as the involvement and commitment of employees at *all* levels *in* the organization *to* the learning organization. The learning organization does not evolve overnight – it is a journey as opposed to a destination. The process is long, ongoing, and developmental in nature. Learning will be the essential factor if organizations are to cope with rapid continuous change and survive in the future.

In the past, organizations could grow, evolve, and survive just by improving production in a totally mechanistic way. However, this is not acceptable as contingencies become more unstable, are rapidly changing, are flexible and decentralized, and information flows are lateral with ongoing consultation from all levels in the organization. The necessary form then is an organic, learning organization. Given the extremely volatile external environments in which organizations now operate, the impetus to develop more flexible, organic structures operating in team-oriented work patterns has been generated at all levels in industry.

Increased competition and rapid technological development means that a significant competitive advantage for organizations in the future will be their ability to create new knowledge which is disseminated throughout the organization and which will, in turn, lead to continuous learning and innovation. Under changing circumstances it appears that elements of organizations must develop an expanded understanding of their roles, to question the appropriateness of what they are doing and press to modify their actions and processes to account for new situations. Also, individuals discover sources of error and attribute them to the operating norms or theory-in-use within the organization. They must then invent new strategies to keep organizational performance within normative ranges, based on new assumptions to correct errors after which they must evaluate the results of the action. In this way, error correction and continuous questioning embodies a complex learning cycle.

Argyris[55] argues that there can be no organizational learning without individual learning, but that individual learning is a necessary but insufficient condition for organizational learning. Until such time as individuals embed their discoveries, challenges and results of their enquiries into the organizational "memory" which encodes the theory-in-use, their work as learning agents is incomplete. This, however, implies that organizational structures, processes, and cultures are receptive to fundamental challenges to established norms and procedures to facilitate learning. Changing such complex, intertwined elements is no easy task even for an organization bent on becoming a learning organization. It remains to be seen if Angiotech pharmaceuticals and QLT Therapeutics Ltd. can or will do this. There were times when it looked as though they would fail and yet they pulled through. CEOs came and went but it appears now that they are more stable and focused and only time will tell if they are going to continue performing.

If organizations are to increase their capacity to learn, by both individual and organizational means, there must be recognition and removal of the barriers they have created which inhibit the processes. A learning organization cannot evolve unless and until such issues are alleviated. What is necessary is the correct structure, culture, and subcultures, a focus on the development of the individual, a commitment to lifelong learning, and a strong commitment by employees, managers, and leaders to accept change, develop interpersonal skills, and accept mistakes as a natural part and main element of learning. Embracing change will be a core tenet of organizational success and leadership must take the lead in ensuring the key elements discussed above are integrated in organizational strategy—the survival of the organization depends on it.

Endnotes

1   F. E. Fiedler, *A Theory of Leadership Effectiveness* (NY: McGraw-Hill, 1967), 11.

2   Bass, *Transactional*, 38.

3   Bass, *Stogdill's.*

    S. Kerr et al., "Toward a Contingency Theory of Leadership Based Upon The Consideration and Initiation Structure Literature," *Organizational Behavior and Human Performance* 12 (1974): 62-83.

    Bass, *Transactional*, 53.

4   Bass, *Transactional.*

5   Chin-Hsien, Hsu, "A Structural Equation Modeling Analysis of Transformational Leadership, Organizational Culture, and Organizational Effectiveness In Taiwanese Sport/Fitness Organizations" (PhD diss., Daphne, Alabama, December, 2010).

6   B. M. Bass and B. J. Avolio, "The Implications of Transactional and Transformational Leadership for Individual, Team, and Organizational Development," *Research in Organizational Change and Development* 4 (1990b): 231-272.

7   B. M. Bass and B. J. Avolio, "Developing Transformational Leadership: 1992 and Beyond," *Journal of European Industrial Training* 4 (1990a): 22.

    Bass and Avolio, *Developing*, 21-37.

8   K. A. Ohman, "The Transformational Leadership of Critical Care Nurse-Managers," *Dimensions of Critical Care Nursing* 19(1) (2000): 47.

9   Bennis, *Why Leaders.*

10 Bass and Avolio, *Developing*, 21-37.

    Ohman, *Transformational*, 46-53.

11 L. Berry, "Strategic Generosity", in *On High-Performance Organizations* by F. Hesselbein and R. Johnston, R. (2002). NY: Jossey-Bass (1999): 125-135.

    E. E. Lawler III, *High-Involvement Management* (San-Franciso: Jossey-Bass, 1986).

M. Morley and N. Heraty, "The High Performance Organization: Developing Teamwork," *Management Decision* 33(2) (1995): 56-64., accessed September 28, 2002, www.apollolibrary.com.

J. R. Hackman and R. E. Walton, "Leading Groups in Organizations". In P. S. Goodman, & Associates (Eds.), *Designing Effective Work Groups* (San Francisco, CA: Jossey-Bass, 1986), 72 - 119.

12 Berry, *Strategic*, 125.

13 Collins and Porras, *Built*.

14 Morley and Heraty, *High*, 56

15 J. R. Katzenbach, and D. K. Smith, "The Wisdom of Teams: Creating The High-Performance Organization," Boston: *Harvard Business School* (1993): 111.

16 Kouzes and Posner, *Leadership*.

17 Bass, *Leadership*.

S. Carless, "Assessing the Discriminant Validity of the Leadership Practices Inventory," *Journal of Occupational and Organizational Psychology*, 74(2)(June, 2001): 233-240, accessed January 4, 2003, PROQuest search, www.apollolibrary.com.

N. Tichy and M. Devanna, *Transformational Leadership* (New York: Wiley, 1986).

18 Harper, *Forward*.

19 Harper, *Forward*, 39.

20 Berry, *Strategic*, 126.

21 Berry, *Strategic*, 128.

22 M. Onken, "Temporal Elements of Organizational Culture and Impact on Firm Performance," *Journal of Managerial Psychology*, 14 (3/4) (1999): 236.

23 J. Robins and M.F. Wiersema, "A Resource-Based Approach to The Multi-Business Firm: Empirical Analysis of Portfolio Interrelationships and Corporate Financial Performance," *Strategic Management Journal*, 16 (1995): 277-299.

24 A. Thompson and A. Strickland, *Strategic Management* (Burr Ridge, IL: Irwin, 1994).

25 K. Boehnke and A. DiStefano, A, "Leadership for Extraordinary Performance," *Business Quarterly* 6(4) (Summer, 1997): 62, accessed October 7, 2002, EBSCOHost, www.apollogrouplibrary.com.

26 Fullan, *Leading*.

Goleman, Boyatzis, and McKee, *Primal*.

De Vries, *Leadership Mystique*.

Kotter, *Leading*.

Schein, *Organizational*.

27 Blumenthal and Haspeslagh, *Toward*.

Kouzes and Posner, *Leadership*.

28 Goleman, *Working*.

29 Goleman, *Working*, 95.

30 Fullan, *Leading*.

Goleman, *Working*.

Heifetz, *Leadership*.

Kotter, *Leading*.

31 Goleman, *Leadership*.

32 Fullan, *Leading*, 131.

33 Fullan, *Leading*, 137.

34 C. Argyris, *Flawed Advice and The Management Trap: How Managers Can Know When They're Getting Good Advice and When They're Not* (Oxford and New York: Oxford University Press, ISBN 0-19-513286-6, 2000).

35 Fullan, *Leading*, 133.

36 Schein, *Leader*, 61.

37 Schein, *Leader*, 64.

38 Heskett and Schlesinger, *Leader*.

39 E. K. Kelloway and J. Barling, J. "What We Have Learned About Developing Transformational Leaders," *Leadership and Organization Development Journal* 21(7) (2000): 355-362.

40 De Vries, *Leadership Mystique*, 60.

41 De Vries, *Leadership Mystique*, 63.

42 Covey, *Leader*, 149.

43 Covey, *Leader*, 149-150.

44 Blanchard, *Leader*, 85.

45 Blanchard, *Leader*, 189 - 190.

46 De Vries, *Leadership Mystique*.

    Schein, *Organizational*.

47 Schein, *Organizational*, 304.

48 Schein, *Organizational*.

49 Lewin, *Frontiers*, 5-40.

50 Schein, *Organizational*, 391-392.

51 Schein, *Organizational*, 68.

52 W. Bennis and B. Nanus, *Leaders: The Strategies for Taking Charge* (NY: Harper & Row, 1985).

    Kotter, *Leading*.

    Schein, *Organizational*.

    Sowell, *Titan*.

53 W. Bennis and B. Nanus, *Leaders: The Strategies for Taking Charge* (NY: Harper & Row, 1985).

54 Kotter, *Leading*, 26.

55 Argyris, *Overcoming*.

Appendix A: Discussion of New Competency Framework for Leading Complex Change and Obtaining Performance

The new framework for leadership, change, and performance is an integration of information put forth by Fullan (2001), Kets De Vries (2001), and Goleman (2000). While each of these authors had presented some of these items separately and did a good job, there was no framework for the integration of all three elements. This book attempted to discuss the importance of dealing with culture, change, and leadership and the implications of the elements on performance. The model created attempts to integrate these critical elements and should result in extraordinary performance if organizational conditions are correct. In this framework, the necessary leadership attributes are: trust, integrity, vision, analytical intelligence, passion and energy, and commitment. These are not all-inclusive but are some of the most important, and they are necessary for leaders to possess. The role of the leaders, managers, and employees (but especially the leaders) is to ensure that the underlying circle elements (refer to the competency diagram for more detail) are present in the organization.

These crucial items are: understanding change and having a clear process; developing knowledge, sharing, and lifelong learning; embracing change and 5C receptivity: building strong teams and relationships; alliances; emotional intelligence and sociability; developing a strong culture; and building an unchanging core ideology. These elements should be important to all stakeholders (employees, customers, investors, and suppliers). The circles are continuously moving, multidirectionally, highlighting the fact that change is continuous, discontinuous, and constant, and the leadership skills and core elements need to move with the change. Finally, if all members clearly understand the change process (the recommendation is a combination of Theory E and Theory O), then the organization has a very good chance of achieving extraordinary performance over a sustainable period of time—maybe even decades.

Appendix B: Life Cycles of Organizational Development

Start-Up. The Childhood Years - you have a vision. During this stage, you develop plan and develop a business idea and start your business.

Validation. The Teen Years - establishing where you fit in. You develop the company's own unique identity and carve out a distinct place in the eyes of customers. Many companies never make it beyond this stage of development because it is the hardest test for most companies. During Validation, you will need to develop a unique value proposition and convert key customers.

Expansion. The College Years - rapid growth and development. You expand your business by pursuing new customers and sales and make a significant investment in your company's future. During the Growth phase, you focus on sales growth and you pursue opportunities to expand your business.

Maximize Profitability. The Adult Years - a period of adjustment and refinement. You continue to add new products and services to grow and expand your business. Each of these new opportunities will create the need to revisit many of the stages of development that you have already experienced. For each new opportunity, your company may revisit the Validation, Growth, and Maximize Profit Stages of Company Development.

Exit. The Senior Years - retirement and moving on. At some point, you will decide to exit your business. You may sell the company, or merge it with another organization. If you have planned properly, you will be able to maximize the value that you receive out of your business.

Source: Retrieved online August 20, 2002 from http://www.thebdc.com/bizstages/

Appendix C: Traditional versus High-Performance Organizations

Dimension	Traditional	High-Performance
Support for innovation and risk-taking	Status quo	Continuous improvement
Emphasis on learning	• Few opportunities • Few rewards • No time set aside • Cross-training viewed as inefficient	• Many opportunities • Learning is highly rewarded • Time regularly set aside • Cross-training is the norm
Job design	• Jobs require almost no skills • People performing the work make no decisions about how the work is performed • People work alone • People do only repetitive, partial tasks • Supervisors problem solve, not workers	• Jobs require many skills that take a long time to learn • People are relied on to make almost all important decisions on how the work will be done • People work in teams • People do a variety of tasks and see the connection to their work and the final product • Problem-solving is an important part of everyone's job

Dimension	Traditional	High-Performance
Role of management	• Managers tell people what to do and watch performance • Managers focus on "own" departments • Rules are followed, and managers are never evaluated by employees • Meetings are one-way communication tools • Strict "chain of command" to be followed • Managers are selected primarily for their technical skills	• Managers explain results and help subordinates "facilitate" solutions • Managers focus on the "system" view • Managers break rules and encourage innovation • Meetings are used to facilitate discussions on improving performance • Communication is two-way • Anyone can speak to anyone at any time about anything • Managers need excellent skills for dealing with people
Organizational structure	• Many levels of management • Functional departments • Clear boundaries between departments/functions • Meetings usually functional and not inclusive	• Flat structure (only a few levels) • Process team • Boundaries are fuzzy • Lots of cross-functional problem-solving and interdepartmental communication

Dimension	Traditional	High-Performance
Customer relations	• Few people talk to customers • Fellow employees not viewed as customers • No one knows the standards used by customers to judge quality of final product or service	• Everyone is constantly striving to determine customer wants/needs and how to meet them • Employees are viewed as "internal" customers • Everyone knows ...
Flexibility	• Slow to respond to changes in its environment • Slow to adapt technology • Adept at producing only a limited number of products and services • Slow to introduce new products and services	• Anticipates changes in its environment and is quick to adapt itself to new demands • Quickly exploits technological advances and is adept at finding innovative ways to use existing technology • Offers a wide variety of products and services • Can easily adapt existing products and services to meet new or changing customer requirements
Teamwork	• People look out for only themselves	• People help one another without being told

Dimension	Traditional	High-Performance
	• There is often destructive competition • Few people can state the values behind decisions that are made • Values, if they exist at all, concern only profit	• Everyone in the organization works together with a goal toward shared accomplishment • Everyone can state their values • The organization values teamwork, participation, innovation, and quality as much as profit
Dedication	• Only a few people at the top feel personally responsible for how well the organization performs • Few people are willing to put out effort above the minimum required to do their own work • People slack off when their supervisors are not present	• Everyone has a sense of personal responsibility for how well the organization performs • People frequently expend effort well above the minimum necessary • Almost everyone performs at a peak level regardless of whether a supervisor is present

Dimension	Traditional	High-Performance
Rewards	• People are rewarded the same whether they perform or not • People are rewarded for seniority • There are large differences in the way managers and their employees are rewarded • Financial gains due to improvements in performance are not shared with employees • People are rewarded on an individual basis	• People are rewarded based upon their performance and/or the performance of their team • People are rewarded for what they know • Managers and their employees are rewarded in similar fashions • Financial gains due to improvements in performance are shared equitably with all employees
Access to information	• Little information about the state of the business is shared with employees • Managers and technical experts withhold information • Information is viewed as a source of power and privilege	• A great deal of information about the state of the business is shared with employees • Managers and technical experts share information freely • Information is viewed as a valuable resource that belongs to the entire organization

Dimension	Traditional	High-Performance
	• Access to information systems and data is tightly controlled	• Information systems are designed to enable the maximum number of people to communicate electronically across boundaries to share data, analysis tools, and information
Socio-technical balance	• Technology is considered more important than people • Technology in use is understood by few and inhibits teamwork • The technology used by the organization is difficult to change	• Technology and people are treated as having equal importance • People are involved in the selection and use of the technology • The technology is designed to support teamwork throughout the organization • The technology used by the organization is easy to change

Source: Adapted from J.Boyett and J.Boyett, 1998, "The Basic Requirements For High Performance", accessed September 28, 2002 from www.apollolibrary. com.EBSCOHost.

Appendix D: QLT Inc. Background and Company Description

QLT Inc. is a world leader in photodynamic therapy (the use of light-activated drugs in the treatment of disease) and has a successful history of drug development, having received regulatory approvals on all submissions made to date. QLT was established in 1981 and is headquartered in Vancouver, British Columbia, Canada. Its two main products are Visudyne, the first biopharmaceutical treatment for age-related macular degeneration (AMD), the leading cause of blindness in people over the age of fifty-five; and Photofrin, the world's first approved photodynamic therapy drug, used in the treatment of a variety of cancers.

QLT's business focus is the discovery, development, and commercialization of innovative therapies to treat cancer, eye diseases, and niche areas for which treatments can be marketed by a specialty sales force.

QLT's vision is to be among the top ten biotechnology companies worldwide in terms of market capitalization by 2010. The company's strategy is to maximize the potential of Visudyne; continue to build a strong pipeline through early-stage development, clinical trials, in-licensing and other expansion opportunities; and manage the business for continuous growth.

QLT's business strategy is to pursue expanded indications for Visudyne therapy and develop and commercialize other products that can be marketed by a focused specialty sales and marketing team in ophthalmology, oncology and other diseases. QLT has expanded its research and development pipeline by acquiring rights to new product candidates and access to new technologies. QLT intends to continue to expand its product pipeline by continuing its in-licensing efforts and pursuing strategic acquisitions.

Appendix E: Angiotech Pharmaceuticals Background and Company Description

Angiotech Pharmaceuticals is a Canadian pharmaceutical company dedicated to the development of medical device coatings and treatments for chronic inflammatory diseases through reformulation of paclitaxel. The company operates in two segments: medical device coatings/implants and therapeutics. Medical device coatings/implants comprise the research and development of pharmaceuticals for the treatment of chronic inflammatory diseases such as rheumatoid arthritis and psoriasis.

Angiotech Pharmaceuticals is dedicated to enhancing the performance of medical devices and biomaterials through the innovative uses of pharmacotherapeutics.

Concluding Thoughts

Beginning in the late 1970s and continuing into the 1980s, studies of leadership moved from describing transactional leadership to focusing on transformational leadership, and perhaps the most significant writer during the latter period was Burns. Burns[1] was one of the first researchers to describe the term "transformational leadership" in his study of political leaders in 1978. Bass[2] expanded upon and augmented Burns's hypotheses of transactional and transformational leadership. Bass defines transformational leadership as a superior form of leadership that occurs when leaders "broaden and elevate the interests of their employees, when they generate awareness and acceptance of the purposes and the mission of the group and when they stir their employees to look beyond their own self-interest for the good of the group."[3]

According to Bass and Avolio,[4] a transformational leader motivates or "transforms" followers to do more than they originally expected to do using several means, including stimulating interest in their work, generating awareness of the mission or vision, developing followers' potential, and motivating followers to work for individual, as well as group, benefit. Burns[5] had a slightly different view that contained some similar elements but with a seemingly higher order or standard for this type of leader. Burns believed that transformational leadership occurred when the leader and the follower raised each other to higher levels of motivation and morality. This may or may not be true; however, what appears to be true is that a transformation between followers and the leaders actually occurs, which is beneficial to both parties.

Some Findings From the Study of Transformational Leadership

A transformational leader motivates or *transforms* followers to do more than they originally expected to do, utilizing one or all of the following methods: (1) stimulates interest among followers to view their work from new perspectives; (2) generates awareness of mission or vision of the organization; (3) develops followers to higher levels of ability and potential;

and (4) motivates followers to work for the group benefit, as well as their own.[6] According to Burns,[7] transformational leadership is really a moral form of leadership that affects leaders and followers in such a way that they raise one another to higher levels of motivation and morality. Transformational leaders go beyond the simple transactional relationship of action–reward to satisfy the higher needs of the follower. This results in a relationship of mutual stimulation.

Link to Motivation

The theoretical basis for transformational leadership is dependent upon Abraham Maslow's hierarchy-of-needs theory, developed in 1954, which later became one of the most frequently acknowledged motivation theories among managers. This theory was discussed in detail in an earlier section, so it will be discussed only briefly here. It needs to be discussed here because it is directly linked to human motivation, and transformational leaders understand well how to motivate followers. The underlying principle of Maslow's theory is that people's needs may be arranged in a hierarchy, ranked from basic physiological needs at the lower level to self-actualization or self-fulfillment needs at the highest level. Consistent with Maslow's hierarchy, the transforming leader is able to raise his followers' needs from concerns for physiological satisfaction, security, and affiliation to interest in achievement, recognition, and self-actualization.[7]

Burns determined that the utilization of transformational leadership skills satisfied the higher-level needs of subordinates by engaging people. Burns perceived leaders as being either transactional or transformational, but Bass[8] proposed that transformational leadership augments the effects of transactional leadership on the efforts, satisfaction, and effectiveness of followers.

Role in Change

Transformational leadership occurs more conspicuously in situations of organizational crisis and change.[9] The typical environment in which transformational leadership occurs is when four variables are present. These variables are: (1) a crisis situation, (2) emotional distress among organization members, (3) a clearly defined leader, and (4) an inspirational message.[10] Individuals involved in a crisis are prepared to make changes,[11] and the emotional distress experienced by these individuals encourages them to look toward a leader to resolve the situation. The transformational leader will appear in times of crisis and create success.[12] It appears from the literature review conducted for this section that transformational leadership is making a comeback as a popular leadership theory/style. The elements that compose transformational leadership are popular in current leadership books and articles, and the conditions in the external environment are such that transformational leadership may indeed be needed. Employees need to be motivated (if they do not have sufficient internal motivation), and transformational leadership appears to be the right style to aid in the motivation of followers to enhance both individual and organizational performance. Also, in this new global economy, change is rapid and often discontinuous. Given the earlier discussions around the rationale for employee resistance to change and the current magnitude and pace of change occurring in organizations and if the theories are correct, transformational leadership may begin to emerge as a dominant leadership style.

Benefits of Transformational Leadership

From the literature review, it appears that transformational leadership is emerging as a popular leadership theory/style. Transformational leadership emerges and is effective when facing change or changing an organization.[13] Transformational leadership can be linked to Maslow's hierarchy of needs and can aid in motivating employees to achieve higher performance.[14] The transformational leadership elements (idealized influence and inspirational motivation) may affect follower performance. Individualized consideration may be important in organizations dealing with change and conflict.[15] Transformational leadership skills lead to a high level of follower satisfaction and increase effectiveness and individual effort.[16]

Endnotes

1   Burns, *Leadership*.

2   Bass, *Leadership*.

3   Bass, *Handbook*, 2.

4   Bass, *Developing*, 21-37.

    B.M. Bass, B.M. and B. J. Avolio, "The Implications of Transactional and Transformational Leadership for Individual, Team, and Organizational Development," *Research in Organizational Change and Development* 4 (1990b): 231-272.

5   Burns, *Leadership*.

6   B.M. Bass and B. J. Avolio, eds., *Improving Organizational Effectiveness Through Transformational Leadership* (Thousand Oaks, CA: Sage, 1994).

7   Burns, *Leadership*.

8   Bass, *Leadership*.

9   G. A. Yukl, "Managerial Leadership: A Review of Theory and Research," *Journal of Management* 15 (1989b): 251-289.

Glossary

Change: when the structure and functioning of a system is altered so as to enable more or different adaptation.

Change process: involves four distinct stages: unfreezing, moving to a new end state, embedding the change in the corporate culture, and refreezing.

Cultural learning: how employees learn the culture of an organization or society; can be transmitted to employees in a number of forms, the most effective being stories, rituals, material symbols, and language.

First-order change: incremental and convergent change; helps firms maintain internal reliability; may involve adjustments in systems, processes, or structures, but does not involve change in strategy, core values, or corporate identity; most likely during times of relative environmental stability and likely to take place over extended periods of time.

High-performance organization: an organization that is a radical departure from the traditional organization, with a continuous focus on innovation, customer orientation, a strong entrepreneurial culture, and work teams.

Organizational culture: a complex system of historical beliefs, values, attitudes, behaviors, assumptions, symbols, and norms that describe how the organization should conduct its business and convey its vision to stakeholders inside and outside the organization; is stable, deeply held, fundamental, difficult to change, rare, and almost impossible to imitate; in conjunction with strong leadership, and a core ideology that embraces change, can be a source of competitive advantage for learning organizations.

Return on assets (ROA): net income divided by total assets.

Return on equity (ROE): net income divided by total common equity.

Return on sales (ROS): net income divided by total net sales.

Second-order change: transformational and radical change that fundamentally alters the organization at its core; difficult and risky, triggered by a change in competitive conditions that may emanate from either the institutional or market contexts, a change in leadership, or a decline in actual, expected, or aspiration-level organizational performance.

Strong culture: when employees buy into the organization's vision, goals, and plans for reaching those goals.

Team: a small number of people with complementary skills, who are committed to a common purpose, set of performance goals, and approach for which they hold themselves accountable; made up of highly committed individuals who seek out what they need to know to get their job done.

Theory E change: change that makes headline news; *hard* approach to change in which shareholder value is the only legitimate measure of corporate success; usually involves heavy use of economic incentives, drastic layoffs, downsizing, and restructuring.

Theory O change: a *soft* approach to change that focuses on developing a corporate culture and human capability through individual and organizational learning of the process of changing, obtaining feedback, reflecting, and making further changes.

Transformational leadership: charisma, and inspirational and intellectual stimulation; display of the following behaviors significantly more than other managers: visioning (communicating a vision of the future that is shared broadly by the organization's members); inspiring (generating excitement and heightening others' expectations through symbols and images); stimulating (arousing interest in new ideas and approaches, enabling employees to think creatively about problems); coaching (advising and helping others to improve their performance by giving challenging and interesting tasks); and team building (building effective teams by selecting team members with complementary skills).

Visionary leadership: leadership with an understanding of change and the change process, developing a picture of an improved state of the organization, encouraging creativity, and managing operations in relation to student learning.

References

Adair, J. "Effective Strategic Leadership: An Essential Path to Success Guided by The World's Greatest Leaders." Pan Macmillan Australia Pty Limited, *Business & Economics* (2002):321.

Adams, J.S. *Inequity in Social Exchange. Advances in Experimental Social Psychology.* New York: Academic Press, 1959.

Allerton, H.E. "High Performance." *Training & Development* 52(7) (July, 1998): 11-13. Accessed July 4, 2003, EBSCOHost, www.apollolibrary.com.

Alvesson, M. *Cultural Perspectives on Organizations.* Cambridge, MA: Harvard University Press, 1993.

Argyris, C. 2000. *Flawed Advice and The Management Trap: How Managers Can Know When They're Getting Good Advice and When They're Not.* Oxford and New York: Oxford University Press, ISBN 0-19-513286-6, 2000.

Argyris, C. *On Organizational Learning.* Cambridge, MA: Blackwell, 1993, 20.

Argyris, C. *Overcoming Organizational Defenses: Facilitating Organizational Learning.* Boston: Allyn & Bacon, 1990.

Argyris, C.and Schon, D.A. *Organizational Learning: A Theory of Action Perspective.* Reading, MA: Addisson Wesley, 1978.

Arie de Gues, In "The Professional Development of Principals: Innovations and Opportunities." Peterson, K. D. *Educational Administration Quarterly* 38(2) (2002): 213-232.

Avolio, B. *Full Leadership Development: Building The Vital Forces* in Badaracco, J. Jr., *Leading Quietly: An Unorthodox Guide to Doing the Right Thing.* Boston, MA: Harvard Business School Press, 2002.

Balasubramanian, V. *Organizational Learning and Information Systems.* Rutgers University Working Paper, 1996.

Bandura A and Butz A. R.In "The Leadership Challenge." Kouzes, J.M. and Posner, B.Z. San Francisco: Jossey-Bass, 1995, 288.

Barney, J. "Organizational Culture: Can it be a Source of Sustained Competitive Advantage." *Academy of Management Review* 11(3) (1986). Accessed June 13, 2002, EBSCOHost from www.appologrouplibrary.com, 658.

Bartlett, C., & Ghoshal, S. "Changing the Role of Top Management: Beyond Systems to People." Boston, MA: *Harvard Business Review* 73(2) (1995).

Bass, B. *Bass and Stogdill's Handbook of Leadership: Theory, Research &Managerial Applications*. New York: The Free Press, 1990.

Bass, B. *Leadership and Performance Beyond Expectations*. New York: Free Press, 1985.

Bass, B. M. "Does the Transactional – Transformational Leadership Paradigm Transcend Organizational and National Boundaries?" *American Psychologist* 52(2) (1997).

Bass, B. M. *Stogdill's Handbook of Leadership*. New York: Macmillan, 1981.

Bass, B.M. & Avolio, B.J. (eds.) *Improving Organizational Effectiveness Through Transformational Leadership*. Thousand Oaks, CA: Sage, 1994.

Bass, B.M. "From Transactional to Transformational Leadership: Learning to Share The Vision." *Organizational Dynamics* (18)3, 1990: 19-36.

Bass, B.M., & Avolio, B.J. "Developing Transformational Leadership: 1992 and Beyond." *Journal of European Industrial Training* 4 (1990a): 22.

Bass, B.M., & Avolio, B.J. "The Implications of Transactional and Transformational Leadership for Individual, Team, and Organizational Development." *Research in Organizational Change and Development* 4 (1990b): 231-272.

Beaven, M.H. *Leadership, Charisma, Personality, and Power*. Townson: ND, 1989.

Beckhard, R. *The Leader of The Future: New Visions, Strategies, and Practices For The Next Era*. San Francisco: Jossey-Bass Publishers, 1996.

Begin, J. *Strategic Employment Policy: An Organizational Systems Perspective*. Englewood Cliffs, NJ: Prentice-Hall, 1991.

Bennis, W. *On Becoming a Leader*. Rev/2nd ed. Addison-Wesley Pub Co, 1995.

Bennis, W. (1989). *Why Leaders Can't Lead*. San Francisco: Jossey-Bass, 1989, 77-78.

Bennis, W. and Goldsmith, J. *Learning to Lead: A Workbook on Becoming a Leader*. New York: Perseus Press, 1997.

Bennis, W. & Nanus, B. *Leaders: The Strategies for Taking Charge*. (2nd ed.). New York: Harperbusiness, 1997.

Bennis, W. & Nanus, B. *Leaders: The Strategies for Taking Charge*. NY: Harper & Row, 1985.

Berry, L., "Strategic Generosity", in *On High-Performance Organizations* by Hesselbein, F. and Johnston, R., 2002. NY: Jossey-Bass, 1999, 125.

Blake, R.R., & Mouton, J.S. *The Managerial Grid*. Houston, TX: Gulf Publishing, 1964.

Blanchard,K. in Hesselbein, F., Goldsmith, M., & Beckhard, R. *The Leader of The Future*. San Francisco: Jossey-Bass, 1996, 85.

Blumenthal, B. & Haspeslagh, P. "Toward a Definition of Corporate Transformation." *Sloan Management Review* (1994).

Boehnke, K. & DiStefano, A. "Leadership for Extraordinary Performance." *Business Quarterly* 6(4) (Summer,1997): 62. Accessed October 7, 2002, EBSCOHost, www. apollogrouplibrary.com.

Boisot, M. "Is your firm a Creative Destroyer? Competitive Learning and Knowledge Flows in The Technological Strategies of Firms." *Research Policy* 24(4) (1995).

Bolt, J. *The Leader of The Future: New Visions, Strategies, and Practices For The Next Era*. San Francisco: Jossey-Bass, 1996.

Bornstein, S. and Smith, A. *The Leader of The Future: New Visions, Strategies, and Practices for The Next Era*. San Francisco: Jossey-Bass, 1996, 283.

Boyatzis, R.E. *The Competent Manager: A Model For Effective Performance*. NY: Wiley, 1982.

Boyett, J., & Boyett, J. *The Guru Guide*. New York: John Wiley & Sons Ltd., 1998.

Brooking, A. *Corporate Memories, Strategies for Knowledge Management*. London: Thompson Business Press, 1999.

Brown, J.S., & Duguid, P. "Organizational Learning and Communities-of-Practice: Toward a Unified View of Working, Learning and Innovation." *Organization Science* 2(1) (1991).

Burns, J. M. *Leadership*. New York: Harper & Row, 1978.

Carless, S. "Assessing the Discriminant Validity of The Leadership Practices Inventory." *Journal of Occupational and Organizational Psychology* 74(2) (June, 2001): 233-240. Accessed January 4, 2003, ProQuest search, www.apolloli-brary.com.

Cascio, W. F. *Managing Human Resources: Productivity, Quality of Work Life, Profits*. McGraw-Hill Ryerson, Limited, 1995.

Chowdhury, S. *Management 21C*. London: Prentice-Hall, 2000.

Chowdhury, S.D. "Turnarounds: A Stage Theory Perspective." *Canadian Journal of Administrative Sciences* 19 (2002).

Collins, J. & Porras, J. *Built to Last: Successful Habits of Visionary Companies*. New York: Harper Business, 1997, 84.

Conner, D. *Leading at The Edge of Chaos*. New York: John Wiley, 1998.

Cooke, R.A., & Lafferty, J.C. *Organizational Culture Inventory*. Plymouth, MI: Human Synergistics, 1994.

Cooke, R.A., & Rousseau, D.M. "Behavioral Norms and Expectations: A Quantitative Approach to the Assessment of Organizational Culture." *Group and Organizational Studies* 13 (1988).

Corporate Structure, www.sobeys.ca, 6.

Covey, S. in Hesselbein, F., Goldsmith, M., & Beckhard, R. *The Leader of The Future*. San Francisco: Jossey-Bass, 1996, 149.

Covey, H. R. *Principle-Centered Leadership*. New York: Simon & Schuster, 1990, 62.

Crainer, S. & Dearlove, D. (2002). "Excellence Revisited." *Business Strategy Review* 13(1) (2002). Accessed July 4, 2003, EBSCOHost, www.apollolibrary.com.15.

Cunningham, J.B., & Gerrard, P. "Characteristics of Well-Performing Organizations in Singapore." *Singapore Management Review* 22(1) (2000): 35-64. Accessed July 4, 2003, EBSCOHost, www.apollolibrary.com.

Davenport, T. H. "Putting The Enterprise Into The Enterprise System." *Harvard Business Review* (July – August, 1998): 5, Reprint 98401.

Davenport, T.H. & Prusak, L. *Working Knowledge*. Boston: Harvard Business School Press, 1998.

De Pree, M. *Leadership is an Art*. New York: Dell Publishing, 1989.

De Vries, M. *The Leadership Mystique: A User's Manual for The Human Enterprise*. Toronto: Prentice Hall, 2001, 186.

Decrane, A., in *The Leader of The Future*, Hesselbein, F., Goldsmith, M., & Beckhard, R. San Francisco: Jossey-Bass, 1996, 254.

Deming, W.E. *The New Economics For Industry, Government, Education*. Cambridge, MA: MIT, 1993.

Denison, D. R. *Corporate Culture and Organizational Effectiveness*. New York, NY: John Wiley & Sons, Inc., 1990, 1.

Dessler, G. (1998). *Management: Leading People and Organizations in The 21st Century*. New Jersey: Prentice Hall, 1998, 335.

Dodgson, M."Organizational Learning," *Academy of Management Review* 10(4) (1993).

Dodgson, M. "Organizational Learning: A Review of Some Literatures." *Organization Studies* (1993): 375–394.

Downey, M. *Effective Coaching.* London: Orion Business Books, 1999, 12.

Drucker, P. In "Peter Drucker on The Profession of Management." Pressly, T. R. and Drucker, P.F., *Ohio CPA Journal,* 58(2) (April/June, 1999): 1-3.

Drucker, P. "The Practice of Management Reflections on Peter F. Drucker's Landmark Book Shaker A. Zahra." *The Academy of Management Executive* 17(3), (Aug., 2003): 16-23.

Drucker, P. F. "The Discipline of Innovation." *Harvard Business Review* (November – December 1998): 3-8, Reprint 98604.

Drucker, P. F. *The Profession of Management.* Boston: Harvard Business Press, 1998.

Drucker, P. In "The Business of The Kingdom." Stafford, T. *Christianity Today,* 43(13) (November15, 1999): 3-8. Accessed July 11, 2003, EBSCOHost, www. apollolibrary.com.

Drucker, P. *The Effective Executive.* New York: HarperCollins, 1999.

Drucker,P. In "Peter Drucker." Galagan, P. A., *Training and Development* 52(9) (September 1998):1-6.

Fiedler, F. E. *A Theory of Leadership Effectiveness,* NY: McGraw-Hill, 1967, 11.

Fiol, C.M., & Lyles. "M.A. Organizational Learning."*Academy of Management Review* 10(4) (1985).

Fleming, A., & Drucker, P. "Innovation by Numbers." *Economist* 367(8329), 1-3, (June 21, 2003): 2.

Fraquhar, C. "People Power." *Canadian Business Review* 23(1) (Spring, 1996): 42

Fullan, M. *Leading in a Culture of Change.* San Francisco: Jossey-Bass, 2001, 34.

Fullan, M."Principals as Leaders in a Culture of Change." *Educational Leadership,* May (2002).

Fullan, M. *Leading in a Culture of Change.* San Francisco: Jossey-Bass, 2001.

Fullan, M. *Principals as Leaders in a Culture of Change.* Ontario Institute for Studies in Education, University of Toronto. Paper prepared for Educational Leadership, Special Issue, May 2002. Revised March 12, 2002.

Fulmer, R.M., & Goldsmith, M. "The Leadership Investment: How the World's Best Organizations Gain Strategic Advantage Through Leadership Development." New York: *American Management Association*, AMACOM, 2001.

Gardner, J. W. *On Leadership*. New York, NY: The Free Press, 1990, 14.

Garvey, R. "Mentoring in The Marketing Place." Unpublished doctoral dissertation, Durham University, England, 1998.

Gephart, M.A. "The Road to High Performance." *Training & Development* 49(6) (June, 1995): 29-39. Accessed July 4, 2003, EBSCOHost, www.apollolibrary.com.

Goleman, D. "Leadership That Gets Results." Boston, MA: *Harvard Business Review* (March/April, 2000).

Goleman, D. *Working With Emotional Intelligence*. NY: Bantam Books, 1998, 95.

Goleman, D., Boyatzis, R. and McKee, A. (2001). *Primal Leadership. The Hidden Driver of Great Performance*. Harvard Business Review Press, 2001, 44.

Goleman, D., Boyatzis, R., & McKee, A. *Primal Leadership*. Boston, MA: Harvard Business School Publishing, 2002.

Goodman, N. "An Introduction to Sociology." In *International Business: Competing in The Global Marketplace* 3rd ed. Hill, C. (Toronto: McGraw-Hill, 2000), 86. Originally published New York: Harper Collins, 1991.

Greenberg, J. *Managing Behavior in Organizations* 3rd ed. New Jersey: Upper Saddle River, 2002, 377.

Gunn, B. "The Performance Edge." *Strategic Finance* 81(11) (May, 2000): 14-16.

Hackman, J. R. & Walton, R. E. "Leading Groups in Organizations". In P. S. Goodman, & Associates (Eds.), *Designing Effective Work Groups*, 72–119. San Francisco, CA: Jossey-Bass, 1986.

Hagberg Consulting Group. (1998). Accessed January 08, 2003, http://209.157.100.6/p-compare.html.

Haines, S. In "Extraordinary Leadership - Creating Strategies For Change," P. Reed (London, UK: Kogan Page Limited, 2001), 131.

Hall, R. (1996). *Developing Capabilities and Managing Knowledge in Supply Chains*. Durham, England: University of Durham Working Paper, 1996.

Handy, C. *The Leader of The Future: New Visions, Strategies, and Practices For The Next Era*. San Francisco: Jossey-Bass, 1996: 9.

Hargrove, R. *Masterful Coaching*. San Francisco, CA: Jossey-Bass, 1995, 100.

Hargrove, R. *E-leader: Reinventing Leadership in a Connected Economy.* Perseus Publishing, 2001.

Harper, S. In "The Forward Focused Organization." Enrico, R. CEO of PepsiCo New York: AMACOM, 2001, 30.

Hartog, D. et al. "Culture Specific and Cross-Culturally Generalizable Implicit Leadership Theories: Are Attributes of Charismatic/Transformational Leadership Universally Endorsed?" *Leadership Quarterly* 10 (2) (Summer, 1999): 219-257.

Hartog, D. N, House, R.J., Hanges, P. J., Ruiz-Quintanilla, S. A., Dorfman, P. W., et al. "Culture Specific and Cross-Culturally Generalizable Implicit Leadership Theories: Are Attributes of Charismatic/Transformational Leadership Universally Endorsed?." *Leadership Quarterly* 10(2), 1999: 219-257.

Heffernan, M.M., & Flood, P.C. "An Exploration of The Relationships Between the Adoption of Managerial Competencies, Organizational Characteristics, Human Resource Sophistication and Performance in Irish Organizations." *Journal of European Industrial Training* 24(2/3/4) (2000): 128-136.

Heifetz, R. *Leadership Without Easy Answers.* Cambridge, MA: Harvard University Press, 1994.

Herzberg, F., Mausner, B., & Snyderman, B.B. *The Motivation to Work.* New York: John Wiley & Sons, 1959.

Heskett, J. & Schlesinger, L. In *The Leader of The Future,* Hesselbein, F., Goldsmith, M., & Beckhard, R. San Francisco: Jossey-Bass, 1996, 119.

Hesselbein, F., Goldsmith, M. and Beckhard, R. *The Leader of The Future* San Francisco: Jossey-Bass, 1996.

Hesselbein, F., Goldsmith, M., & Sommerville, I. *Leading Beyond The Walls.* San Francisco: Jossey-Bass, 1999, 46.

Hill, C. (2000). *International Business: Competing in The Global Marketplace* (3rd ed.). Toronto: McGraw-Hill, 2000, 82.

Hilmer, S. & Karney, D. "Towards Understanding The Foundations of Deming's Theory." *Journal of Quality Management* 2(2), 1997, 20.

Hock, D. *The Birth of The Chaordic Organization of Turning Chaos and Order Into Money and Meaning in The New Millenium.* Bantam Doubleday: Dell Publishing Group, 1998.

Hofstede, G. *Cultures and Organizations: Software of The Mind* 1st ed. McGraw-Hill: USA, 1997, 179.

Hofstede, G., "The Cultural Relativity of Organizational Practices and Theories," *Journal of International Business Studies* 14 (1983): 75- 89.

Howell, J. M and Avolio, B.J. "Transformational Leadership, Transactional Leadership, Locus of Control, and Support for Innovation: Key Predictors of Consolidated- Business-Unit Performance." *Journal of Applied Psychology,* 78(6) (1993):891- 902.

Hsu, Chin-Hsien. "A Structural Equation Modeling Analysis of Transformational Leadership, Organizational Culture, and Organizational Effectiveness in Taiwanese Sport/Fitness Organizations." PhD diss., Daphne, Alabama, December, 2010.

J. Bolt, In *The Leader of The Future,* Hesselbein, F., Goldsmith, M., & Beckhard, R. San Francisco: Jossey-Bass, 168.

Jacobs, R. *Real Time Strategic Change: How to Involve an Entire Organization in Fast and Far-Reaching Change.* San Francisco: Berrett-Koehler Publishers, 1997.

Kanter, R. *Evolve!: Succeeding in The Digital Culture of Tomorrow.* Boston: Harvard Business School Press, 2001.

Katz, J. H., & Miller, F. A. "Coaching Leaders Through Culture Change." *Consulting Psychology Journal*: Practice & Research 48(2) (1996): 111.

Katzenbach, J.R. & Smith, D.K. *The Wisdom of Teams: Creating The High-Performance Organization.* Boston: Harvard Business School, 1993, 111.

Keller, R.T. "Transformational Leaders Make a Difference." *Research Technology Management* 38(3) (May –June, 1995): 41. Accessed June 30, 2003, http://proquest. umi.com/pqdweb, 41.

Keller, R.T. "Transformational Leaders Make a Difference." *Research Technology Management* 38(3) (May/June, 1995).

Kelloway, E.K., & Barling, J. What We Have Learned About Developing Transformational Leaders. *Leadership and Organization Development Journal* 21(7) (2000): 355-362.

Kerr, S., Schriesheim, C.A., Murphy, C.J. and Stogdill, R.M. "Toward a Contingency Theory of Leadership Based Upon the Consideration and Initiation Structure Literature." *Organizational Behavior and Human Performance* 12 (1974): 62-83.

Kilburg, R. "Forward: Executive Coaching as an Emerging Competency in The Practice of Consultation." *Consulting Psychology Journal*: Practice and Research 48(2) (1996).

Kilmann, R.H., & Saxton, M.J. *Kilmann-Saxton Culture-Gap Survey*. Tuxedo, NY: Xicom, 1991.

Kim, D. In *The Basic Requirements For High Performance*, J. Boyett, and J. Boyett, 1998, 93. Accessed September 28, 2002, EBSCOHost, www.apollolibrary.com.

Kinlaw, D. *Coaching, Winning Strategies For Individuals and Teams*. England: Gower Publishing Ltd, 1997.

Kogut, B. and U. Zander. "Knowledge of the Firm, Combinative Capabilities, and The Replication of Technology." *Organization Science* 3(3), 1992.

Kopelman, R., Brief, A. and Guzzo, R., "The Role of Climate and Culture in Productivity." In *Organizational Climate and Culture*, Schneider, B. (San Francisco: Jossey-Bass, 1990): 282-318.

Kotter, J. P. *Leading Change*. Boston: Harvard Business School Press, 1996.

Kotter, J. P. "Leading Change: Why Transformation Efforts Fail." *Harvard Business Review* (1995).

Kotter, J.P. "John P. Kotter on What Leaders Really do." Boston: *Harvard Business Review* (1999).

Kotter, P. In "The Corporate Culture Connection." Dumaine, B. *Fortune* 125(9) (May 4, 1992): 1-2.

Kouzes, J. M. and Posner B.Z. *The Leadership Challenge*. 2nd ed. San Francisco: Jossey-Bass, 1995.

Kouzes, J. M. and Posner B.Z. *The Leadership Challenge: How to Get Extraordinary Things Done in Organizations:* San Francisco, CA. Josssey-Bass, 1990.

Kouzes, J. M. and Posner B.Z. *Credibility: How Leaders Gain and Lose it, Why People Demand it*. Reissue. Jossey-Bass. Simon and Schuster Books, 1993.

Kouzes, J. M., Posner B.Z. and Peters, T. *Credibility: How Leaders Gain and Lose it, Why People Demand it*. San Francisco: Jossey-Bass, 1995.

Kouzes, J., & Posner, B. *Encouraging the Heart: A Leader's Guide to Rewarding and Recognizing Others*. San Francisco: Jossey-Bass, 1999.

Kouzes, J., & Posner, B. *The Leadership Challenge: How to Get Extraordinary Things Done in Organizations*. San Franscisco: Jossey-Bass, 1987.

Krames, J.A. *The Jack Welch Lexicon of Leadership.* New York: McGraw-Hill, 2002, 28.

Laiken, M.E. *Models of Organizational Learning: Paradoxes and Best Practices in the Post-Industrial Workplace.* NALL Working Paper #25, 2001.

Landry, J. "Information Characteristics as Constraints to Innovation," (paper from proceedings of the Twenty-Fifth Hawaii International Conference on Systems Sciences, CA: IEEE Press, 1992).

Langan-Fox, J. & Tan, P. "Images of a Culture in Transition: Personal Constructs of Organizational Stability and Change." *Journal of Occupational & Organizational Psychology* (70)3, Sep, 1997:1-2.

Latham, J. *Personal Comments in Comprehensive Paper Answers.* Vancouver, BC: Unpublished, 2003.

Lawler III, E.E. *High-Involvement Management.* San-Franciso: Jossey-Bass, 1986.

Leadership, Special Issue, May 2002. Revised March 12, 2002.

Leider, R. In *The Leader of The Future,* Hesselbein, F., Goldsmith, M., & Beckhard, R. San Francisco: Jossey-Bass, 189-190.

Lewin, K. "Frontiers in Group Dynamics. Concept, Method and Reality in Social Science." *Human Relations* 1(1) (1947): 5-40. Accessed October 15, 2002, http://www.apollolibrary.com.

Loblaws *Annual Report,* 2001, 1.

Loblaws, *Annual Report,* 2012, 4.

Loblaws, *Annual Reports,* 2010, 2011, 2012.

Mann, R. D. "A Review of The Relationship Between Personality and Performance in Small Groups." *Psychological Bulletin* 66(4) (1959): 241-270.

Maslow, A.H. "A Theory of Human Motivation. " *Psychological Review* (July, 1943).

Maxwell, J. *The 21 Indispensable Qualities of a Leader. Becoming the Person Others Will Want to Follow.* Nashville, Tenn: Thomas Nelson, Inc., 1999, 58-59.

Maxwell, J. *The 21 Indispensable Qualities of a Leader. Becoming the Person Others Will Want to Follow.* Nashville, Tenn: Thomas Nelson, Inc., 1999, 53-54.

Mercer, T. "Study Confirms It: Corporate Culture Matters." *Crain's Detroit Business* 12(48) (1996). Accessed May 15, 2002, http://ehostvgw2.epnet.com.

Mink, O., Owen, K., & Mink, B. *Developing High-Performance People: The Art of Coaching.* Boston, MA: Addison-Wesley, 1993.

Mintzberg, H., Ahlstrand, B., & Lampel, J. *Strategy Safari: A Guided Tour Through The Wilds of Strategic Management*. New York: Free Press, 1998, 324.

Morgan, G. *Images of Organization*. Thousand Oaks, CA: SAGE Publications, Inc., 1997, 150.

Morley, M. & Heraty, N. *The High Performance Organization: Developing Teamwork*. Management Decision 33(2)(1995): 56-64. Accessed September 28, 2002, www.apollolibrary.com.

Morrison, M. *Leadership and Management Skills for Practical – Vocational*. Mosby Incorporated, 1993.

Myerson, D. "Radical Change, The Quiet Way." *Harvard Business Review* 79(9) (October, 2001): 92.

Nonaka, I. "A Dynamic Theory of Organization Knowledge Creation." *Organization Science,* 5(1), 1994.

Nonaka, I. and Konno, N. "The Concept of "Ba": Building a Foundation for Knowledge Creation." *California Management Review* (Spring,1998).

Nonaka, I. In "Knowledge is Power," Grecco, J., *The Journal of Business Strategy,* (March/April, 1999). Originally published in *The Knowledge Creating Company* 69(6) (Boston: Harvard Business Review, 1991):96-104.

O'Hara, H.T., Lazdowski, L., Moldovean, C., & Samuelson, S.T. "Financial Indicators of Stock Price Performance." *American Business Review* 18(1) (January, 2000): 90-100. Accessed EBSCOHost, July 4, 2003, www.apollogrouplibrary.com.

O'Toole, J. *Leading Change: The Argument for Values-Based Leadership*. New York: Ballantine Books, 1996.

Ohman, K.A. "The Transformational Leadership of Critical Care Nurse-Managers." *Dimensions of Critical Care Nursing* 19(1) (2000): 47.

Onken, M. "Temporal Elements of Organizational Culture and Impact on Firm Performance." *Journal of Managerial Psychology* 14 (3/4) (1999): 236.

Pascale, R., Millemann, M., & Gioja, L. *Surfing The Edge of Chaos*. New York: Crown Business Publishing, 2000, 6.

Pietersen, W. "The Mark Twain Dilemma: The Theory and Practice of Change Leadership." *Journal of Business Strategy* 23(5) (2002).

Pietersen, W. *Reinventing Strategy*. New York, NY: John Wiley & Sons Ltd, 2002.

Porter, M. E. *Competitive Advantage: Creating and Sustaining Superior Performance.* NY: Free Press, 1985.

Prahalad, C. K. and Hamel, G. "The Core Competence of The Corporation." *Harvard Business Review* (May-June, 1990): 79-91.

Quinn, J.B., Anderson, P. & Finklestein, S. "Leveraging Intellect." *Academy of Management Executive* 10(3), 1996.

Reed P. *Extraordinary Leadership - Creating Strategies For Change.* London, UK: Kogan Page Limited, 2001.

Reed, P. *Extraordinary Leadership.* London, UK: Kogan Page Limited, 2001.

Robbins, S. & Langton, N. *Organizational Behavior: Concepts, Controversies, Applications.* Toronto: Prentice-Hall, 2001, 587.

Robins J, Wiersema M. F. "A Resource-Based Approach to The Multi-Business Firm: Empirical Analysis of Portfolio Interrelationships and Corporate Financial Performance." *Strategic Management Journal* 16 (1995): 277-299.

Rowden, R.W. "High Performance and Human Resource Characteristics of Successful Small Manufacturing and Processing Companies." *Leadership & Organization Development Journal* 23(1/2) (2002): 79-83. Accessed EBSCOHost, July 4, 2003, www.apollogrouplibrary.com.

Sashkin, M. *Pillars of Excellence: Organizational Beliefs Questionnaire.* PA: Bryn Mawr, 1984.

Schein E. In "The Leader of The Future," Hesselbein, F., Goldsmith, M., & Beckard, R. San Francisco: Jossey-Bass, 1996, 64.

Schein, E. *Organizational Culture and Leadership.* Reprint. San Francisco: Jossey-Bass. 1997, 391-392.

Schein, E. *Organizational Culture and Leadership.* 2nd ed. San Franciso: Jossey-Bass, 1992, 209.

Schein, E. H. "Organizational Culture." *American Psychologist* 45(2) (1990): 109-119.

Schermerhorn, J. Jr., Hunt J. & Osborn, R. *Organizational Behavior.* 7th ed. New York:Wiley & Sons, 2000, 44.

Schneider, B., "Organizational Climate and Culture," in *The Steal Motive: Managing the Social Determinants of Employee Theft,* Greenberg, J. San Francisco: Jossey-Bass, 1990, 307. In *Antisocial in Organizations,* Giacalone, R. A. and Greenberg, J. (Eds.), (Thousand Oaks: Sage Publications), 1997.

Senge, P. (1990). *The Fifth Discipline: The Art and Practice of The Learning Organization.* New York: Doubleday Currency, 1990.

Senge, P. In "Extraordinary Leadership - Creating Strategies For Change," P. Reed (London, UK: Kogan Page Limited, 2001), 131.

Senge, P. M. *The Fifth Discipline: The Art and Practice of The Learning Organization.* New York: Doubleday Currency, 1993.

Senge, P. *The Fifth Discipline.* New York: Doubleday Currency, 1990.

Senge, P. *The Fifth Discipline: The Art and Practice of The Learning Organization.* New York: Doubleday Currency, 1990, 4.

Sims, H., & Manz, C. *Company of Heroes: Unleashing The Power of Self-Leadership.* NY: Wiley and Sons, 1996.

Skinner, B.F. *Science and Human Behavior.* Boston: Houghton Mifflin Company, 1953.

Sobeys, *Annual Report,* 2001, 2.

Sobeys, *Annual Reports,* 2010, 2011, 2012.

Sowell, T. "Titan Problems in Academe." *Forbes* 82 (November, 1998): 5.

Stannack, P. "Perspectives on Employee Performance." *Management Research News* 19(4/5) (1996): 38-40.

Stevens, G. "The Art of Running a Business School in The New Millennium: a Dean's Perspective." *SAM Advanced Management Journal* 65(3) (2000).

Stogdill (1974,18) in Yukl, G. *Leadership in Organizations.* New Jersey: Prentice Hall, 1998, 236.

Stogdill, R. "Personal Factors Associated With Leadership. A Survey of Literature." *Journal of Psychology* 25 (1948): 35-71.

Stogdill, R. *Handbook of Leadership.* New York: The Free Press, 1974.

Stone, F. *Coaching, Counseling and Mentoring.* NY: AMACOM, 1999.

Stowell, S., & Starcevich, M. "The Coach, Creating Partnerships for a Competitive Edge." OK: *Centre for Management and Organization Effectiveness,* 1998, 3.

Sveiby, Karl. *The New Organizational Wealth,* San Francisco, CA: Berrett-Koehler, 1997, 29.

Terpstra, D.E. "Theories of Motivation: Borrowing The Best." *Personnel Journal* 58 (1979): 376.

Thompson, A., & Strickland, A. *Strategic Management*. Burr Ridge, IL: Irwin, 1994.

Tichy, N., & Devanna, M. *Transformational Leadership*. New York: Wiley, 1986.

Tobias, L. "Coaching Executives." *Consulting Psychology Journal* 48(2) (1996): 88.

Ulrich, D., Zenger, J. and Smallwood, N. *Results-Based Leadership*. Boston, Mass.: Harvard Business School Press, 1999.

University of Phoenix, *Annual Report*, 2001, 1.

Vroom, V. H. *Work and Motivation*. New York: Wiley, 1964.

Weber, M. *On Charisma and Institution Building: Selected Papers*. Chicago: University of Chicago Press, 1952.

Wheatley, M.J. *Leadership and The New Science*, 2nd ed. San Francisco: Berrett-Koehler, 1999, 110.

Whitmore, J. *Coaching For Performance*. CA: Nicholas Brealey Publishing Ltd, 1998.

Willingham, R. *The People Principle: A Revolutionary Redefinition of Leadership*. New York: St. Martin's Press, 1997.

Willner, A.R. *The Spellbinders: Charismatic Political Leaders*. New Haven: Yale University Press, 1984.

www.loblaw.com

www.sobeys.ca

Yukl, G. *Leadership in Organizations*. New Jersey: Prentice Hall, 1998.

Yukl, G. *Leadership in Organizations*. (3rd.ed.). Englewood Cliffs, NJ: Prentice-Hall, 1998, 9.

Yukl, G. *Leadership in Organizations*. New Jersey: Prentice-Hall, 1981.

Yukl, G.A. "Managerial Leadership: A Review of Theory and Research." *Journal of Management* 15 (1989b): 251-289.

Zaleznik, A. "Managers and Leaders: Are They Different?" Boston: *Harvard Business Review*, 1992.

Zaleznik, A. "The Human Dilemmas of Leadership." *Harvard Business Review*, 1963.

www.ingramcontent.com/pod-product-compliance
Lightning Source LLC
Chambersburg PA
CBHW031830170526
45157CB00001B/253